HOUSEHOLD WORKERS UNITE

Josephine Hulett (right), field officer for the National Committee on Household Employment, recruiting household workers. (Mary McLeod Bethune Council House National Historic Site, National Archives for Black Women's History)

HOUSEHOLD WORKERS UNITE

THE UNTOLD STORY OF
AFRICAN AMERICAN WOMEN
WHO BUILT A MOVEMENT

Premilla Nadasen

BEACON PRESS
BOSTON

BEACON PRESS
Boston, Massachusetts
www.beacon.org

Beacon Press books
are published under the auspices of
the Unitarian Universalist Association of Congregations.

18 17 16 15   8 7 6 5 4 3 2 1

This book is printed on acid-free paper that meets the uncoated paper
ANSI/NISO specifications for permanence as revised in 1992.

Text design and composition by Kim Arney

Chapter 4 was adapted from Premilla Nadasen, "Power, Intimacy, and
Contestation: Dorothy Bolden and Domestic Worker Organizing in Atlanta in the
1960s," in *Intimate Labors: Cultures, Technologies, and the Politics of Care*, 204–16,
ed. Eileen Boris and Rhacel Salazar Parreñas. © 2010 by the Board of Trustees of
the Leland Stanford Jr. University. All rights reserved. Reprinted by permission
of the publisher, Stanford University Press, sup.org.

Chapter 6 was adapted from Premilla Nadasen, "Citizenship Rights, Domestic
Work, and the Fair Labor Standards Act," *Journal of Policy History* 24, no. 1
(January 2012): 74–94. Reprinted with permission © Donald Critchlow
and Cambridge University Press, 2012.

Library of Congress Cataloging-in-Publication Data
Nadasen, Premilla.
Household workers unite : the untold story of African American
women who built a movement / Premilla Nadasen.
pages   cm
Includes bibliographical references and index.
ISBN 978-0-8070-1450-9 (hardback)
ISBN 978-0-8070-1451-6 (ebook)
1. Women household employees—United States—History—20th century. 2. African
American household employees—History—20th century. 3. Household
employees—Labor unions—United States—History—20th century.
4. Women labor leaders—United States—History—20th century. 5. African
American labor leaders—United States—History—20th century. I. Title.
HD6072.2.U5N33 2015
331.4'78116408996073—dc23
2015003720

CONTENTS

INTRODUCTION

What matters in life is not what happens to you but
what you remember and how you remember it.

—GABRIEL GARCÍA MÁRQUEZ

In 2007 a landscape contractor in the exclusive New York City suburb of Muttontown, on Long Island, was sitting in his truck after purchasing a box of doughnuts when a malnourished, bedraggled woman approached him. Barely speaking English, the woman pointed frantically to her stomach and begged him to give her a doughnut. The woman, as was later learned through media accounts, was a household worker—one of two live-in Indonesian workers who had been virtually imprisoned and literally tortured by their employers for five years. They were beaten with rolling pins, scalded with boiling water, force-fed chili peppers, required to sleep on the floor in a closet, and only allowed to leave the house to take out the garbage. The employers—a wealthy married couple—were eventually brought to trial, convicted, fined, and sent to jail.[1] This widely publicized case, an extreme but not isolated incident, rightly drew condemnation from many quarters and became emblematic of the vulnerability of private household workers: their isolation, their status as marginalized (and in this case noncitizen) workers, and the vastly unequal power relations that characterize the occupation.

Buried in the sensational news coverage was the fact that an organization of South Asian workers—Andolan—had learned of the case and begun to advocate on behalf of the workers. Andolan collaborated with Domestic Workers United (DWU) to organize a public demonstration in front of the courthouse as the trial took place. Founded in 2000 and composed of nannies, cleaners, and elder-care workers, DWU is a multiracial organization that adopted the slogan "Tell Dem Slavery Done!" Based in New York City, it holds rallies, organizes picket lines, lobbies legislators, and brings lawsuits on behalf of workers to improve labor conditions.

Andolan, DWU, and other organizations in this active and vocal household-workers movement are frequently overlooked in the media, while the victimization stories—like that of the Indonesian workers— dominate. Stories of domestic workers who need rescuing often appear in the popular press and circulate through the Internet. In short, the image of the disempowered and abused domestic worker is a common one, evoking pity and outrage.

The victimization theme plays out in the best-selling book and popular 2011 film *The Help*. Although the story is set in the turbulent decade of the 1960s, the workers profiled are not embroiled in the heroic efforts to overturn Jim Crow segregation or transform southern race relations. In fact, they need prodding and encouragement from the young white protagonist to speak out about their hardship. The story of *The Help* is one about black domestic life told from the perspective of a white employer and, in the end, reinforces dominant stereotypes of passive household workers. Rarely do we see such workers as agents of history. They exist on the sidelines, serve as a backdrop for the stories of others, or, when they are cast as the main actors, give voice to victimization and oppression. They remain nameless stereotypes, like the elderly black woman who, tired but determined, heroically walks to work rather than ride a segregated bus, or one of the thousands of African Americans filling church pews at a mass meeting in support of civil rights.

Although over one-third of employed black women in the United States labored as domestics in 1960, household workers are oddly invisible in histories of postwar social movements. Many Americans are familiar with iconic stories of political struggles, whether it is Rosa Parks's refusal to relinquish her seat on a racially segregated bus in Montgomery, Alabama, in 1955, or the so-called bra burning at the Miss America Pageant in Atlantic City, New Jersey, in 1968, where women's liberationists threw symbols of gendered oppression into a "freedom trash can." These stories are often told in a particular way, with a clear political purpose: to illustrate the dignity in acts of civil disobedience as practiced during the early civil rights movement, in the case of the former; and in the latter, to demonstrate the women's liberation movement's opposition to women's objectification. Preachers and students, sanitation workers and sharecroppers, are all given their due in such stories, but not domestic workers.

This book tells the story of household-worker activism from the 1950s to the 1970s, a pivotal period during which domestic workers established a national movement to transform the occupation. It is a story of women, primarily women of color, who have for the most part operated in the shadows of the formal labor movement, on the margins of the struggle for black freedom, and under the heels of the mainstream women's movement. It challenges widespread assumptions about the passivity of domestic workers and paints a markedly different picture of household workers—one in which they do not need a savior. But it does more than that. It analyzes their strategies of mobilization and explores how storytelling was central to the way they organized and developed a political agenda. Household-worker activists shared stories that were passed down to them and told stories of their own experiences as workers. Their stories, which they connected to the struggle for black liberation, highlighted the racial exploitation of the labor and were part of a collective remembered history in the African American community. Storytelling was a form of activism, a strategic way to make sense of the past as well as the present and to overturn assumptions about domestic workers.

This book contributes to histories of labor and political organizing and makes a claim for how the voices and analytical perspective of working-class black women, as understood through their stories, can help us rethink the basic contours of the postwar period. *Household Workers Unite* is intended to intervene in the discipline—that is, offer a new way to think about how storytelling helps construct identities and how social movements create historical narratives and put them to use.

The stories recounted here are not stories told *about* domestic workers, but stories that domestic workers articulated themselves. The half-dozen African American women activists profiled in these pages were exceptional leaders and participants in a powerful social movement that sought to improve the lives of their fellow domestic workers. In the process of organizing, they shared stories of abuse and exploitation that drew on examples from history—especially the history of slavery and the notorious "slave markets" of the 1930s—to make their case for why they deserved rights. For them, slavery was a trope that connected past and present, illuminated power relations, and spoke to kin, community, and a legacy of racism. Consequently, invoking these stories served a political purpose: to mobilize other household workers and forge a collective political identity as workers. In the 1950s, the notion of an identity as a domestic worker—as opposed to domestic work simply being the work that one did—was not self-evident and had to be constructed. The movement eventually brought together twenty-five thousand women to fight for basic labor protections and transform relationships with their employers.

I begin in the mid-twentieth century, a critical moment in the history of domestic work, by tracing the powerful symbolic association of domestic labor with black women's oppression, recounting the stirrings of a grassroots movement of domestic workers that evolved into a mass movement which fundamentally redefined black women's relationship to the world of work. The occupation both reflects and ushers in dramatic changes in race relations. Domestic work, so representative of white racial oppression for the African American community, became an important platform for the politics of black liberation.

Organizing by domestic workers was distinctly different from other forms of labor organizing. As "invisible" work that took place in private households behind closed doors and was not always recognized as "real" work, household labor has been marginalized within the labor movement and, for many decades, was excluded from key labor laws. A central goal for domestic-worker organizers was to revalue social reproductive labor—paid and unpaid household work. Through their campaigns for respect and recognition of their work, they brought attention to labor in the home and expanded the definition of work that characterized much of the history of labor and labor organizing. This radical redefinition offered possibilities of alliance with feminists, since women, whether paid or not, were traditionally responsible for housework. But demands for higher wages also created tensions as greater numbers of middle-class women entered the paid labor force and increasingly hired household workers in order to pursue careers outside the home. In this case, their "freedom to work" led to further exploitation of private domestic workers.

There is a long history of individual, covert, day-to-day resistance among household workers. The women in this book, however, engaged in overt, collective, and public forms of opposition. They were vibrant middle-aged or elderly black women, very often mothers and grandmothers, who took multiple risks, made enormous personal sacrifices, and offered powerful critiques of the status quo. And it is in this context that the stories and crafting of an identity become important. Beginning in the 1960s, household workers organized forums, spoke publicly, circulated pamphlets, gave testimonials, and lobbied legislatures. Their political identity was bound up with the politics of race, gender, culture, and ethnicity, as their stories of the "mammy" image, the history of slavery, and patterns of servitude that shaped domestic labor illustrate.

Their class consciousness was also shaped through the inequality that characterized domestic work. The legal exclusions from labor rights such as minimum wage and workers' compensation inform how and why an identity of "household workers" begins to develop in the postwar period. The broader cultural patterns and legal practices that degraded their labor led domestic workers to question whether employers should always be their primary target, and in some cases, they saw employers as potential allies. The intimacy of the work, where personal contact with employers was the hallmark of the occupation, also discouraged them from establishing an antagonistic relationship with their bosses. This form of worker consciousness, which didn't necessarily make the employer-employee relationship the central contradiction, also distinguishes this movement from other forms of labor organizing.

Additionally, domestic workers advocated training programs, professionalization, fair wages, benefits, and model contracts. They formulated detailed and clearly defined work expectations and renamed themselves "household technicians." Most of these women took pride in their occupation—in some cases organizing "Maids' Honor Days" to bring respect and public recognition to their work. They wanted their work to be valued the same as all other work and they fought for the legal protections and collective bargaining rights to which other workers were entitled. Their political program included individual and collective empowerment strategies; they targeted both the households in which they worked and state policies that constrained them or devalued their labor.

The women domestic workers highlighted in this book claimed rights as workers. They drew attention to the home as a workspace, to the gendered labor of social reproduction, and to work that many claimed was invisible. Dorothy Bolden, Geraldine Roberts, Josephine Hulett, and others proved that domestic labor is not invisible, even if it is unrecognized. Unlike a factory worker who toils in a distant location that consumers rarely visit, domestic labor is hypervisible, taking place in front of our eyes, every day. As such, the degradation of domestic labor is less about visibility than the way in which the work is perceived—as a labor of love—or the way in which workers are cast—as either "one of the family" or as less than human.

Because domestic workers were considered difficult to organize and neglected by most labor organizers, they had no choice but to strike out on their own. The African American women who led this movement in the 1970s utilized public spaces as centers of organizing, modeled alternative strategies of achieving worker power, and drew attention to the domestic sphere as a site of work. They reached out to immigrant and native-born workers, both the documented and the undocumented. Although they didn't build the racially diverse movement they envisioned, they nevertheless had significant victories. While there were many previous efforts to reform and improve the circumstances of domestic workers, the movement of the 1970s was the first one to put the issue of domestic workers' labor rights on the national political agenda.

Political identity is not given or fixed. It is forged through political struggle, through collective and individual stories, through narrative. The social world of domestic workers in this period was constructed through their words, stories, and silences. Although we don't have access to every narrative, we do have access to some, which can help us understand the social reality of domestic labor for these particular individuals. This book is an attempt to piece together narratives of African American women in private household labor in the postwar period who came to develop the category of domestic workers as rights-bearing citizens engaged in socially and economically valuable work.

Since this struggle of the 1950s through 1970s, domestic workers' representation in both the labor force and in the discourse of the labor movement has assumed enormous significance. In the past two decades, the dramatic rise in the number of household workers worldwide and several well-publicized instances of abuse and exploitation have drawn attention to the occupation. In response, another political movement of domestic workers has emerged under a different set of circumstances to insist on labor rights and occupational safeguards, claims that resonate with the movement of a half century ago.[2]

In this new historical moment, the ranks of labor are under attack and union leaders grapple with how to move forward; capital increasingly treats workers as interchangeable or indispensable; the number of manufacturing jobs continues to dwindle and the number of service-sector jobs expands; and a critical mass of workers in industrialized countries find themselves in precarious situations and struggle to make ends meet without state support or protection.

In this moment, the lessons of domestic-worker organizing might prove to be more important than just a correction of the historical record.

CHAPTER 1

———

"CONVERSATIONS" ABOUT DOMESTIC LABOR

I think Georgia Teresa Gilmore was one of the unsung heroines of the Civil Rights Movement. She was not a formally educated woman, but she had that mother wit. She had a tough mind but a tender heart.

—THOMAS E. JORDAN

In 1956 African American playwright and actress Alice Childress published *Like One of the Family: Conversations from a Domestic's Life,* a searing commentary on the status of black domestic workers. The book was a compilation of stories Childress had written in the early 1950s for the African American press, including Paul Robeson's *Freedom* newspaper and the *Baltimore Afro-American.* These "Conversations from Life" were reflections by Mildred, a sassy and self-confident domestic, shared with her friend Marge in the intimate space of a black working-class home. They conveyed in colorful terms her dissatisfaction with domestic work. Mildred, who is thirty-two, single, and childless, recounts her experience as a day worker in white homes with wit and humor, in the storytelling tradition. In one case, Mildred's employer effusively tells a visiting friend that Mildred is "like one of the family" and how much they love her. When the guest leaves, Mildred asks to have a word with "Mrs. C.," her employer.

"In the first place," she chastises the woman, "you do not *love* me; you may be fond of me, but that is all. . . . In the second place, I am *not* just like one of the family at all! The family eats in the dining room and I eat in the kitchen. Your mama borrows your lace tablecloth for her company and your son entertains his friends in your parlor, your

8

daughter takes her afternoon nap on the living room couch and the puppy sleeps on your satin spread. . . . So you can see I am not *just* like one of the family."[1]

As an activist affiliated with the American Communist Party, Alice Childress was part of a black left cultural community focused on the plight of working-class black women. This network of activists had supported the organizing of household workers in the 1930s, and many had subsequently written political tracts about the exploitation of these workers. Although in later years Childress would attempt to distance herself from her radical past, in the 1950s this political sensibility and her own personal experience undoubtedly influenced her writing of *Like One of the Family*.[2] Before she became a successful playwright, Childress had worked briefly as a domestic, and she reportedly based the character of Mildred on the life of her aunt. In its portrayal of a witty, sharp-minded domestic worker in 1950s New York, the book debunked myths about domestic service and exposed the dark underside of the occupation.[3] The stories' inclusion in African American newspapers around the country ensured a wide readership among household workers, some of whom reached out to Childress. As she described it: "Floods of beautiful mail came in from domestics . . . telling me of their own experiences."[4] The popularity of the essays helped foster a critique of the working conditions of African American household workers.

The publication of Childress's book marked a critical moment in the history of domestic labor. Childress's commentary on household labor seemed to echo a growing sentiment among black domestic workers— of a desire for recognition of their humanity and assertion of rights— that had bubbled beneath the surface for years but would soon achieve full expression. Domestic work had for decades been steeped in a racialized portrayal of African American women as the servile "mammy" figure. In part because of political organizing in the 1930s and changing views about race during World War II, new ideas were germinating. Black women's household labor became a contested terrain on which racial politics played out in the postwar era. The emerging civil rights movement—and household workers' participation in campaigns like the Montgomery bus boycott—provided a forum in which household workers could speak out, creating their own "conversations" about domestic labor. Their voices were critical to reshaping not only Jim Crow segregation and the dominant stereotypes of black domestics, but African American women's status as marginalized and invisible workers.

DOMESTIC WORK AND THE POLITICS OF RACE

Prior to World War II, domestic work was one of the few occupations open to African American women and was weighted with a long history of slavery, servitude, and racial oppression.[5] Black women labored in the homes of white southerners, serving a cultural as well as economic function in that their subordination reinforced white racial power. Black women's work in white homes was characterized by economic and sexual exploitation, as well as the denial of black women's humanity and motherhood. Predatory white male employers wielded their power to sexually abuse or harass black women employed in their homes. White female employers maintained nearly complete control over the outward behavior and actions of domestics, determining what they wore, what they ate, where they ate, which bathrooms they used, and the specific ways they carried out their responsibilities. Both live-in and day workers put in extremely long hours, thus inhibiting their ability to effectively parent their own children. Moreover, the low pay, lack of benefits, and master-servant character of the relationship degraded the economic value of African American women's labor.

The story of domestic labor in the United States is not solely an African American one. During the nineteenth and into the twentieth centuries, native-born white and immigrant European women, including those of Irish, German, and Scandinavian descent, comprised a significant portion of the domestic labor force in the Northeast and Midwest. For them, as for all domestic help, the household was a site of exploitation. Irish Catholic immigrants, in particular, experienced discrimination and social marginalization stemming from stereotypes of Irish workers as uncivilized and insolent. Native-born white domestics, on the other hand, were highly desired by white employers. For most native-born and European immigrant women, however, domestic work was a temporary occupation, engaged in prior to marriage.[6] Women of color—African American, Latina, Asian, and Native American—denied access to other jobs, worked as domestics out of necessity even after they had their own families. They experienced household labor as an "occupational ghetto."[7] Throughout the former slave South, African American women were the primary domestic-service labor force. In the Southwest, Mexican and Mexican American women, and in the West, Japanese and Chinese women, as well as some Asian men in the nineteenth century, were employed as household servants.[8]

During the first two decades of the twentieth century, industrialization and the rise of the service sector generated more opportunities for working-class white women, who rapidly exited domestic work for jobs in garment factories, department stores, the telephone industry, and offices.[9] The curtailment of European immigration in the 1920s further limited the number of domestics available from across the Atlantic. These trends resulted in a shortage of white and European-immigrant domestic workers, and women of color became the vast majority of domestic workers in all regions of the country. From 1900 to 1950 the number of white female household employees declined from 1.3 million to 542,000. The number of nonwhite domestic workers increased from 567,000 to 796,000.[10] Attempts to recruit working-class white women as well as migrant domestic workers from Jamaica, Puerto Rico, the Bahamas, and Barbados were only marginally successful. Northern employers more commonly turned to agencies that recruited African American women from the South.[11] As the number of private household workers declined overall, African American women became a greater proportion of the workforce. In 1900 black women constituted 28 percent of domestic workers; by 1950 they were 60 percent.[12]

African American women's predominance in the field of household labor tied the occupation more closely to the history of race and slavery, and this fueled a battle between black and white communities to define the racial politics of domestic labor.[13] Southern whites—and many northern whites—romanticized the mammy figure, an African American woman who represented the ideal loyal servant and embodied a harmonious view of race relations.[14] Dominant white society used the stereotype of the mammy to justify African American women's status as household laborers and to reconstitute racial hierarchies. For the black community, domestic service became a powerful symbol of racial exploitation and a platform for the assertion of black women's rights. Middle- and working-class African Americans challenged both the constellation of ideas that associated African American women with household labor and the social and economic arrangements that confined African American women to this occupation. Household workers themselves turned to both the legacy of slavery and the nature of their work to formulate critiques of black working-class life. Thus black domestic-worker organizing had its own strategic legacy: it did not merely play a supportive role in the struggle for black freedom but generated new tactics and ideas of black activism in resisting the fundamental arrangements of white supremacy. The divergence in perspectives between blacks and whites with respect to domestic labor reflected and shaped broader discourses on race.

In the early twentieth century, when a Ku Klux Klan march of twenty thousand people paraded through the streets of the nation's capital, when African Americans were systematically denied the right to vote through poll taxes, literacy tests, and overt threats, and when white mobs rampaged through black communities inflicting terror and deadly violence, some white southerners sought to rewrite the history of slavery and race relations through the elevation and reverence of the mammy figure. Indeed, the period from the 1890s through the 1940s experienced a "Mammy craze," in the words of the scholar Cheryl Thurber.[15] The mammy became a source of comfort when racial strife was heightened, and provided concrete evidence for whites that the paternal southern order made African Americans happy. A white construction emerging from the defense of slavery in the 1830s, the mammy symbolized a content and loyal household worker who nurtured and protected white children. As historian Kimberly Wallace-Sanders puts it, "mammy" was "a code word for appropriately subordinate black behavior."[16] The mammy figured prominently in advertising, the arts, and literature at the beginning of the twentieth century, as white northerners and southerners attempted to put the divisiveness and resentment of the Civil War behind them and mask contemporary racial violence. The black mammy issued from a fictionalized tale of stable race relations marked by mutual dependence and familial love. In 1936, Margaret Mitchell's novel *Gone with the Wind* generated a national commercial audience for the stereotyped figure; the character of Mammy is a caricatured, heavyset black servant who demonstrates unwavering loyalty to the O'Hara family over three generations. The astounding success of the book and film suggests how comfortable white Americans were with the idealized image of the black maid.

White southerners paid homage to the mammy figure in countless ways. The United Daughters of the Confederacy, an organization of white southern women whose name implies a commitment to the vision of a slave South, went so far as to launch a campaign in 1924 to build a federally funded national "black mammy" monument in the nation's capital. African American activists, many of whom were part of the New Negro cultural movement promoting racial pride, furiously opposed the congressional bill, claiming that the proposed monument glorified slavery and black subservience.[17] For them the mammy figure was a distortion of the historical record, reflecting a paternalism that continued to shape domestic worker–employer relations into the twentieth century. African American activist Mary Church Terrell, one of the most outspoken opponents of the proposed monument, wrote that if it were built, "there are thousands of colored men and women who will fervently pray that on some stormy night the lightning will strike it and the heavenly elements will send it crashing to the ground."[18] African American opposition to the legislation carried the day. The bill passed the Senate but died in the House, and the monument was never built.

THE 1930s AND 1940s: "EVERY DOMESTIC WORKER A UNION WORKER"

As difficult as the economic collapse of 1929 and subsequent Great Depression was for many Americans, the situation for black domestic workers was dire. With twenty-five percent of the nation unemployed, work was especially hard to come by and, for those lucky enough to find a job, exploitation was rampant. As family incomes dwindled, employers fired domestic workers, reduced rates of pay, or simply squeezed more work out of their employees.

Through their writing and activism, a group of radical black women drew public attention to the plight of African American women working as day laborers during this period. In 1935 investigative journalist Marvel Cooke and activist Ella Baker coauthored a widely circulated article about what they called the "slave market" of domestic labor. The article, published in the NAACP's magazine, *Crisis*, cast light on an estimated two hundred informal markets in New York City—essentially street corners—where African American women waited in hopes of being hired for the day by white employers. "Rain or shine, cold or hot, you will find them there—Negro women, old and young—sometimes bedraggled, sometimes neatly dressed . . . waiting expectantly for Bronx housewives to buy their strength and energy." Cooke and Baker highlighted the vulnerability of these workers: "Often, her day's slavery is rewarded with a single dollar bill or whatever her unscrupulous employer pleases to pay. More often, the clock is set back for an hour or more. Too often she is sent away without any pay at all."[19]

Over the next several years, Cooke, often posing as a domestic worker, wrote a series of articles in the *New York Amsterdam News* exposing the harrowing experiences of the city's black domestic workers. Because of public attention to the condition of household laborers, New York mayor Fiorello La Guardia established the Committee on Street Corner Markets, outlawed the hiring of women off the street, and opened two employment offices to combat exploitative practices. In the postwar period, Cooke carried on her crusade to document the ongoing abuses of domestic workers, writing a five-part series on domestic work in 1950 for the leftist newspaper the *Daily Compass*. Despite modest gains made during the war years, Cooke argued that slave markets had reappeared and that African American women were once again experiencing declining job opportunities.[20]

Street-corner markets became a graphic example of racism and the legacy of slavery. The image of poor African American women being

Bronx Slave Market, 170th Street, New York City, 1938
(Smithsonian American Art Museum, photograph by Robert McNeill)

subjected to a latter-day slave market and mistreated by white employers with impunity fueled a commitment to reform. Stories about the
abuses were repeated and passed down in African American families.
Some three decades after the 1930s slave markets, these stories would be
claimed and retold by household workers who were developing a mass
movement to transform the occupation.

Cooke was part of a network of African American women activists
that included Alice Childress and Claudia Jones, a journalist with the
Communist Party USA's newspaper the *Daily Worker*. Esther Cooper
Jackson, who had worked with the Southern Negro Youth Congress and
wrote a master's thesis challenging the widespread belief that household
workers could not be unionized—the first study of its kind—also participated in this circle of activists; as did Louise Thompson Patterson, a
central figure in the Harlem Renaissance who led a group of black artists
and intellectuals to the Soviet Union in 1932. These mostly middle-class

black women, politicized during the economic turmoil and mass mobilization of the 1930s, were members of the Communist Party.[21] They
established friendships and collaborated on building organizations for
social change such as Sojourners for Truth and Justice, a short-lived early
1950s black radical feminist group that made domestic work central to
its agenda. They worked with the National Negro Labor Council, which
was committed to organizing domestics, and formulated an intellectual
analysis of domestic labor that challenged the strictly class-based Marxist
analysis. These black feminists produced a body of work that theorized
the place of domestic labor in working-class politics and social change.
In 1936 Patterson, examining the interconnections of race, class, and
gender, published a groundbreaking essay in the Communist Party magazine *Woman Today*. "Toward a Brighter Dawn" analyzed the "triple
exploitation" domestic workers experienced, "as workers, as Negroes,
and as women," and called for unionization.[22] Similarly, Jones, in a 1949
article, "An End to the Neglect of the Problems of the Negro Woman!"
argued that "Negro women . . . are the most oppressed stratum of the
whole population." She insisted that slave markets and mammy stereotypes that trapped African American women in a cycle of exploitation "must be combatted and rejected." She also argued that household
workers exhibited the revolutionary and leadership potential necessary
for political organizing.[23] The historian Mary Helen Washington believes
that Childress's *Like One of the Family* was a literary response to Jones's
call for thinking about household workers as political agents.[24]

Cooke, Jones, and other black feminists supported groups such as
the New York–based Domestic Workers Union (DWU) led by Dora
Jones, an African American domestic worker from Sunnyside, Queens.
Formed in 1934, the DWU was part of a spate of domestic-worker organizing in the 1930s, one of dozens of such formations around the country.[25] With bases in several New York City neighborhoods, the DWU
had an estimated one thousand African American and Finnish members, but soon became almost entirely black. They organized in public
parks, apartment buildings, and in the "slave marts" to establish decent wage rates and pressure other workers to refuse to work for less.

According to historian Vanessa May, organizing was an opportunity for household workers to speak for themselves, and union members created a "community of shared experience and suffering."[26] DWU campaigned to pass state legislation to provide minimum wage and workers' compensation protections for household workers. Participation seemed to have a tangible effect on those women who joined. Esther Cooper, in her 1940s master's thesis on domestic-worker organizing, recounted the views of union members: "Before I belonged, I quit two jobs 'cause I couldn't stand it, and then spent a month on the 'slave market' working by the day for 25c an hour. . . . I ain't never been sorry that I'm a Union member and I'll fight for the Union all I can."[27] In 1936 DWU affiliated with the Building Service Employees International Union (BSEIU), a member of the American Federation of Labor (AFL).[28] Under the slogan "Every domestic worker a union worker," DWU opened a hiring hall, required nonunion workers to join the union, and insisted that employers sign contracts with its members. The union built alliances with labor and civil rights groups and with the Women's Trade Union League to lobby for minimum wage and workers' compensation for domestic workers in New York State. It advocated for individual workers and organized mass meetings. Although hampered by a shortage of funds, opposition from white housewives, and a competitive labor market, DWU continued to operate until at least 1950, after which there is little information about its activities.

The DWU prefigured the upsurge of domestic-worker organizing that would transform the political landscape in the postwar era. Domestic work assumed an important place in the politics of black left feminists of this period.[29] Although few were domestics themselves, they were immersed in a world where the dividing line between the African American middle class and working class was easily traversed; many, like Alice Childress, had family members who were household workers or were working class themselves. These activists wrote about the importance of domestic work for African American women, but also articulated the radical potential of this workforce, helping to foster in domestic workers a subjectivity of dignity and resistance. They unequivocally rejected the mammy stereotype and placed domestic work firmly within discussions of class, race, and gender. They suggested that, as the most oppressed labor sector, domestic workers' mobilization offered the possibility of liberating the entire working class. These black feminists saw black domestic labor not simply as evidence of exploitation, but as an avenue for political mobilization. The political and cultural connections between black activists and intellectuals and their working-class and poor counterparts formed the basis of an alliance as the domestic workers' rights movement burgeoned in the postwar period.

The black household workers that made up the domestic workers' rights movement in the 1960s and 1970s probably hadn't read Claudia Jones or Marvel Cooke. They may not even have heard of them. Indeed, Cold War repression and witch hunts for Communists and Communist sympathizers ensured the marginalization of these black women activists and blunted their connection to the emerging civil rights movement.[30] But domestic workers who organized in the postwar period drew on the same history and collective knowledge.

A NEW ERA: "MY FEETS IS TIRED, BUT MY SOUL IS RESTED"

Although the postwar period brought the Cold War and a stifled political climate, it also generated critiques of the racial status quo. World War II ushered in dramatic political and economic changes and new sensibilities about race that shaped the politics of domestic labor. A newfound sense of freedom and political possibility—no doubt bolstered by anticolonial movements and the rhetoric of self-determination—became evident among African Americans who engaged in the black freedom movement in the 1950s. And domestic workers were a critical component of that movement. Although many of its vignettes were written earlier, Alice Childress's *Like One of the Family* was published in 1956, in the midst of the Montgomery bus boycott, a campaign that showcased the power and resistance of domestic workers.

Perhaps no civil rights protest in the 1950s better reflected emerging domestic worker agitation than the Montgomery bus boycott. Thousands of working-class black women in Montgomery, Alabama, many of whom were household workers, participated in and supported the boycott, a protest campaign to end racial discrimination in the city's public transportation system. According to one study, at the start of the protest over half of black women workers in Montgomery were employed in white homes.[31] These women relied on public transportation on a daily basis to get to their places of employment. Without their support, the bus boycott, quite simply, would never have succeeded.

Middle-class black women were critical to initiating and sustaining the protest. The Women's Political Council, a civil rights group founded in Montgomery, had been meeting for years and discussing a possible citywide bus boycott. It had a distributional network in place and was ready to launch such a protest at a moment's notice.[32] Martin Luther King Jr. would become the primary spokesperson of the yearlong boycott, bringing him to national attention. Less prominent in the boycott's retelling are the working-class and poor black women who were the grassroots base of the movement, whose voices are often muted. The iconic black maid dutifully supporting the boycott by refusing to ride the buses after a long and exhausting workday is an image closely associated with the national narrative of the boycott. In some ways the representation of the maid in the movement fed popular stereotypes of the loyal black mammy—although in the service of the movement rather than the white family. She is strong but not confrontational; tired but determined, as evidenced in the oft-repeated quote attributed to Mother Pollard, a poor elderly black woman who, when asked if she was tired, replied: "My feets is tired, but my soul is rested."

In reality, domestic workers played a significant and complicated role in the boycott. They filled the pews at mass meetings and served as the foot soldiers that made the boycott a success, and they also exhibited leadership by raising money and mobilizing others in the community to support the campaign. They used their domestic skills in the service of the protest (by selling food they had cooked to raise funds, for example), and the political leverage they gained from civil rights activism in their day-to-day dealings with their employers. The disruptions of the boycott transformed their relationships with their employers, emboldening the workers and fostering a sense of militancy.

"STOP TREATING US LIKE DOGS"

With the arrest of Rosa Parks, most Montgomery maids knew their time had come. In early 1956, a couple of months after the boycott began, researchers from Nashville's historically black Fisk University conducted interviews of household workers in Montgomery under the supervision of African American sociologists Preston and Bonita Valien. The racial background of the interviewers is not specified, but the recorded black vernacular of the interviewees, seemingly exaggerated in the original transcripts, reflects class or intellectual bias. Nevertheless, the content of the interviews is an important window into a sector of the African American community and captures the sentiment of household workers at the start of the boycott.

One of the workers interviewed, Allean Wright, a cook in her late forties, spoke of her joy upon hearing about the boycott: "I felt good, I felt like shoutin' . . . because the time had come for them to stop treating us like dogs."[33] The hardship of domestic labor as well as ongoing mistreatment had taken its toll. "This stuff has been going on for a long time," remarked Beatrice Charles, a forty-five-year-old maid. "To tell you the truth, it's been happening ever since I came here before the war. . . . But . . . in the last few years they've been getting worse and worse."[34] Another domestic worker, in her late sixties, explained: "Honey, I have washed and iron[ed] clothes till my legs and body ached. . . . [What] does it matter if . . . I still ache, 'cause my mind is now at peace with God, 'cause we're doing what's right and right always win out."[35] Gussie Nesbitt, a fifty-three-year-old domestic and a member of the NAACP, echoed this sentiment. "I walked because I wanted everything to be better for us. Before the boycott, we were stuffed in the back of the bus just like cattle. And if we got to a seat, we couldn't sit down in that seat. We had to stand up over that seat. I work hard all day, and I had to stand up all the way home, because I couldn't have a seat on the bus. And if you sit down on the bus, the bus driver would say, 'Let me have that seat, Nigger.' And you'd have to get up."[36] Irene Stovall had ridden the buses for fifteen years and had been at the bus stop talking about the poor treatment of African American riders when she first heard about the boycott. "When I got home," she recalled, "Junior came runnin' [in] with the paper, 'Momma they say don't ride the buses.' I said, Lord you . . . answered my prayer."[37] So despite the physically taxing nature of their labor and the sacrifices they would have to make to participate in the campaign, domestic workers expressed unequivocal support for the boycott.

Rosa Parks, whose arrest initiated the boycott, became the symbol of the mistreatment of African American women in the segregated South. One domestic worker observed that they were boycotting the buses because Montgomery was a "Jim Crow" town, and they "put one of our [re]spectable ladies in jail." She continued, saying that she could only take so much and "soon you [get] full."[38] Beatrice Charles explained: "I had heard about Rosa Parks getting put in jail because she would not get up and stand so a white man could sit down. Well, I got a little mad, you know how it is when you hear how white folks treat us." After she heard about the boycott, Beatrice recalled: "I felt good. I said this is what we should do. So I got on the phone and called all my friends and told them, and they said they wouldn't ride."[39]

The boycott demonstrated a level of cross-class alliance between the protest's middle-class organizers and leaders, who saw their fate tied to the larger black community, and the workers whose support for the boycott was critical to its success. Dealy Cooksey, a domestic worker about forty years old, described the tension this alliance created in her relationship with her employer. "Dealy, why don't you ride the bus?" her employer, who drove her home most days after work, asked her shortly after the boycott began. Reverend King is "making a fool out of you people." Dealy replied angrily: "Don't you say nothing about Rev. King. . . . He went to school and made something out of hisself, and now he's trying to help us. Y'all white folks done kept us blind long enough. We got our eyes open and ain't gonna let you close them back. I don't mean to be sassy, but when you talk bout Rev. King I gets mad. Y'all white folks work us to death and don't pay nothing." Her employer retorted: "But Dealy, I pay you." Dealy challenged her: "What do you pay, just tell me? I'm ashamed to tell folks what I work for." Dealy was not about to be swayed by her employer's words: "I walked to work the first day and can walk now. If you don't want to bring me, I ain't begging, and I sure ain't getting back on the bus and don't you never say nothing about Rev. King."[40]

Dealy's no-nonsense attitude toward her employer is echoed by many of the domestic workers interviewed. In speaking about the protest, domestic workers were less constrained by notions of decorum and propriety than the middle-class leaders of the boycott. In contrast, the question of respectability occupied the minds of boycott leaders from the outset, especially regarding who would become its symbol. This had to be, they argued, an upstanding citizen of the community, someone beyond reproach. Despite her working-class status, Rosa Parks's genteel and soft-spoken demeanor more easily fit into traditional standards of respectability and she was carefully cultivated to become that symbol even to the point of rewriting her own personal history.[41] And she was chosen at the expense of others who had been arrested for violating local segregation laws. Claudette Colvin was a young black teenager who was arrested several months before Parks for violating the city's segregation laws. Even though Colvin was a straight A student, she was visibly pregnant at the time of the arrest and that, coupled with her working-class status—her mother was a maid and her father a yard worker—made her a less-than-ideal symbol of black protest. Although city leaders decided not to call a boycott, Colvin's arrest garnered a wellspring of support within Montgomery's black community. A few months later, in October 1955, Mary Louise Smith, an eighteen-year-old maid, was arrested and fined for refusing to give her seat to a white woman.[42] Smith's working-class status also proved to be an obstacle to her becoming a symbol of black resistance in Montgomery. These decisions reflected the politics of respectability that shaped the Montgomery bus boycott and the civil rights movement more broadly.[43]

The upstandingness of Rosa Parks, the dignified restraint of Martin Luther King, the self-possession of well-dressed college students taking part in lunch counter sit-ins—all are examples of movement leaders making their public claim to political rights.[44] But domestic workers and other activists at the grassroots level provided an important counterpoint to their middle-class counterparts: they didn't hesitate to tell it like it is, and their testimony reveals an awakening political sensibility.[45]

The experience of Willie Mae Wallace, a store cleaner in her thirties, may not have been typical, but it is indicative of the fed-up attitude of some working-class people who rode the buses in segregated Montgomery. She explained: "One morning I got on the bus and I had a nickel and five pennies. I put the nickel in and showed him the five pennies. You know how they do you. You put five pennies in there, and they say you didn't. And do you know that bastard cussed me out. He called me bastards, whores and when he called me a mother F—, I got mad and I put my hand on my razor. I looked at him and told him 'Your mammy was a son-of-a-bitch, that's why she had you bitch. And if you so bad, get up out of that seat.' I rode four blocks, then I went to the front door and backed off the bus, and I was just hoping he'd get up . . . but he didn't say nothing. Colored folks ain't like they use to be," she went on to say. "They ain't scared no more. Guns don't scare us. . . . I don't mind dying, but I sure Lord am taking a white bastard with me."[46]

The militant attitudes of domestic workers carried over into their work relationships. The boycott emboldened them to speak out. The conventional wisdom among white employers held that domestic workers were meek and submissive and that the boycott was a result of outsider agitation. Employer interviews seem to confirm this. As Mrs. H. N. Blackwell, for example, asserted, "I can tell you that the Negroes I have talked to about it aren't interested in the issue and say they wish it hadn't come up. . . . Certainly none of the maids who work out here would cause any trouble." She was convinced that refusal to ride the buses was not their own decision: "You know they are superstitious, emotional people and if their preachers tell them something will happen if they ride the buses I believe that many of them might be afraid."[47] According to Mrs. Lydia S. Prim, "Everything was all right before those radicals came in and started stirring up trouble."[48] This attitude was also reflected in certain sectors of the black community. In the days after Rosa Parks was arrested, civil rights leader E. D. Nixon charged black ministers to publicly support the boycott when he told them, "It's time to take the aprons off."[49] The gendered language was intended to shame African American men into taking a stronger stand against white oppression. Fear was a powerful force that shaped what many, including King, described as complacency within Montgomery's black community. Interviews with domestic workers suggest that concerns over losing their jobs had discouraged some from adopting a more visible role.

As the Montgomery protest garnered national attention, domestic workers who had been hesitant to speak out gained strength from the community mobilization. Willie Mae Wallace, a store cleaner, experienced ongoing harassment during the boycott from a white woman who worked with her. When her coworker asked if she rode the bus, Willie Mae responded that she did not and was not going to. The woman gave her a hard time all day. Finally, Willie Mae confronted her. "I told her if she didn't like the way I did it to do it herself. She didn't hire me and, she sure couldn't fire me. She bristled all up like she wanted to hit me. I said, 'Look, my ma was black and she's resting [deceased] and the white woman ain't been born that would hit me and live. The police might get me, but when they do, you'll be three D: Dead, Damned and Delivered.'"[50]

The husband of Irene Stovall's employer was a city bus driver. One evening the employer told her to come by and pick up some bacon grease, but "she told me don't let her husband see it because he had instructed her not to give Irene anything else." Then, she asked: "Irene, what happened at the meeting last night?" When Irene responded that they sang and prayed, her employer got angry and called her a liar. "Now listen, I know we [sang] and prayed, and if you don't believe me, YOU go to the meeting for yourself." Irene was furious that her employer would try to get information out of her and said to herself: "She must take me for a fool—think I'll come back here and puke everything my folks says to her, and then for some little old stinking bacon grease." Her employer shot back: "Irene, I didn't know you was so damn stupid. . . . I didn't know you were scared to ride the bus." Irene was so infuriated, she told her employer off. "I told her that I was not scared to ride the bus, I'd ride if I want to, but her husband never would get a dime from me no more." She explained that she joined the boycott because she wanted to, and that she remained in the South in order to help her people. Her employer responded: "You know we could starve y'all maids for a month." Irene, using the full weight of her words as well as her two-hundred-pound frame to her advantage, retorted: "I pity anybody who waits fur me to starve. They'll be waiting for a long time." Despite the heated exchange, Irene's boss continued to pay her wages and bus fare, but Irene decided, "I better quit before I have to beat her . . . She heard me say [a] heap of time that if you hit me, I hit back and I ain't big for nothing."[51]

The complexity of the mistress-maid relationship came to the fore during the boycott. In their actions, domestic workers disproved the loyal mammy myth of popular culture, agitating and maneuvering to improve their lot. The boycott created an opening for workers to express their political views and to question the terms of their employment. White employers expressed surprise at the dissatisfaction vocalized by domestics. And many were taken aback by the overt militancy exhibited by their workers. At the same time, many employers inadvertently aided the boycott by driving their maids to work or giving them cab fare, because they depended upon domestics to keep their households running. This became evident when the mayor of Montgomery, Tacky Gayle, urged white housewives not to drive their maids to and from work. White employers responded angrily and suggested that the mayor come do their household chores for them.[52] Even at the expense of aiding the boycott, employers were not willing to do without their maids. Domestic workers were indispensable to the white community and played a pivotal role in the effort to establish a new politics of race relations in Montgomery.

The interviews of Montgomery's domestic workers make clear black domestics' desire to challenge the status quo. The boycott, which proved an overwhelming success, emboldened domestic workers in their workspaces as well as in public spaces, even though they were isolated employees. The key issues that plagued them in the workplace— unfair treatment and denial of their humanity—were also in play on the city buses. Domestic workers not only supported the boycott and made it part of their own struggle, but, as Georgia Gilmore's story illustrates, they also provided leadership.

Georgia Gilmore: "We Rather Walk"

Georgia Gilmore, who moved to Montgomery in 1920, became a leading advocate for household laborers. She lived in Centennial Hill, a middle-class African American community with a thriving black business sector on Montgomery's east side, near the state capitol. A large woman who weighed over three hundred pounds, Gilmore was a single mother of six. Like most black women in the South, she earned her living through her knowledge and skill as a domestic—although she did so in multiple settings. Gilmore worked as a nurse and a midwife, delivering babies in the black community. She was employed as a cook in a cafeteria and also a maid in private households.[53] She put those skills to use during the Montgomery bus boycott, raising money, feeding demonstrators, and creating meeting spaces, yet her name is relatively unknown today.

Gilmore understood that household workers' refusal to ride the buses was indispensable to the boycott's success. "Because you see they were maids, cooks," she said. "And they was the one that really and truly kept the bus running. And after the maids and the cooks stopped riding the bus, well the bus didn't have any need to run."[54] Her support for the boycott was rooted in part in her own experiences on the city buses. As was typical for working-class black people in Montgomery, Gilmore didn't own a car. She was a regular bus rider with few other transportation options. Gilmore shared her experience of riding on the city buses when she testified at the 1956 trial of Martin Luther King: "Many times I have been standing without any white people on the bus and have taken seats, and when the driver sees you he says, 'You have to move because those seats aren't for you Negroes.'"[55] Gilmore's elderly mother also encountered difficulties. Gilmore recounted one experience that not only demonstrated the callous disregard for her mother's physical limitations, but the vicious racial insults that accompanied it: "She was an old person and it was hard for her to get in and out of the bus except the front door. The bus was crowded that evening with everybody coming home from work. She went to the front door to get on the bus, and this bus driver was mean and surly, and when she asked him if she could get in the front door he said she would have to go around and get in the back door, and she said she couldn't get in, the steps were too high. He said she couldn't go in the front door. He said, 'You damn niggers are all alike. You don't want to do what you are told. If I had my way I would kill off every nigger person.'"[56]

In October 1955, before Rosa Parks's arrest, Gilmore had another in a long series of unpleasant encounters with city bus drivers, which prompted her to begin her own one-woman boycott. During Friday-afternoon rush hour, Gilmore boarded a packed Oak Park bus. There were two white passengers; the rest were African Americans. Although she didn't know the driver's name, she recognized him. "This bus driver is tall, hair red, and has freckles, and wears glasses. He is a very nasty bus driver." After she paid her fare, the driver told her to get off the bus and enter through the rear door. She pleaded with him to let her stand there, since she was already on the bus and most of the riders were African Americans in any case. The driver refused. "So, I got off the front door and went around the side of the bus to get in the back door, and when I reached the back door and was about to get on he shut the back door and pulled off, and I didn't even ride the bus after paying my fare. So, I decided right then and there I wasn't going to ride the busses any more. . . . And so I haven't missed the busses because I really don't have to ride them. . . . I haven't returned to the busses—I walk."[57] This kind of individual protest was not unheard of among black women in Montgomery before the bus boycott.

THE CLUB FROM NOWHERE

A few months after her decision to stop riding the city buses, Gilmore heard a radio broadcast announcing the arrest of Rosa Parks. At the time, she was working at a white-owned segregated restaurant in Montgomery, the National Lunch Company. After a hugely successful one-day boycott of Montgomery's buses the Monday after Parks's arrest, a community meeting was convened to discuss a course of action. Gilmore was one of several thousand people who attended the evening gathering at Holt Street Baptist Church. Organizers had to set up speakers to accommodate the overflow crowd. Gilmore was moved by what she heard, especially the speech by the young Reverend Martin Luther King, who declared in his address, "There comes a time when people get tired of being trampled over by the iron feet of oppression." Gilmore was impressed: "I never cared too much for preachers, but I listened to him preach that night. And the things he said were things I believed in."[58] The community members in attendance overwhelmingly supported the decision to continue the boycott indefinitely under the leadership of the newly formed Montgomery Improvement Association (MIA).

Gilmore, of course, had no intention of riding the buses. She was fed up, and welcomed the opportunity to engage in collective protest. She explained: "Sometime I walked by myself and sometime I walked with different people, and I began to enjoy walking, because for so long I guess I had this convenient ride until I had forgot about how well it would be to walk. I walked a mile, maybe two miles, some days. Going to and from. A lot of times, some of the young whites would come along and they would say, 'Nigger, don't you know it's better to ride the bus than it is to walk?' And we would say, 'No, cracker, no. We rather walk.' I was the kind of person who would be fiery. I didn't mind fighting with you."[59]

The Monday- and Thursday-night meetings, part organizing committee, part solidarity rally, became a regular occurrence in Montgomery as the boycott dragged on. The large crowds, led by middle-class ministers but made up overwhelmingly of black working-class women, were enthusiastic and lively. Gilmore showed up almost without fail to the gatherings.

As became clear early on, the boycott was expensive to run and maintain. Coordination was a massive undertaking and included fundraising, publicity, legal representation, security patrols, as well as the providing of alternative transportation in the form of an organized carpool for protesters. The Montgomery Improvement Association needed money to operate the carpool and assist people who had been arrested, fined, or fired for participation in the protest. The carpool was an extensive citywide network with three hundred vehicles and forty-two pickup and drop-off points. Coordinators rented or borrowed vehicles, hired drivers, and paid for gas and insurance. Gilmore looked for a way that she could best help out. According to Johnnie Carr, a member of the Women's Political Council and longtime friend of Rosa Parks: "Georgia just got it into her mind that she was going to raise money for the Movement. And if Georgia was raising money, she was doing it through food."[60] Gilmore recounted: "We collected $14 from amongst ourselves and bought some chickens, bread and lettuce, started cooking and made up a bundle of sandwiches for the big rally. We had a lot of our club members who were hard-pressed and couldn't give more than a quarter or half-dollar, but all knew how to raise money. We started selling sandwiches and went from there to selling full dinners in our neighborhoods and we'd bake pies and cakes for people."[61]

Gilmore founded the Club from Nowhere, an organization of maids, service workers, and cooks seeking to aid the boycott. The name was an attempt to shield members from the consequences of openly supporting the boycott. "Some colored folks or Negroes could afford to stick out their necks more than others because they had independent incomes," Gilmore explained, "but some just couldn't afford to be called 'ring leaders' and have the white folks fire them. So when we made our financial reports to the MIA officers we had them record us as the money coming from nowhere. 'The Club from Nowhere.'"[62] Only Gilmore knew who made and bought the food and who donated money. The underground network of cooks went door-to-door selling sandwiches, pies, and cakes, and collecting donations. The proceeds were then turned over to boycott leaders. Donations came from whites as well as blacks. That "was very nice of the people because so many of the people who didn't attend the mass meetings would give the donation to help keep the carpool going."[63]

The campaign spread to other neighborhoods. According to Gilmore: "Well, in order to make the mass meeting and the boycott be a success and that keep the car pool running, we decided that the peoples on the south side would get a club and the peoples on the west side would get a club."[64] The various groups competed, each trying to raise more money than the other. "When we'd raise as much as $300 for a Monday night rally, then we knowed we was on our way for $500 on Thursday night."[65] Gilmore offered the money at the Monday-night mass meetings to wild cheers and thunderous applause.

When Gilmore's boss at the National Lunch Company learned of her activism, she was fired and blacklisted. Unfortunately, retaliation was not uncommon during the boycott; both E. D. Nixon and Martin Luther King had their homes bombed, and Rosa Parks lost her job at the department store where she worked as a seamstress. Gilmore had little choice but to turn these impediments into opportunities. Martin Luther King encouraged her to cook out of her own home and even helped her financially.[66] When the city tried to shut her down, King helped her remodel her kitchen to meet city standards. Gilmore awoke at four o'clock in the morning and, in her small kitchen, began preparations to make stuffed pork chops, meat loaf, barbecued ribs, fried fish, spaghetti in meat sauce, collard greens and black-eyed peas, stuffed bell peppers, corn muffins, bread pudding, and sweet potato pies. She cooked lunch daily out of her kitchen for people involved in the boycott, including King.[67] Although she had no restaurant seating, people showed up at her house to eat, squeezing around the dining room table or sitting and eating on the couch. King, who called her Tiny, frequented her house, often bringing guests or holding clandestine meetings at her home.[68] According to Reverend Al Dixon: "Dr. King needed a place where he could go. You know, he couldn't go just anywhere and eat. He needed someplace where he could not only trust the people around him but also trust the food. And that was Georgia's."[69] Gilmore's dining room table became a meeting space connecting blacks and whites, working class and middle class in the civil rights movement: professors, politicians, lawyers, clerical workers, police officers. She served such well-known figures as Morris Dees of the Southern Poverty Law Center, Lyndon Johnson, and John Kennedy. In this context, cooking became a conduit for political connections.[70]

Reverend Thomas E. Jordan, pastor of Lilly Baptist Church, reflected on Gilmore's role in the boycott: "I think Georgia Teresa Gilmore was one of the unsung heroines of the Civil Rights Movement.

She was not a formally educated woman, but she had that mother wit. She had a tough mind but a tender heart. You know, Martin Luther King often talked about the ground crew, the unknown people who work to keep the plane in the air. She was not really recognized for who she was, but had it not been for people like Georgia Gilmore, Martin Luther King Jr. would not have been who he was."[71]

Like other domestic workers, Gilmore was less constrained by social niceties than movement leaders. As Alabama State professor Benjamin Simms, who served as head of the MIA's transportation committee, commented: "She's a sweet woman, but don't rub her the wrong way. Would you believe that this charming woman once beat up a white man who had mistreated one of her children. He owned a grocery store, and Mrs. Gilmore marched into his place and wrung him out."[72]

Black domestic workers like Gilmore were service workers with a particular set of skills that could be utilized for political mobilization. Thus they exhibited the political agency that Claudia Jones anticipated. Their struggle, however, was not for class overthrow, as the black radical feminists of the 1930s and 1940s predicted, but transformation of the power structure, on city buses and in their workplaces. They sought to build cross-class alliances and carve out spaces of autonomy and mutual respect for the South's working-class black women. Household workers were the quintessential "outsiders within," to use Patricia Hill Collins's term—privy to the most intimate details of white family life yet not a part of that family.[73] Their social status and proximity to the white domestic sphere enabled them to wield a different kind of power in engaging in community action. Their intimate relationship with white households granted them access and knowledge unavailable to others. During the Montgomery bus boycott, maids surreptitiously gathered information from the white community. Bernice Barnett argues: "The maids, cooks, and service workers of the [Club from Nowhere] also had access to information in the homes of their White employers. As they went invisibly about their domestic work, the [members of the Club] were alert to news about the strategies and tactics of the White opposition."[74] Domestic workers used the very elements of domestic work— their marginalization, their insider status, their access to the white domestic sphere, their culinary skills—as a basis for subversive activity. They were instrumental in unsettling the white community and pushing for more egalitarian race relations. They made clear that the boycott was not only about equal rights, but about respect.[75] Their claim for respect and political engagement posed a fundamental challenge to the long-standing "mammy" stereotype. Even though they had few labor rights, black domestic workers possessed power within their workplace that enabled them to exercise leverage over their employers.

In one of her "conversations," Alice Childress writes about the benefits of unionization and the need for domestic workers to band together. "Honey," says Mildred, her protagonist, "I mean to tell you that we got a job that almost nobody wants! That is why we need a union! Why shouldn't we have set hours and set pay just like busdrivers and other folks, why shouldn't we have vacation pay and things like that?" And if employers don't like the terms of the work and want to hire a nonunion person? "Well, then the union calls out all the folks who work in that buildin', and we'll march up and down in front of that apartment house carryin' signs which will read 'Miss So-and-so of Apartment 5B is unfair to organized houseworkers!' . . . The other folks in the buildin' will not like it, and they will also be annoyed 'cause their maids are out there walkin' instead of upstairs doin' the work. Can't you see all the neighbors bangin' on Apartment 5B!"[76]

In her writings, Childress foreshadowed a new kind of resistance among black domestic workers. While the Montgomery bus boycott encouraged household workers to mobilize in support of the boycott and created a space to express dissatisfaction to their employers, it also prompted household workers in other parts of the country to organize independently—as workers—to transform an occupation that was central to working-class black women's lives and the history of race in modern America.

CHAPTER 2

WOMEN, CIVIL RIGHTS, AND GRASSROOTS MOBILIZATION

The domestic worker has been the kind of worker that has been overlooked and ignored—what I refer to as an invisible worker.

—GERALDINE ROBERTS

One December evening in 1955, Dorothy Bolden was sitting in her two-story bungalow in Vine City, an all-black section of Atlanta, watching television as she sewed clothes for her children, when she learned of Rosa Parks's ordeal in Montgomery, Alabama. Parks's story resonated deeply with Bolden, who like many African American domestics was often mistreated on her daily bus ride, a fact that compounded the disrespect she experienced in the workplace. As Bolden later recalled in an interview, "There had been some hard days with us women riding the buses trying to get to the houses to clean them up, work. . . . Georgia Tech students, Emory students would stand over you and take their elbow and hit you in the head. You would get up and move and then, he got the seat 'cause you didn't want him bopping your head. . . . You would just get up and move and get on farther back. You would be packed back there, but you'd squeeze in there some kinda way."[1]

Like other black working-class women, domestic workers relied heavily on public transportation to get to and from their places of employment. The journey home could be made more difficult if the domestic worker carried a "tote pan" containing leftover food, which employers sometimes gave workers to supplement their meager wages. While the offering might help feed the families of domestic workers, carrying it on a crowded bus was no easy task. "If you bring a pan home sometimes, [they] would knock you down, knock the pan out of your hand with food in it."[2]

Bolden was riveted as she watched the footage of Parks that night. In her mind, Parks's act was powerfully courageous. Drawing on a wellspring of empathy, strongly identifying with the yearning for freedom that had inspired such an act, Bolden began speaking to Parks: "I was telling her to sit there. I know she couldn't hear me, but I said 'sit on down honey, don't move. You tired, I know you is.'"[3] Ultimately, Parks's protest and arrest galvanized civil rights activists and sparked the yearlong Montgomery bus boycott. A turning point in civil rights history, Parks's act and the resilience of the mostly working-class participants of the Montgomery boycott would have a lasting impact on Bolden.

Inspired by Rosa Parks, Bolden became involved in civil rights activism in Atlanta, going on to form the Atlanta-based National Domestic Workers Union of America (NDWUA), which was part of a larger movement for domestic workers' rights. NDWUA would become one of the largest and most active local domestic workers' rights groups. It pioneered strategies of organizing in public spaces, worked to enhance the individual and collective power of household workers, and sought to remake the public image of domestic workers.

Bolden wasn't alone—the civil rights movement nurtured, trained, and inspired a generation of African American women domestic workers who mobilized to reform household labor. Civil rights discourse tended to focus on voting and educational access, but poverty and job discrimination were widespread. For domestic-worker activists, civil and economic rights were inextricably linked. Many believed that economic security was the foundation upon which black freedom should be built. In advocating for domestic workers, activists and reformers would address both racial inequality and poverty.

The domestic workers' rights movement brought a new dimension to black working-class struggles. This was not a struggle for equal opportunity or individual access to previously closed occupations, but a broader campaign for economic rights for African American domestic workers and for a new definition of labor. Poor black women who worked as domestics were often considered outside the boundaries of "labor." Excluded from most labor law protections, such as minimum wage and the right to organize and bargain collectively, domestic work was, in some ways, not considered "real work," because of its location in the home, the low status of women of color, and the job's association with women's unpaid household labor. Because of this history, domestic workers were considered by some to be "unorganizable."[4] The occupation had few ties to unions or mainstream labor. Consequently, when domestic workers began to mobilize, they found their most reliable allies among civil rights, black power, and women's organizations. They developed an alternative class and gender model for civil rights leadership by highlighting the voices and experiences of poor black women. Domestic workers in the 1960s and 1970s brought attention to undervalued household and reproductive labor, claimed their rights as workers, and in the process redefined the very meaning of work.[5]

Dorothy Bolden was born in 1920 in Atlanta to Raymond Bolden and Georgia Mae Patterson.[6] Her family lived in Vine City, where her father worked as a chauffeur and her mother as a maid and washerwoman.[7] As a child, Dorothy and her older brother helped their mother by picking up other households' dirty laundry in a wagon and returning it clean and pressed after her mother washed it. Dorothy was very close to her grandparents, who often brought canned goods, bacon, eggs, and ham to the family when food was scarce. Despite her parents' straitened circumstances, she had fond memories of childhood, and recalled a community filled with love and support, and a collective spirit—especially around child rearing and food. "They looked out for each other and looked out for the children. You didn't have no problem with people taking care of your children. . . . Everybody looked after everybody's child. When they feed one child, they feed all."[8]

An accident when she was three years old left Dorothy with poor eyesight that would plague her throughout her life. Despite her impaired vision, Dorothy began working as a domestic at the age of nine to help support her family. After attending a split-day session at school that ended at noon, she babysat, washed diapers, and did light cleaning for a Jewish family. Dorothy dropped out of Booker T. Washington High School in the eleventh grade and worked for another family from 8:00 a.m. until after dinner, earning three dollars a week.[9]

Like many African Americans who came of age during the Great Migration of the 1930s and 1940s, Bolden was curious about the world and eager to escape the South.[10] The relentless violence, limited economic opportunities, and unforgiving day-to-day life under Jim Crow, combined with restrictions on European immigration and the wartime expansion of the economy, prompted six million African Americans and many poor whites to travel North.[11] Intrigued by stories of personal freedom and economic advancement, Bolden, too, wanted to see the so-called promised land. Through her job as a domestic, she met white northerners who were visiting the South and, impressed with her work, agreed to pay her fare and a higher salary to come work for them.[12] For Bolden, the offer was an opportunity to travel and explore the country. She remembered her first journey, riding a train to Chicago at the age of seventeen. "They can tell when you are from the South 'cause you are scared to get on the train, you know, you are waiting for your turn. When somebody is being polite to you, you are kinda scared to accept it 'cause from being down South. . . . Southern people don't treat you that way."[13]

As a young adult, both in Atlanta and elsewhere, Dorothy held various jobs but always returned to domestic work. For a few years she attended a school for dress designers in Chicago, but was forced to drop out because of her poor eyesight.[14] During the war, she worked in the Sears, Roebuck mailroom and for four years at National Linen Service. Bolden recalled the struggle for unionization at the latter company: "I felt very good after we heard the presentations they made to us about how much we could be getting and how it could go up and up, and it did go up and up."[15] It's not clear if Bolden was directly involved in the unionization effort, but it's safe to assume that what she witnessed firsthand demonstrated to her the power of collective organizing. After traveling to Illinois, North Carolina, New York, Virginia, Michigan, and Alabama, she returned to Atlanta and started working at the railway. It was there that she met Abraham Thompson, a fellow railroad employee.

They married in 1944, settled in Atlanta, and together had nine children, three of whom died. Shortly after she married, she began doing household work again as a live-in, earning eighteen dollars a week. Bolden stayed home when her children were young, but returned to work when they got older.[16]

Atlanta was a center of civil rights activity in the postwar period. Just as the city served as the air and rail transportation hub for the Southeast region, it also provided the connective tissue for the civil rights movement, linking together activists throughout the South. Atlanta's historically black colleges and universities and substantial black middle-class population produced a group of civil rights leaders with both a vested interest in toppling segregation and the skills and resources that poorer, less educated black southerners did not have. The city was the base of operations for the Southern Christian Leadership Conference (SCLC) and the Student Nonviolent Coordinating Committee (SNCC), and the birthplace of Martin Luther King Jr. King, who, in 1960, moved back to Atlanta to co-pastor with his father at Ebenezer Baptist Church. Ella Baker, longtime civil rights activist and intellectual mentor for students in SNCC, also moved to Atlanta in 1958 to serve as the first executive director of SCLC.[17]

During the 1960s, former mayor William Hartsfield deemed Atlanta "the city too busy to hate"—helping to foster an image of a progressive metropolis distinct from other southern cities. In some ways, Atlanta seemed worlds apart from places like Birmingham, Alabama, where notorious police chief Bull Connor turned water hoses on schoolchildren, or Albany, Georgia, where civil rights demonstrators were arrested en masse. Atlanta initiated gradual and peaceful desegregation of public schools, and city leaders, at least publicly, expressed support for equal accommodations, even if behind the scenes they attempted to stymie the efforts of more militant civil rights activists. Despite the veneer of civility, Atlanta saw its share of civil rights showdowns and urban unrest. In the spring of 1960, black students in Atlanta, like thousands of other students throughout the South that year, initiated sit-ins at segregated lunch counters. Their direct-action tactics sparked a new, more militant phase in the black freedom movement, as young activists, unwilling to wait for legal decisions or institutional sanction for their demands, insisted on an immediate end to racial segregation, a goal for which they were willing to get arrested. Although a compromise between the city and black leaders was worked out without the students' consent, the sit-ins led to complete desegregation of lunch counters by the fall of 1961. But students in Atlanta had an expansive notion of what their struggle was about, and eradicating Jim Crow was only part of their agenda. Broadly framing their struggle as one of "human rights," they incorporated the goals of ending poverty and empowering the community, and in this they had many allies in the city.[18] Throughout the 1970s, Atlanta had a vibrant cadre of black power and neighborhood activists who addressed issues from voting rights to public education to welfare rights.[19] Domestic-worker organizing was one component of this range of political mobilization.

Bolden's early attempts to organize workers wasn't unprecedented, and in fact was informed by a long history of domestic-worker organizing in Atlanta. In July 1881, twenty African American laundresses formed a "Washing Society" and wrote an open letter to the mayor demanding higher wages. Eventually three thousand women went on strike for better wages and more autonomy. They garnered citywide support from black churches, mutual aid societies, and fraternal organizations. The strike illustrates the ways in which laundresses, although employed individually, were able to utilize collective workspaces to form an association and organize a citywide demonstration. Although short-lived and presumably unsuccessful, the 1881 strike is a powerful example of black women household workers organizing to claim their rights.[20] During World War II there was renewed interest in the plight of domestic workers. Ruby Blackburn, a former domestic, organized the Negro Cultural League in Atlanta to train domestic workers and help them find employment. The league took as its motto "A fair day's pay for a fair day's work." Under the leadership of Blackburn, domestic workers in Atlanta participated in the voter-registration drive in 1946.[21]

Bolden would build on this history of organizing black household workers in the context of the civil rights activity swirling around her both in
Atlanta and across the United States. "Civil rights was a plate of food to
us," she recalled. "It fed our soul. It strengthened our bodies. Built our
minds. It was everything to us."[22] This sentiment was echoed by one of
the cofounders of the NDWUA, Louise Bradley, who observed that the
movement "gave these people the motivation to speak out."[23] Bolden's
close contact with civil rights leaders fueled her political activism. Martin Luther King Jr. lived in Bolden's Vine City neighborhood, and she
had periodic encounters with him. "I marched with Dr. King every time
he came to town," she stated. "I went to rallies, I was the most vocal
person there."[24]

A longtime community leader, Bolden was recognized and respected
as someone who knew every inch of her working-class neighborhood.
Vine City produced some of Atlanta's most important politicians, including Maynard Jackson, who would become the first black mayor
of Atlanta in 1974. Jackson, in fact, attended several early meetings of
NDWUA and credited the support of maids in Vine City with his elec-
toral success.[25] Bolden worked most closely with the SNCC, which es-
poused a philosophy of long-term organizing rather than short-term
mobilizing and aimed to establish sustained relationships with community members, build institutions, and empower the poor.[26] SNCC had
reached out to community leaders such as Dorothy Bolden.[27] "Dr. King
sent SNCC and all the rest of them: 'Look Ms. Bolden up down there,
she'll help you.'"[28] Julian Bond, a founding member of SNCC who subsequently served multiple terms in the Georgia legislature, described
Bolden as a neighborhood activist with "good connections" and sought
her help in his 1965 campaign for the state House of Representatives.[29]
His campaign employed a "new kind of politics" that called attention
to grassroots political engagement and housing, sanitation, welfare,
and medical care for the poor, as well as a minimum wage for domestic workers. In February 1966 SNCC formally launched its short-lived
Atlanta Project to emphasize grassroots urban organizing. Although
SNCC's shift to black power later that year diminished its attention to

local organizing, the group nevertheless had a lasting impact locally and nationally. Bolden truly appreciated the community organizing that SNCC engaged in: "I don't think anybody really knew what [SNCC] meant to low-income people."[30]

Bolden's earliest civil rights activism was a campaign to ensure equal educational access for black children. Although Atlanta had formally desegregated public schools in 1961, inequality persisted. In 1964, as one of her daughters was about to begin eighth grade at Booker T. Washington High School, the district, because of overcrowding, decided to transfer seventh- and eighth-grade students to Central Junior High School, where they would be assigned to a condemned building. Along with other community members and SNCC students, Bolden opposed overcrowded conditions and inadequate facilities, and fought the plan to bus children downtown, demanding that the city build another neighborhood school. According to Bolden, participation of the SNCC students "was excellent. They helped me boycott the school board. We stayed up all night some nights. I would go home so sleepy, then go on to work."[31] As a result of their efforts and Bolden's tenacity, six years later, John F. Kennedy Middle School opened in Vine City.[32]

Although equal access to education was important to her, Bolden's overwhelming passion was for organizing domestic workers. Bolden had worked for several different white families in Atlanta, earning between fifty and sixty dollars a week, and had her share of run-ins with employers. In one case, in early 1940, she was working for a woman in the Peachtree area of Atlanta. After her day's work was done and she was ready to leave, her employer ordered her to wash the dishes. Bolden refused and walked out. When she was several blocks from the house, the police picked her up and took her to the county jail "because I had talked back to a white woman."[33] By the time she formed NDWUA she had worked her way up to what she called a "home manager," supervising other employees for ninety dollars a week.[34]

"There used to be so many hardships, being a maid. Children disrespecting you, mother disrespecting you. You were nursing the children and they were being taught the maid wasn't as good as you and she's not your mother so you don't have to do so-and-so, and they would call you nigger. And we had to take all that stuff. That was the time, you know, blacks were humble, didn't have anything to say. Now they have more pride in themselves."[35]

Despite toiling for years as a domestic, Bolden deeply valued her work. "I love this work. I really love this work," she stated in one interview.[36] "You were doing the cooking, the cleaning, staying after the babies and the children. . . . You were playing the role of a mother as well as the cook as well as the laundry lady as well as the housekeeper as well as guiding the children."[37] But she did believe that how she was treated as a domestic mattered greatly. There were employers who were decent and fair. And there were those who were not.

Without decent working conditions, respect, and fair pay, she argued, many of the goals of the civil rights movement—especially that of legal integration—meant very little. She had come to believe that poverty and economic deprivation were critically important and that you couldn't integrate schools if children didn't have shoes to wear. She resolved to organize household workers as a way to improve the economic status of the poorest African Americans. In seeking assistance, she first spoke to Dr. King. "I had talked with him several months before then that I wanted him to help me organize. . . . He told me 'You do it, and don't let nobody take it.'. . . I did."[38]

Bolden heeded King's advice, although he never lived to see the results. Ironically, King's death in 1968 and the ensuing social upheaval fostered a climate that encouraged a shift in political strategy away from a narrow focus on legal integration. After King's assassination, impoverished black communities in dozens of cities around the country, including Washington, DC, Chicago, and Baltimore, were hotbeds of racial strife, revealing deep-seated tensions around housing, education, and poverty. Although many black activists had addressed economic issues for years, even while simultaneously working to tear down Jim Crow, the widespread urban unrest in the mid- to late-1960s in regions of the country where overt segregation laws were no longer on the books made the goal of "equality as a fact" imperative.

Bolden launched her initiative at a moment that seemed ripe for change. Public transportation, where domestic workers mingled on their way to work, was an important location for organizing. Most cities were racially segregated and the typical pattern was for domestics to board buses in black neighborhoods early in the morning to make the journey to white areas. Domestic-worker organizers handed out flyers at bus stops and initiated conversations with other workers while riding the buses to work.[39] There was, according to Julian Bond, a "network of maids" created by the transportation routes. Maids from around the city boarded buses going downtown, where they transferred to get to their places of employment. This transfer point became a meeting ground, a hub of organizing, and "Dorothy Bolden was in the center of it."[40]

To galvanize support, Bolden rode every city bus line and spoke to hundreds of maids.[41] "I would go around in the bus and ask maids how they would feel about joining if we could organize, and they would say 'I'm for that.'"[42] City buses became impromptu mobile meeting grounds. These "freedom buses" were comparable to the rural freedom schools of the 1960s, sites for political education and organizing as well as consciousness-raising. They were venues where poor women could share grievances and concerns, trade stories of abuse, exchange information about wages and workload, and learn about their rights. In this way, individual domestic workers, engaged in labor that was private in nature, became part of a very public effort.

Shortly after King's assassination in 1968, domestic workers in Atlanta met to talk about reforming paid household work. Bolden's group was not the only one in Atlanta that convened, however. Charles Stinson of the Atlanta Urban League had also brought together a group of domestic workers. The two groups soon merged their efforts, and named Bolden president of the organization.[43] This cadre of seventy women, with aid from the National Urban League and the Georgia Council on Human Relations, met weekly, and continued promoting their efforts to build membership.[44] They ushered in what Bolden called a "new birth" of social activism among this sector of black women workers.[45] That summer they formed the National Domestic Workers Union of America (NDWUA)—a misnomer on two counts, since it was neither national nor a union. Bolden along with Martha Parker, Theresa Ragland, Louise Scott, and a handful of other women formed a charter, established several offices, and opened an employment and training center with set wages. Each member paid dues of one dollar and they met every Thursday at Wheat Street Baptist Church, just two blocks away from Ebenezer.[46]

Bolden led the NDWUA for the next twenty-eight years, maintaining an unswerving commitment to improving working conditions for domestic workers, despite ongoing harassment from hostile whites. Once she received a phone call from a Ku Klux Klan member who threatened to "whip her ass," to which she responded fearlessly. "I told them any time they wanted to, come on over and grab it. You've got a chubby ass to whip."[47] Bolden's husband helped with raising their six children, enabling her to devote herself to the cause. "I had to have somebody that I could trust with my children," she stated. "I trusted my husband."[48] Deeply religious, she had a strong moral sensibility that permeated both her personal and professional life. "I wasn't a money lover. I am that way now, I don't love money, never have."[49] She was also fiercely independent: "I have never been a person who had to take orders from any man."[50] Her respect for King notwithstanding, she was keenly aware that the civil rights movement relied on the participation of women. "Dr. King would always stand out in my mind, he's the strongest one of them. [But] he had help, he had women like me," along with such leaders as Rosa Parks and Fannie Lou Hamer: "Strong women that didn't back down."[51] Bolden and her allies were not the first domestics to organize, nor the first activists to try to reform domestic service, but they did succeed in reaching thousands of Atlanta women—both employers and employees—whom they educated about the rights and responsibilities of domestic work.

Geraldine Roberts: "No Real Hope for a Better Life"

Around the time Dorothy Bolden was pondering how to bring together domestic workers in Atlanta, Geraldine Roberts had already done so in Cleveland, forming the Domestic Workers of America (DWA) in 1965. Roberts started the first documented domestic workers' rights group in the postwar period, built strong alliances with civil rights and black power organizations, and mobilized household workers in Cleveland to fight for job training and higher wages. She overcame the obstacles of limited formal education and single motherhood to become one of the most well-respected leaders in Cleveland, even testifying before the US Commission on Civil Rights in 1967. Through DWA she established a name for herself in local civil rights circles, as well as in national women's rights activism and labor policy debates.

Roberts was born in 1924 in Pawhuska, Oklahoma; her paternal grandmother was reportedly Choctaw Indian and periodically left the reservation to visit Geraldine as a child. Geraldine's father didn't have steady employment, and her mother worked six days a week as a domestic for white families. After a few years of marriage, Geraldine's mother left her father. The family was extremely poor, living on her mother's meager income in a house so small and with such inadequate furnishings that Geraldine slept under a table.

When Geraldine was around five, her mother and father died a few months apart. She and her younger sister Elizabeth were separated from their five brothers and sisters from their mother's previous marriage and went to live with Ella, their maternal grandmother, in Ola, Arkansas. Ella was a well-off landowner and somewhat independent from Ola's largely white community. She was a strong woman, a head of household who took in needy relatives like Geraldine and Elizabeth and one of their cousins. Her economic success was due in part to her multiple entrepreneurial ventures, including running a boardinghouse, washing clothes, catering, and farming. Ella taught—and expected—her children, and those she took in, to work hard. Geraldine started picking cotton when she was six or seven, assisted other sharecropping families harvesting their crops, and catered meals for white families with her grandmother. By the time she was eight she had her first experience as a domestic worker.

Despite the expectation that she work, getting an education had long been a priority for Geraldine. Her step-grandfather, a schoolmaster, encouraged her dream of someday attending Fisk University to become a teacher or a principal. Ola, however, had few educational opportunities for black children. Beginning school at age seven, Geraldine attended a segregated one-room schoolhouse—an unpainted building with no windows and a snake-infested outhouse—that was open only three months a year. The teacher split her time between older and younger children. When in the mid-1930s the town declared it had no money to support the black school, the teacher, a member of the African Methodist Episcopal Church, tutored the children in their homes for nearly two years without pay.

Even when the school was in session, Ella's reliance on her labor made it difficult for Geraldine to attend full-time. After helping her grandmother with the laundry and other chores, most of the school day was over.[52] She longed for a time when she would be able to pursue her education. Her limited opportunity became evident to her when she befriended a white girl named Frances, whom she met through her grandmother's laundry business. The two were the same age and shared a birthday, and they developed a close bond. When Geraldine saw Frances's beautiful whites-only school, she was dismayed by the obvious racial inequities for African Americans.

As Geraldine faced the dawning reality of constraints imposed on her in the Jim Crow South, she began, like Dorothy Bolden, to consider leaving the region altogether. Ironically, her grandmother's relative financial success made migration more complicated. Unlike sharecroppers, who had few economic investments and could easily pick up and move on, "We weren't able to do that then, myself and my sister Elizabeth, [because] . . . my grandparents were property owners. It wasn't that easy to leave at all if you owned property."[53]

At twelve, Geraldine ran away from home to join a traveling colored minstrel show, a bold move for a young African American girl in 1936. Although her initial impetus was to seek educational opportunity, she ended up doing service work for the show—preparing food for the employees, setting the table, and washing dishes. Eventually one of the performers taught her to dance and she began earning three dollars a week as a performer. When the show was on the road in Iowa, Geraldine met James Roberts, a musician. They married, eventually settled in Cleveland, and had three children.

After moving to Cleveland in 1944, Geraldine Roberts tried once more to achieve her lifelong dream of attending school. She saw her lack of a formal education as a handicap that hindered her ability to help her children with their homework, limited her job opportunities, and made her self-conscious at social gatherings. She tried repeatedly, but with little success, to look for well-paying work. "I was told after fillin' out the application I couldn't do very well, that I would, could be hired as a domestic worker."[54] She enrolled in adult reading classes at the Woodland branch of the Cleveland Public Library and East Technical High School. Although an eager learner, as a mother of young children she found night school taxing. Her husband couldn't manage taking care of the kids in her absence, so she stopped attending. But she never lost her passion and desire for education. "There was always this fear that someone would know that I couldn't read and I lived with that through the period of my children growin' up."[55] Several years later, when her children were older and after her eleven-year marriage ended, she would once again go back to school.

After separating from her husband, Roberts was a single mother of three in her twenties living in the Carver Park Housing Projects. She went on welfare for a short time, "then I was told to get a job as a domestic worker."[56] Welfare recipients were frequently pushed into the paid labor force, even when the only jobs available were poorly paid and lacked benefits. Initially, Roberts did day work, cleaning for five dollars a day.[57] But the work was unpredictable. She then got a job as a hotel maid working seven days a week for nineteen dollars. Despite full-time employment, she and her children were desperately poor. She spent the next several years working, raising her children, and trying to make ends meet. After illness forced her to leave her hotel job, she spent some time on welfare before returning to domestic labor.

In the early 1960s, she heard radio broadcasts of civil rights protests and speeches by Martin Luther King and found that the issues, especially school segregation, "seemed to be a part of my life." Roberts, like Bolden, was deeply moved and inspired by civil rights organizing. She saw parallels between her own life and African Americans living in the

Jim Crow South. For Roberts, the campaign for racial equality resonated with her experiences as a black woman of the South and as a domestic worker. "The civil rights reminded me of all the terrible things I learned about in the South, why I couldn't go to school . . . why I wasn't able to attend the all-white school that Frances went to."[58]

Roberts worked in several different white homes and had experiences that shaped her thinking about racial equality and opportunity. Seeing her limited job opportunities as a result of a segregated southern educational system, and her employment as a domestic worker as a product of a similar racial order in the North, Roberts recognized herself as among the disempowered. "The domestic worker has been the kind of worker that has been overlooked and ignored—what I refer to as an invisible worker," she explained. "No one really sees that worker in the labor market and whatever benefits other workers are thinking of or attemptin' to get or are gettin' the domestic worker has not been included."[59] They were routinely treated as inferior to their employers. Although domestic workers occupied the most intimate spaces of the family home, and were entrusted with preparing meals and bathing children, employers often designated separate eating and bathroom facilities for them. "There was a back room that was the bathroom, that would be the bathroom for myself and . . . other household employees . . . all black, and we were all told to use that bathroom, and to *never* use the family bathroom."[60] As Roberts explained, this separation enabled employers to maintain a racial hierarchy.

She was equally disturbed by the quality and quantity of food she was served because it seemed to signify employers' disregard and disrespect for workers. She remembered working for one "very nice lady" in Cleveland. Every morning when she arrived at work, breakfast and a small glass of milk would be sitting on the table for her. One day, noticing that someone had drunk from the glass that had been set out for her, she learned that it had first been offered to the woman's child, who had taken only a few sips.

"I got real sick over that . . . it was something I never forgot. . . . I began to realize something . . . that hey, I wasn't very much of anything, drinkin' left over milk, piece of steak that my husband had last night and he couldn't eat all, he saved it for you. Don' worry, we cut off the part where he was eatin'. He could never eat it all, and it had been sliced off and warmed over from the supper before and the very idea to tell me that meat was on her husband's plate made me sick. I began to think he could have coughed on it and all sorts of things went through, but I didn't dare tell her because she could tell me not to come back any more and I needed the money."[61]

In addition to these strained day-to-day interactions with employers, Roberts began to notice that her experience was not an isolated one; hundreds, perhaps thousands, of African American women in Cleveland seemed to be living similar lives. Her daily bus ride to and from work served as the most visible manifestation of this collective experience. If domestic work took place behind closed doors, the bus route fully exposed the racialized nature of the work. "There was something that I felt that was terribly wrong and very unfair and I began to look at the buses which taken the women into the heights and what I seen." During her morning commute, Roberts took note that all the buses going east early in the morning were filled with black women carrying bags and ready for work wearing their "flat heeled shoes," while "all the buses headed west" carried "painted up dressed up women with white skin."[62]

While these on-the-job experiences formed the basis of a critical perspective for Roberts, growing black activism in Cleveland enabled her to move from critique to action. Local black leaders, especially Ruth Turner of the Congress of Racial Equality (CORE) and Lewis G. Robinson of the Freedom Fighters proved to be instrumental in Roberts's politicization and subsequent campaign to organize household workers. Turner was a public school teacher who quit her job to become executive secretary of Cleveland CORE in the early 1960s.[63] Robinson, a city housing inspector and well-known community activist, founded the Freedom Fighters in 1960 and two years later joined the United Freedom Movement (UFM), an umbrella organization that brought together civil rights groups in Cleveland. A context of heightened racial

tension that advocated greater community empowerment was the backdrop for Roberts's call for household workers to organize themselves.

During the postwar period, the African American community in
Cleveland, like elsewhere around the country, began to transgress the
boundaries of race and power that defined the black urban experience.[64] Cleveland was a primary destination for many who took part in
the Great Migration, both black and white. They flooded the booming
city hoping to secure jobs in the expanding auto, war production, and
steel industries. Unlike their white counterparts, black migrants like
Roberts experienced rampant discrimination in both employment and
housing. Cleveland's black population grew dramatically from 85,000
in 1940 to 250,000 in 1960, leading to a chronic shortage of housing,
poor living conditions, and overcrowded schools in the predominantly
black East Side. White Cleveland residents blocked, sometimes vio-
lently, racial integration of neighborhoods, and those areas where African Americans did eventually make inroads, such as East Cleveland
and Hough, saw rapid white flight.[65] In response, black activists and
their white supporters organized boycotts, pickets, sit-ins, marches,
and community meetings to break the patterns of de facto segregation
and racial inequality in Cleveland. They targeted schools, lunch counters, public facilities, segregated neighborhoods, and businesses that
refused to hire African Americans.[66]

By the early 1960s the battle lines in Cleveland were clearly drawn
around school segregation. On April 7, 1964, several dozen members
of CORE and UFM were at the construction site of Stephen E. Howe
Elementary School in Glenville, a largely black area. The school was being built to assuage black demands for equal access to education. With
rapid demographic change, Cleveland schools were both segregated and
inequitable: white schools had vacant seats, while black schools were
overcrowded and children were forced to attend split-day sessions. The
school board, unwilling to counter white residents' vehement refusal to
integrate schools, settled on building more black schools in largely black
areas. Civil rights activists opposed this plan, believing it reinforced racial segregation. They therefore came out to prevent the building of
Howe Elementary. As protesters formed human barricades to block

construction vehicles, twenty-seven-year-old Reverend Bruce Klunder, a white member of Cleveland CORE and father of two, was accidentally crushed to death by a bulldozer as it backed up. A few weeks later, in response to Klunder's tragic death, as well as the school board's inability to enact meaningful reform, black activists launched a reportedly successful one-day school boycott with students attending freedom schools that taught black history and black culture.[67]

The Klunder death proved pivotal. Activists seized on it as evidence of the failure of city leadership. The incident, along with a lack of response from city officials, who refused to even meet with civil rights activists, led many to feel disaffected. In 1964, Robinson, a longtime advocate of self-defense, formed the Medgar Evers Rifle Club with the intention of protecting civil rights activists when the police failed to do so.[68] He was especially critical of the double standard applied by police, who arrested peaceful black protesters while ignoring violent white agitators. CORE leader Ruth Turner, who had witnessed Klunder's death, found herself increasingly skeptical of nonviolence as an effective political strategy.[69] To Turner and Robinson, community empowerment seemed the most obvious solution, and they proved to be two of Roberts's most ardent supporters. Roberts's commitment to organizing poor black women dovetailed with this desire to empower black inner-city residents.[70]

Roberts was drawn into the movement, attending demonstrations and picketing. "And there I was with a picket sign for the first time," she said, "and not really knowin' that meanin' of even carrying a picket sign"—nor could she read their slogans, "Down with Segregation" and "Discrimination in Employment," though she fully embraced their message. Acutely aware of the risks associated with activism, Roberts believed the danger was outweighed by the obstacles and limited opportunities she had long confronted. "And if it meant me carryin' a picket sign, if it also meant that I could get injured or die, I didn't think it meant much difference because I had already mentally, or I was dead. I couldn't read; I was sort of trapped in society; the best I could do was to help someone else."[71]

Like Bolden, Roberts's involvement in the civil rights movement proved transformative as she experienced the vast gulf between the movement's calls for human dignity and self-worth and her daily life as a domestic worker. She began to ascribe her exploitation as a household worker to the legacy of slavery. Roberts worked for six weeks for one family that seemed perfectly satisfied with her work. One day the employer asked her to clean the chandelier and the outside of the windows, tasks that she did not see as part of her job description and refused to do. The employer fired her without pay. Roberts angrily charged that she was being treated like a slave, perhaps aware that it would strike a chord in the context of racial strife in Cleveland. Her employer denied that race had anything to do with it and claimed the issue was one of obedience: "I don't only throw out black girls. I throw out white girls, too. You're not the first one I threw out of my house. It's not because you're black . . . we don't have that racial stuff in here. If you don't do what we tell you to do, then you get the hell out of here."[72]

In 1965, when she started organizing household workers, Roberts was employed part-time as a cleaner at a penthouse in Shaker Heights for nine dollars a day, and worked alongside two full-time employees— a cook and a maid. The work environment was meticulously managed and controlled, with separate servants' quarters, restricted telephone usage, and an intercom system that the employer used to monitor employees and prohibit them from speaking to one another, even during lunch.[73] "I got kind of an opinion that she was like a white mistress or something over black workers," Roberts said.[74] "I felt as if I was probably the size of an ant or something. An ant, say, talking to a person who's standing in the door of a fifty or a hundred thousand dollar home and I had absolutely nothing, and to tell this person something was pretty hard to do."[75] At this job it dawned on Roberts how employers viewed household workers: "I wasn't aware that persons looked upon household employment as dumb people or people who didn't get an education, that there was something wrong with us. . . . I realized more and more, that there was something wrong with me, what was I? Why was I treated like this?"[76]

That particularly difficult work environment served as an entry point for Roberts's commitment to organizing domestic workers. "I felt it was an unusual and terrible place to work. . . . Maybe it's good that I had the experience because I think out of that very home grew the idea, a very strong idea to do something about workin' conditions for household employees. I think it inspired the whole idea out of that particular penthouse."[77] Roberts mustered her courage and began to speak up and assert her rights. She had conversations with her two coworkers, telling them they deserved better and that it was time to organize and form a union.[78] One of them agreed wholeheartedly: "Well, Gerry, we need to get a union or somethin'. You need to do something about it," she said, and handed her a dollar. The other maid also donated a dollar.

With her two-dollar donation in hand, Roberts began to consider how to establish an organization to rally other domestic workers. Ruth Turner encouraged Roberts to take the lead, and helped plan and publicize an initial meeting. Roberts and her cofounders passed out five hundred leaflets announcing the new organization. Twenty-one people showed up to the first meeting in September 1965 at St. James AME Church and testified about their working conditions.[79] Bolden recalled of that historic day, "The women came wide eyed and proud that such a meeting had been called. They were so ready and couldn't believe. Different ones said it was long overdue. They were so glad that somebody decided to do something about this."[80] Subsequent meetings had much higher attendance rates, sometimes with over two hundred people.[81] The organization they founded, Domestic Workers of America, sought to expose and reform the unfair working conditions of private household workers. As Roberts put it: "If we get sick or lose a job, our only recourse is welfare. We have no hospitalization, no transportation, no real hope for a better life."[82]

DWA opened an office on 5120 Woodland Avenue at the Bruce Klunder Freedom House, named after the martyred clergyman. Members were interested in raising wages to fourteen dollars a day, improving job standards, and gaining respect for workers. As Lula Primas, secretary of DWA explained, "Many times [employers] don't know your name or where you live, and don't care."[83] DWA opened a placement office to help workers obtain jobs and launched a clothing drive for needy schoolchildren.[84] Roberts worked in the DWA office part-time, while still engaging in domestic work. She believed her work with

DWA filled an important gap in labor organizing by focusing on a neglected sector of the workforce. She wanted to illuminate how domestic workers had been "completely overlooked" by labor unions.[85] Despite its agenda of organizing workers, DWA received little financial support from donors, foundations, or mainstream unions. At its peak, about six hundred women of different racial backgrounds were involved in DWA in Cleveland.[86]

Shortly after she began to organize, Roberts was fired from her job in Shaker Heights.[87] Because of her notoriety, it was difficult to find employment, and she faced various forms of harassment. "Some said they wouldn't hire colored ones anyway and are there any white domestic workers in the Greater Cleveland area."[88] Others retorted with common stereotypes that African American household workers were lazy, prone to theft, and didn't bathe.[89] Once, at two o'clock in the morning, she received a threatening call: "Hey, nigger, why don't you get out of town. We don't need your kind around here."[90] According to Roberts, "They were opposed to activities and I was tryin' to build a union."[91] In spite of these demoralizing setbacks, others showed their support. A woman engaged in organizing nurses offered her a job. Notably, she asked Roberts to name her salary.

Roberts's leadership role placed her in the national spotlight, which in turn heightened her anxiety about her lack of education and class background. She worried that her illiteracy would prevent her from being an effective leader. "I had a fear after I got into it. I seemed like I wanted to run from the whole thing. I felt how could I do all this when I couldn't even read very well."[92] She began attending evening classes at East Technical High School to improve her reading, and ultimately, her confidence grew as she earned a reputation as an advocate for poor women. Her organizing efforts were in addition to her responsibilities at her job and taking care of her own household. She found herself "stayin' up late in the middle of the night ironing and gettin' necessary things" completed. But she had no regrets.

In 1966, Roberts joined a contingent of the Cleveland NAACP to participate in the Meredith March in Jackson, Mississippi. James Meredith, the first African American admitted into the University of Mississippi, had organized a "March Against Fear" from Memphis, Tennessee, to Jackson, Mississippi, to encourage African Americans to vote. During the course of the march, Meredith was shot by Klansmen. In response to the shooting, thousands of civil rights activists from around the country pledged to go to Mississippi to continue the march. It became a milestone in civil rights history, where Stokely Carmichael popularized the phrase "black power" and signaled a shift in the strategy and goals of many civil rights activists. Roberts was filled with anxiety, but also optimism, as she embarked on her first major civil rights protest outside Cleveland. "I considered [it] one of the most exciting points in my life in that particular demonstration with Dr. King and the thousands upon thousands of demonstrators and the planes overhead and the fear [that] hung over that area as if no one knew what would happen."[93] "I had felt," she continued, "that I was leaving Ohio, going into the state of Mississippi to give my life as something that I felt was right, that every man, every woman, every child on earth had a right to freedom and pursuit of happiness."

The emerging black power movement provoked wider concern among policymakers and government officials about how to empower the poor. The War on Poverty included as part of its goals community-action programs that mandated maximum feasible participation of the poor, providing resources and intellectual support for the underprivileged. DWA's agenda overlapped with these broader concerns, but put its energies specifically into mobilizing poor black women.

Although she had been deeply involved in the black power movement, and the politics of race profoundly shaped her understanding of domestic work, Roberts and DWA made a commitment to including white women in the organization. Roberts understood that poverty and a lack of education pushed women into domestic service and kept them there. Although only a small number of white domestics joined DWA, it remained committed to interracial organizing. "We did accept white domestic workers on the far West Side. They accepted us when they read about us. Her being poor realizing that even though her skin was white it didn't make any difference. She was a poor woman in the United States and so it didn't make any difference."[94]

Through their participation in DWA, domestic workers experienced a newfound level of respect both on and off the job. Their collective efforts led to a greater understanding that their labor was essential to the running of the household and that they deserved recognition. "You begin to build an inward pride that you never had before. Poor people can say something; women can say something; a poor woman can say something and it will be meaningful and the lady who has everything, we learned for the first time, that they really needed us." DWA members worked to cultivate and nurture relationships with the women who hired them. They saw employers as an important constituency: "We need the cooperation of the employers. We need the good will of the housewives who hire us."[95] Roberts believed that because of this effort many employers changed their "hard tough looks," were amenable to domestic-worker requests and willing to discuss wages, working conditions, and responsibilities.[96] The building of alliances with employers would continue to shape the struggle for household rights over the life of the movement.

Forming a Movement

Bolden and Roberts were in many ways ordinary working-class African American women. They were not a part of the African American elite—or the "talented tenth," to use the phrase popularized by W. E. B. Du Bois—nor were they self-appointed leaders of the black community. They had little formal education and spoke in a southern black vernacular, which was distinct from the polished, well-schooled oratory of Martin Luther King. Their political sensibility was crafted in the black neighborhoods where they encountered civil rights activists, on the public transportation system where they mingled with other domestic workers, and in the white homes where employers treated them as servants. They had dreams, and sometimes followed those dreams far from the towns where they were born. But they were also hindered by disability, illiteracy, and limited opportunities, and struggled with the push and pull of everyday life. Most domestic workers who became local leaders were longtime community activists involved in a range of issues, from housing to education to economic justice. Thus their activism was often neighborhood-based rather than occupation-based.

Black domestic workers had for generations engaged in covert day-to-day resistance—what James Scott calls the "hidden transcript"—as a way to maintain their dignity in an occupation that aimed to degrade and disempower.[97] The emergence of an organized, visible, and vocal campaign marks a shift in how domestic workers asserted their rights. The passion for social change exhibited by women like Dorothy Bolden and Geraldine Roberts and their deep desire to improve the lot of other women like themselves grew out of the civil rights movement, which inspired them with its example of courage and tenacity and also created a network of support.[98] They learned, perhaps most importantly, that there was strength in numbers.

The struggle for domestic workers' rights brings a new angle and greater nuance to the meaning of black freedom and labor organizing. Household workers advocated racial equality, women's rights, and raising occupational standards. Their concern for economic autonomy echoed the goals of liberal antipoverty warriors, civil rights activists, and black power advocates. But DWA's focus on working-class black women also distinguished it from many other efforts. And while they might be "labor feminists," as Sue Cobble identifies them, they had little tangible connection to other women's labor activists or union leaders.[99] Much of their organizing was outside the union movement. They modeled a grassroots working-class leadership and an approach to organizing that relied on community building. Theirs was a class-based struggle that centered on an analysis of race and gender. They recognized the labor of social reproduction as racialized work that had often been considered outside the boundaries of legitimate employment. They reached out to domestic workers of all racial backgrounds, as well as middle-class women, to support them in their campaigns. Motivated by the civil rights movement, they came to believe that black freedom could best be achieved by mobilizing domestic workers to press for improvements in their occupation. And that resolve led them down a path that would result in the formation of the first national organization of domestic workers, the Household Technicians of America, which would push for reform of this age-old occupation.

Black domestic workers such as Dorothy Bolden and Geraldine Roberts, who were rooted in this black working-class culture, embraced their status as domestic workers. Rather than reject or deny this identity, they claimed it and sought to bring recognition and respect to the work they did. Their organizing, and the organizing of other women like them, was part of a process of crafting a new identity for domestic workers.

CHAPTER 3

A New Day for Domestic Workers

We refuse to be your mammies, nannies, aunties,
uncles, girls, handmaidens any longer.

—EDITH BARKSDALE SLOAN

Born in the Bronx into a working-class African American family, civil rights activist Edith Barksdale Sloan had never been employed as a domestic when she was chosen in January 1969 to head the National Committee on Household Employment (NCHE), an organization of mostly middle-class women committed to reform. Despite having little firsthand experience of the occupation, Sloan's family had a long tradition of domestic work. As a child she had heard stories about her own family history and about the slave market of the Great Depression, which connected her to the history of domestic-worker exploitation as head of the NCHE.

Individuals, such as Sloan, with a family history of domestic work shared their stories as they set out to build a movement. The stories of past injustices, especially those of the household-labor slave market, resonated with and were reclaimed by African American household-worker activists in the 1960s and 1970s. They were repeated in testimonies and informal gatherings, and illustrated the vulnerability of domestic workers as well as the occupation's racial character and ties to the history of slavery. In the context of civil rights and black freedom organizing, references to the slave market proved to be particularly powerful. Storytelling became a form of activism and a means of political mobilization.

In a feature article in *Essence* magazine in 1974, Sloan wrote about the stories she was told as a child about the "Bronx Slave Market" of the

1930s: "It resembled a slave auction with the prospective buyers looking over the workers like so many head of cattle; looking for the strongest and sturdiest."[1] The stories merged with her personal and family history. "Although I never actually saw the 'Slave Market,' I do remember seeing the women from our neighborhood on their way to cleaning someone else's house. One of them was my great-aunt Rie. She would leave every morning about 7:30 with her housedress in a satchel, on her way to Mrs. So-and-So's house to do her 'day's work.' She would return before dark with her satchel stuffed full of leftover matzos, chicken fat and gefilte fish, and maybe a garment or two that her employer had given her. . . . Aunt Rie always looked forward to her sixty-fifth birthday so she could retire and draw her deceased husband's social security. She did retire at age 65—and died the next year with every ounce of strength worked out of her."[2] "I don't ever remember her arriving home with a bonus or her ever receiving paid sick leave or a paid holiday or a paid vacation."[3] Her aunt's story was one of years of hard labor, long days, and very little pay-off at the end; her life seemed to have been given over to her employers.

Education and opportunity ultimately ended this occupational quagmire for Edith's mother and herself. Her mother was raised in Laurens, South Carolina, by her grandmother, Adoline. Adoline, a household worker, was raped repeatedly by her employer when she was a teenager and bore two children by him. At the age of twenty, she quit domestic work and started her own catering business.[4] Edith's mother was sent to New York when she was fourteen to live with her aunt Rie and her husband, "with hopes of breaking the domestic cycle by attending college." Edith's mother went to vocational school and became an expert dressmaker. Both her mother and her father, a postal worker and electrician, exposed her to prominent African American political leaders such as Mary McLeod Bethune and Ralph Bunche, instilling in her a political and cultural sensibility. According to Edith, "She and my father vowed that their children would all have the opportunity to go to college. And we did."[5]

Edith Barksdale attended Hunter College of the City University of New York, one of the city's premier public institutions, graduating in 1959 with a degree in international affairs. Filled with passion to help the less fortunate, she taught in Lebanon for a period and then traveled to the Philippines to work with sick and disabled children under the auspices of the Peace Corps.

While she was abroad, two events in 1963 changed the course of her life: the Ku Klux Klan bombing of the Sixteenth Street Baptist Church in Birmingham, Alabama, that killed four African American girls attending Sunday school, and the assassination of President John F. Kennedy. These brutally violent events prompted Sloan to return to the United States and join the burgeoning civil rights movement. After a brief internship at the Eleanor Roosevelt Memorial Foundation, she worked with the New York Urban League to register people to vote and address housing violations. In 1965 she married attorney Ned Sloan and moved to Washington, DC. The couple had four sons. Edith Sloan earned a law degree from Catholic University School of Law and continued her commitment to activism, working as a public information specialist with the US Commission on Civil Rights; in 1967 she helped organize the commission's National Conference on Race and Education.[6]

Edith Barksdale Sloan speaking at the first national conference of household workers, in 1971. (Mary McLeod Bethune Council House National Historic Site, National Archives for Black Women's History)

Under her leadership beginning in 1969, the NCHE brought together workers such as Dorothy Bolden and Geraldine Roberts at a national convention that led to the establishment of the Household Technicians of America (HTA), the first-ever national organization of household workers. Sloan shifted the political orientation of the NCHE from the needs of employers to the rights of domestic workers. Less interested in training domestic workers to expand the pool of available employees than on empowering workers in the workplace, Edith Sloan's family history and personal connection to domestic work proved to be significant in her leadership. Her family stories of domestic work and those of other domestic workers were central to building the movement for household workers and helped frame her understanding of the occupation. These narratives became the starting point for arguments for reform.

REFORMING DOMESTIC LABOR

The NCHE, perhaps the most important middle-class organization committed to reforming domestic labor throughout the twentieth century, had two incarnations. The first, lasting from 1928 to 1942, advocated voluntary employer contracts as a way to improve working conditions and increase the number of low-wage domestic laborers.[7] The second grew out of the President's Commission on the Status of Women (PCSW) established under President Kennedy in 1961. Esther Peterson, head of the Women's Bureau in the Department of Labor, was instrumental in planning the commission. The commission's report, issued in 1963, drew attention to the poor conditions of household employees and the need for "the reorganization of home maintenance." The report advocated training, specialization, and placement of workers by private companies, in addition to the extension of unemployment insurance to household workers.[8] In June 1964, the Women's Bureau called a meeting of national organizations to discuss the status of household employment, which formed the basis of a newly constituted NCHE. The new NCHE was concerned not only with recruiting and training workers, but improving their status and compensation, and it was at the forefront of efforts to reform domestic work in the 1960s. It consisted of a group of liberal professional women—many of whom employed household workers—committed to upgrading the occupation. They were driven by both social justice concerns about the workforce as well as the perceived needs of the growing numbers of women who wanted to hire household help. Although emerging out of the 1961 commission, the NCHE was more broadly a result of decades of labor activism by women like Esther Peterson, Dorothy Height, Frieda Miller, Pauline Newman, and others. Much like the radical black feminists of the 1930s, these labor feminists had written about and lobbied for reform of household labor.[9]

Frieda Miller, a longtime white labor activist and economist, had since the Depression advocated reforming domestic labor. Appointed New York State industrial commissioner in 1938, she helped establish employment offices for domestic workers in 1941 to eliminate the notorious slave markets.[10] When Miller headed the US Women's Bureau from 1944 to 1953, she pushed for minimum wage and social security coverage for domestic workers. She also brought an international perspective to this work. She spent the war years in London as a labor advisor to the ambassador and, while abroad, was impressed by government programs and policies that protected both paid and unpaid household workers. She was also a US delegate to the International Labor Organization, a United Nations body that established international labor standards, and in that forum pushed to address the inequities in domestic work. In 1951, in an essay on the shortage of domestic workers in the United States for the journal *International Labour Review*, Miller argued that the growing number of women in the workforce necessitated an expansion of the number of available domestic workers. "The provision of a sufficient number of well-trained, well-qualified household workers is therefore a matter of grave and widespread concern in the United States. Equally important are measures to assure to this larger group of workers social status, economic security, pay, and working conditions comparable to those of other workers."[11] Miller had come to believe that addressing the glaring inequality in household labor was essential for justice and fairness and for meeting the needs of all women. This goal was summed up in a 1946 article she wrote for the *New York Times* titled, "Can We Lure Martha Back to the Kitchen?"[12]

Esther Peterson, a white labor leader who had worked for the AFL-CIO, was a longtime advocate of racial equality and civil rights. For her, like Miller, international reforms, especially in Europe, deeply influenced her thinking. In the late 1940s, Peterson traveled to Sweden with her family and remained in Europe for nearly a decade. Intrigued by domestic worker organizing there, she hoped to use the Swedish case as a model for upgrading US domestic labor. The Swedish Domestic Worker Act of 1944 made employment contracts standard, regulated hours, wages, and living and working conditions, and created a structure for mediating disputes. Based on her experience in Sweden, Peterson wrote a lengthy report for the US Women's Bureau that recommended vocational training and legal standards. In 1961 she was appointed head of the Women's Bureau and assistant secretary of labor and made the plight of low-income women a priority.

Peterson collaborated with Dorothy Height, of the National Council of Negro Women (NCNW), a prominent leader in the African American community.[13] Height's mother had worked as a nurse in a black hospital in Richmond, Virginia. In 1916, when Dorothy was four years old, her family moved from Virginia to Rankin, Pennsylvania, in search of economic opportunity. Her father worked as a building and painting contractor. But her mother, unable to find a job in a hospital, did domestic work instead, earning three dollars a day plus carfare. "I remember best a family named Johnston, for whom my mother worked over the longest period. My mother felt very close to Mrs. Johnston and her daughter Mary, but my feelings were decidedly mixed: I both liked and hated Mary Johnston. On the one hand, it seemed that during every important event in my life, my mother had to be at Mary's house, and that bothered me. On the other hand, Mary was about my age and size and had beautiful clothes, many of which I inherited."[14] In 1957 Height assumed leadership of the NCNW, which had in the 1930s called for minimum wage protection for domestic workers and supported unionization. Height continued the organization's commitment to issues of concern to working-class black women and was also key in the formation of the NCHE. Two decades later, the NCNW would be instrumental in preserving the archival material of the movement of household workers.

In the 1950s and 1960s, these female activists spearheaded efforts to alleviate the shortage of domestic labor and improve working conditions for household workers. They criticized the exclusion of domestic work from New Deal labor legislation and the widening gap between protected and unprotected labor, especially as organized labor won more benefits for its members. They considered professionalization, unionization, training, and improving pay and working conditions their top priorities. Peterson, Miller, and Height helped form the NCHE, which eventually represented twenty-three organizations with an interest in domestic labor, including the National Urban League, the YWCA, the National Association of Colored Women's Clubs, the National Council of Catholic Women, the American Public Welfare Association, the National Council of Jewish Women, and the National Council of Negro Women. It held its first annual meeting in September 1965, and two years later Frieda Miller was elected chairman.[15]

One of the central preoccupations of the NCHE was the increasing number of women entering the workforce, which generated the need for a reliable pool of domestic workers. Women's labor force participation rate increased steadily in the postwar period from 34 percent in 1950 to 38 percent in 1960 to 43 percent in 1970.[16] Perhaps more important is the employment rate of married women with children under the age of six. While 12 percent worked in 1950, by 1970 30 percent worked.[17] Reforming domestic work, the NCHE argued, was essential to meet the needs of working women. Linking the occupation to women employed outside the home framed paid domestic labor not as a luxury or a status symbol but a necessity. Indeed, the occupation had evolved since World War II. As US society modernized, so too did domestic labor and the employer-employee relationship. Victorian notions of women defined by the domestic sphere were less applicable, as were idealized images of corseted, elaborately dressed women attended by a staff of servants. By the mid-twentieth century, assumptions about the role of middle-class women were changing. The boundaries confining women to the home had weakened with women's increasing access to education and entry into the workforce.

But even middle-class women not entering the labor force hired help for cleaning and child care in response to changing expectations of motherhood and pressure to devote attention to children and engage in civic and charity work. Postwar ideologies of motherhood and family drew firm boundaries around the private household. With the expansion of suburbs, the middle-class home became more isolated and was cast as a refuge from the demands of work and the market. Middle-class women were expected to devote more time to caring for their children, perhaps best illustrated by the 1946 publication of Benjamin Spock's best seller, *The Common Sense Book of Baby and Child Care*, which encouraged mothers to be more nurturing and establish strong bonds with their children. These ideologies affected the lives of domestic workers as well, since they were more often relegated to cleaning and less often to nurturing and were similarly isolated in white suburbs. Although many domestic workers still engaged in child care, the celebration of domesticity in the 1950s fostered middle-class women's interest in the nurturing aspects of domesticity and led to a growing demand for household help to carry out other household responsibilities.[18]

In the postwar period, domestic labor was less about serving tea to society ladies, and more about completing essential household chores. The availability of paid domestic labor was essential for maintaining the middle-class gendered social order. Women could take jobs outside the home and engage in civic activities as long as domestic duties were taken care of. This arrangement left intact the basic breadwinner ideology and gendered division of labor—men could still provide for the family and didn't have to do "women's work"—but women could push the circumscribed gender boundaries. Although social status may have been less important for hiring household labor, romanticized notions of the racialized past and patterns of servitude still sometimes seeped into the occupation. Because the workforce was largely women of color, unequal notions of gender justified and informed domestic labor.[19]

Coupled with these cultural shifts was a change in the character of the work itself. Over the course of the twentieth century, domestic work became widespread, with more households hiring part-time domestic workers and fewer maintaining a large staff of employees. Domestic workers were more likely to be a single employee in a household taking on multiple roles as cook, housecleaner, and child care worker or working for a family one or two days a week. Technological advances that eased the burden of maintaining a home contributed to this change. It was no longer necessary, for example, to hire someone to do only laundry with the invention of the automatic washing machine. Along with this came a process of de-skilling and multitasking. Household workers were also changing the character of the occupation by insisting on day work. Most household workers in the postwar period continued to work after having families of their own. These largely women-of-color workers began in the 1920s to refuse live-in work. Domestic workers more commonly went home to their own families at the end of the day, and may even have worked for several families in a given week.[20]

Middle-class women's demand for workers, combined with continuing inequality and low wages, prompted many to leave the occupation and resulted in a shortage of workers. There was a growing sense among employers that domestic workers in the United States were too demanding, very costly, or not properly trained.[21] Popular magazines were filled with stories of middle-class women unable to find household help. Employers were not, according to *Life* magazine in 1961, "rich or idle," but working wives and mothers of large families who "desperately need help around the house." One mother wrote in her diary, which was later published in a magazine, about her frustrating attempt to hire help: "There were some who would not scrub floors. Some couldn't cook. Some would only cook. Some wanted ridiculous salaries or wouldn't work weekends."[22]

Training became one solution. The call for training emerged in part from perceptions about the cultural distance between employers and employees, who it was believed didn't share the same values, ethics, or knowledge as middle-class employees. Mrs. Brooks Wiley Maccraken, a former social worker living in Cleveland Heights, was so exasperated by the lack of "good" help, she started her own domestic-worker training program. One evening after hosting a party, she heard the cleaning woman dump all her precious silver into the sink. "So, I began think-ing, and I guess because I'm a former social worker I thought about the possibility of training women to care for fine things like silver and china and linen, of teaching them how to set and serve a table, so they would be of real help to women giving parties. It seemed to me if women acquired a specialty like this they would earn more money—and both groups would be happier."[23] In 1960 Maccraken established the Party Aide Training Program at the Jane Addams Vocational School in Cleveland to create a better-prepared pool of workers for middle-class homes.[24] The view that the needs of both middle-class women and poor women would be met through domestic-service training programs gained currency.

The mutual dependencies of middle-class and poor women were perhaps best illustrated in a 1967 *Woman's Day* magazine article called "Help Wanted!" It began by profiling a young mother who took a job as a school librarian but needed help taking care of her children. It also featured a woman who had been on welfare for eighteen years and was placed as a domestic in the librarian's home by the welfare employment agency. This "matching" was deemed to be ideal. According to the li-brarian: "I just love my work! I'm doing what I was trained to do. Yet the house and our children aren't neglected either." The former welfare recipient, equally happy, explained: "Now I'm off welfare and we're all doing fine. I work for some real nice people." In this scenario, encour-aging women, especially women on welfare, to enter the field of do-mestic service would be universally beneficial. They would move off the unemployment or welfare rolls and into permanent jobs. And middle-class women would get much-needed help.

The arguments for moving poor women from welfare into domestic service were part of a larger anti-welfare discourse that saw welfare as a social ill, rather than an important source of support for single mothers, as was the case when it was established in the 1930s. The growing num-bers of middle-class women entering the workforce bolstered critiques of welfare, since the idea that women should stay home with children was weakening. But the anti-welfare discourse in the 1960s was also cast through a racial and gendered lens, where women of color in particular were considered undeserving of state assistance and expected to work—especially when there was a shortage of domestic workers. According to one report: "This demand [for domestic labor] is not being met, although there are millions of unemployed and underemployed people who are seeking decent jobs."[25]

The NCHE believed that improving working conditions and making domestic service more attractive would simultaneously reduce the welfare and unemployment rolls and enable middle-class women to enter the workforce. Mary Dublin Keyserling, appointed head of the Women's Bureau in 1964 after Esther Peterson stepped down, explained at a 1967 NCHE conference on household labor: "The great growth in the employment of women and our rising living standards have increased the demand for household assistance. Many women whose services are needed as doctors, social workers, and teachers and in other essential occupations cannot combine work and family responsibilities unless they can count on competent, trained people to give them a hand at home. Many others also need household services, now inadequately available, if they are to make larger contributions as volunteers or in other types of needed community activity."[26] In conjunction with the Women's Bureau, the NCHE created a pamphlet for employers that summed up this goal of meeting the needs of employed middle-class women: *If ONLY I Could Get Some Household Help!* It advised training workers as well as ensuring fair wages, defined hours, and mutual respect.[27]

The status of the occupation—the stigma, low wages, and poor working conditions—the NCHE argued, deterred women from entertaining it and resulted in a shortage. African Americans, they maintained, would return to domestic service if job standards were improved and the master-servant character of the relationship redefined. This meant, in particular, revaluing the labor. Dorothy Height called for the need to recognize that there was "glory" in the work.[28] "Some of these words like 'maid' and 'domestic' are demeaning and I think we must use more professional terms. . . . Let's treat household employment as a profession in which workers have a contract and are assured fair hours and compensation, as well as coverage by our protective labor laws." In addition, the norms and expectations governing the occupation seemed outdated. Peterson suggested: "Household employment is one of the last holdouts against modernization" and must be transformed by encouraging specialization and professionalization and enabling domestic workers to assert their rights.[29] She argued: "This [change] is possible if we bring this occupation into the 20th century, if we give it dignity, provide training for it, and educate employers to recognize the hiring of household help as a business proposition."[30] Elizabeth Koontz, appointed as the first African American woman to head the Women's Bureau in 1969, summed up the goals of the NCHE most succinctly when she said, "We must change the workers; we must change the conditions of the industry; and we must change the attitudes of the employers."[31] The NCHE adopted a program of education, training, and a voluntary Code of Standards for employers that called for a minimum wage of $1.60 an hour, overtime pay, a written agreement of work responsibilities, paid holidays, vacations, sick days, social security, and a "professional working relationship." The Code, which was also the basis for a model contract, became one way to establish a more businesslike employer-employee relationship.[32]

The NCHE launched eight demonstration projects underwritten by the Ford Foundation and the US Department of Labor's Manpower Development and Training Program in 1966 to experiment with ways of reforming domestic service.[33] The main goal was to create worker-run cooperatives or corporate entities with the hope that the "business model will transform the occupation."[34] The NCHE's pilot projects were run by social service agencies, nonprofit organizations, advocacy groups, business leaders, or middle-class individuals with "local expertise" and designed to raise the status and pay of domestic workers and to provide trained, reliable, and professional service to employers. The YWCA-sponsored Household Employment Project based in Chicago, for example, ran seminars for employers on maintaining a professional relationship and training employees in homemaking skills. Another project, Household Management in New York, employed workers and sent them out to private individuals as needed for elder care, catering, child care, or cleaning. Workers were guaranteed full-time work, workers' compensation, unemployment, sick leave, and a paid vacation. The Homemaker Service Demonstration Project at Kansas State University ran a four-week, live-in training program for women over age forty-five that prepared them to work for a family during periods of crisis. They were trained for "infant and child care, personal care, accident prevention, working with children, home nursing, understanding needs of the elderly, dealing with death, meal planning, buying, and money management."[35] SURGE, a Virginia-based employee-owned cooperative, sent out teams of workers for cleaning jobs. The range of projects the NCHE supported reflected the multiple ways it hoped to transform domestic work: from offering higher wages and benefits, to educating employers, to training workers, to introducing a third party into the employer-employee relationship. While the entrepreneurship model had the potential to put the power in the hands of household workers, most of the NCHE demonstration projects were not owned or managed by household workers but by middle-class advocates.

In the mid-1960s, the NCHE designed programs with the needs of employers at the forefront and offered a narrative of domestic work that linked the fate of middle-class and poor women. The popular press reflected concerns about the shortage of good domestic help, which hindered women's ability to mother and constrained their options to enter the workforce. Rather than advocating a cheap, compliant, and deferential workforce, the NCHE's solution was one of a modern workforce with guaranteed basic rights and labor protections. Although their emphasis bent slightly toward the needs of middle-class women, theirs was a progressive vision that sought to shed the culture of servitude that some employers aimed to re-create.

At the same time, the NCHE's reforms reflected a degree of paternalism. In most of the early projects and campaigns, the power to define the terms of reform was in the hands of middle-class advocates. One NCHE-funded project, for example, in addition to pushing for higher wages, taught black women grooming, personality development, and proper diction through repetition of the phrase "The rain in Spain stays mainly on the plain," an approach that seemed to emerge from employers' desire for ideal servants.[36] Household workers themselves played only a minimal role in discussions of how to transform domestic labor. This top-down approach would be replaced with a grassroots one, however, which was prompted by the upsurge of domestic-worker organizing and the growing calls among activists and reformers for empowerment and participation. The NCHE would soon find itself on an altered course as it brought together the local domestic workers' rights groups in 1971 into a national organization, the Household Technicians of America.

SHIFTING POLITICS OF THE NCHE

A turning point for the NCHE came in 1969, with the hiring of Edith Barksdale Sloan as executive director and the establishment of a committee of household workers. Two years later, a Ford Foundation grant enabled the NCHE to convene a national meeting of local household-worker groups. Interest in reaching out to household workers was not entirely new. Conversations about a membership arm of domestic workers were first raised in 1967, although initially little came of this.[37] But Edith Sloan's leadership proved decisive in moving the organization in this direction. Unhappy with NCHE's previous emphasis, she believed that "unless the women had a really strong group to support their demands, the gains of better wages and benefits would be lost."[38]

At its annual meeting in March 1970, the NCHE board formally requested a conference of household workers. In the long term the NCHE hoped to see an independent national organization of workers.[39] It had come to believe that reforming domestic service could best be achieved by placing power in the hands of workers to determine for themselves how the occupation should be changed. This was the beginning of an effort to involve domestic workers and middle-class reformers and involve workers in the transformation of household labor. And most NCHE members expressed enthusiasm for this shift. According to one board member, Uvelia Bowen of HEART in Philadelphia, this initiative would mobilize a "cadre of household workers to decide their destiny in America . . . and this Committee [should] be ready to stand behind them and to make sure that they move in the proper channels to decide their destiny." Anna Halsted, chairman of the NCHE board, concluded: "I believe that this is one of the most significant and exciting assignments which the National Committee on Household Employment could undertake in our program to improve the social and economic status of household workers."[40]

The NCHE's turn to organizing domestic workers was part of a larger political sensibility in the late 1960s and early 1970s that advocated empowerment and self-determination of ordinary people. Anticolonial movements, the struggle for black power, poor people's campaigns, the student movement, and women's organizing all articulated a need for people to act on their own behalf rather than be acted upon. The civil rights movement was one model of how masses of people could participate in social change. Acknowledging people's agency and giving them the opportunity to take control of their own futures was rooted in the idea that those experiencing a problem understood it best and could offer the most appropriate solutions. This sentiment was also reflected in the federal government's War on Poverty, launched in 1964, which mandated "maximum feasible participation" of the poor in constructing programs to combat poverty.

The NCHE's decision to ally with and support the self-empowerment of domestic workers by bringing them together into a separate organization fundamentally altered the political and intellectual direction of the NCHE. Edith Sloan and other advocates of this shift looked at domestic work not in terms of the persistent problems experienced by employers, but in terms of the history of black women and inequities in the labor market. Their new framework in thinking about domestic work drew out a longer historical thread between the occupation and black women's struggle for dignity, equality, and justice and it created the space for domestic workers to speak out. Earlier black women activists like Marvel Cooke and labor feminists like Frieda Miller had waited for this development for years. In fact, Miller had written in 1951: "I hope to see the day when household workers will come together in an organization, and elect delegates and take a conscious pride in their skilled specialties."[41] That day had come.

Under Sloan's leadership, these hopes turned to reality and the NCHE increasingly centered the voices, stories, and leadership of domestic workers to reform the occupation. On the national level, it facilitated the circulation and dissemination of domestic-worker stories, which strengthened organizing on the local level and enabled domestic workers to develop a collective identity. Sloan's story, and others like it, became an important component of domestic-worker organizing because it created a shared history and helped build solidarity, political consciousness, and emotional ties among African American domestic workers. Domestic-worker stories disrupted dominant narratives and offered an alternative history of domestic work, the intimate sphere, and labor organizing. They dispelled the "mammy" stereotype, exposed the power imbalance between employer and employee, and vividly described a life of hardship. The occupation's roots in the history of slavery and racism, and the ways in which household workers used this history, enabled them to form a collective identity as a group of workers lacking protections, rights, and dignity but empowered to fight for them.[42] Josephine Hulett's role in the movement illustrates this.

Josephine Hulett: "Say It Like It Is"

In May 1970 Sloan hired Josephine Hulett as a field officer. Hulett was a household worker who had formed a domestic workers' rights group in Youngstown, Ohio. After she started the group, Hulett wrote to President Lyndon Johnson's wife, Lady Bird Johnson, about the terrible conditions of domestic work. Her letter was forwarded to the Labor Department and then to the NCHE, which put her in touch with Edith Sloan and propelled her into the national circles of domestic-worker organizing. After receiving Hulett's letter, Sloan went to Youngstown in 1969 and asked Hulett to become an organizer for the NCHE and help implement its plan to establish a national organization of domestic workers. Hulett represented Youngstown on the board of the NCHE.

Then, in May of 1970, she took Sloan up on her offer and became a full-time field organizer for the committee.

Hulett's charge was to reach out to and serve as a liaison between local household-workers rights' groups and the NCHE. In some ways, Hulett was the ideal person for the job. She had worked as a domestic for twenty years and understood perfectly the hardships and constraints of the occupation. Hulett's willingness to share her story became her signature strategy for organizing domestic workers.

Hulett was born in 1937 near Portland, Arkansas, and raised on a white-owned farm that functioned more like a plantation. Although her family had been "adequately clothed and housed," their situation deteriorated rapidly when the original owners died and the farm was passed down to their sons. When Josephine was thirteen, her mother died and her father sent her to live with her oldest sister in Ohio. Life wasn't much easier at her new home. Her sister's husband was a coal-yard worker, and the couple had a young daughter. Josephine was lonely and couldn't shake the feeling that she was a financial burden to the family. "Many nights, I used to cry myself to sleep because I was so homesick. I wanted so much to go back home with my father." To escape this unhappy situation, she dropped out of high school and got married. By the time she was twenty, the couple had divorced and Hulett was supporting a baby boy on her own.[43]

As a high school dropout with few job opportunities, Hulett turned to domestic work to support herself. Because she couldn't afford paid child care, she left the baby with her ex-husband's family during the day, and ventured out from her home in Girard, Ohio, near Youngstown, in search of day work. At her first job she earned twenty-five dollars a week for five and a half days. She paid eighty cents for bus fare, walking two and a half miles each way to avoid paying for an additional bus. Her employer's husband owned a produce company, yet she was given only a hot dog for lunch every day. She cared for four young children and cleaned a large house from top to bottom. Although she frequently worked late, she was never paid for overtime. One day, when she left thirty minutes early to take her son to the doctor, her employer docked her pay. The next day she left at five o'clock and informed her boss she would never work overtime again. The following week, she was fired.[44]

At her next job, Hulett accepted a meager salary of $22.50 a week, working for an elderly couple who had no small children living in the home. Despite the anticipated lighter workload, she cooked for the entire extended family on Friday nights and sometimes babysat grandchildren—all for no extra pay. On top of that, when she arrived at work on Monday morning the house was filthy—the sink full of dishes, dirty clothes strewn all over the house, and overflowing ashtrays. In order to make ends meet, Hulett took on extra household work on the weekends. She worked for the family for ten years, fearful that if she demanded more money she would be fired. When she finally got up the nerve to ask for a raise, her pay was increased to $25 a week. But a few days later the family announced they were moving to Florida. They gave her no severance pay, no prior warning, and no benefits.[45]

Committed to improving her economic situation, Hulett studied part-time to earn her high school diploma. She then spent a year and a half and $285—three months' salary—taking a correspondence course to become a practical nurse. After completing it, she was shocked to learn that the course wasn't accredited and she couldn't practice in a medical facility. Hoping to find work in the health-care field, she looked for home-based nursing work—caring for an infant or an elderly or a disabled person. Hulett encountered yet another obstacle, recalling, "I soon discovered that being a companion or baby nurse were jobs mostly for white women." She eventually found a job working for a young doctor, his wife, and their two babies, earning $35 a week for five days. In many ways it was a good position and a vast improvement from her previous jobs. She received wage increases, thoughtful gifts, paid vacations, and sick leave. "They regarded me as a professional and an adult. They didn't pretend that I was a 'member of the family' nor did they intrude on my life." She worked for them until 1970, when she took the position with the NCHE.[46] They remained friends long after that. Hulett's story of her "good" employer also became important symbolically because it illustrated the possibility for just and

respectable work and confirmed that there was nothing about the occupation that made it inescapably oppressive.

Hulett's story resonated with other black domestic workers. She
shared her struggles of living in the rural South and how her treatment
on the job pegged her as separate and highly unequal. As a single mother,
Hulett had to balance care for her son with full-time employment. She
spent as much time with her son as she could and carved out one day a
week to go out to lunch with him, "and that was an occasion he loved
and looked forward to." As she explained later, "A mother's going to
find a way to support her child at all costs. . . . I know that is the only
reason I took some of the conditions I did."[47] As a black woman, she
had few other job opportunities. And in those situations when she tried
to assert her rights, she found herself unemployed. On a few occasions,
she was fired without warning or severance pay, and in her painstaking
efforts to improve her economic situation she found that racial barriers prevented her from taking advantage of better opportunities. Hulett
was often expected to do cooking, cleaning, and child-care work that
was clearly not part of her job description. She was deeply concerned
about the status and dignity of domestic workers and her treatment as
a servant rather than a worker. "Just because a worker lives in doesn't
mean she should be at someone's beck and call 24 hours a day. Even
for a day worker, sometimes it seems the employer feels he or she owns
you. If you're sick, some employers will call up the doctor to make sure
you're not lying."[48]

Hulett's encounter with another household worker sparked her political activism, underscoring how the sharing of stories and communal connection among household workers laid the foundation for this
movement. One morning at 4:30 a.m., Hulett was on her way home
from dropping off her employers at the airport when she saw an older
black woman walking to work and offered her a ride. The woman had
injured her hip while at work and had no sick leave or insurance. She
couldn't afford to take time off. According to Hulett, her "employers refused to accept the fact that her injury had occurred while at work, and
they refused to aid her in any way."[49] Although she completed most of
her work—sitting on a stool to wash dishes—she couldn't take the child

out for a walk. The employer, who was a stockbroker, hired a babysitter to do it for $2 a day and deducted the amount from the employee's weekly wages of $42.[50] This woman's story prompted Hulett to contact several other household workers and encouraged them to form the Youngstown Household Technicians in 1968.

After meeting Edith Barksdale Sloan and joining the staff of the NCHE in 1970, Hulett reached out to domestic workers around the country and helped organize the national conference the following year. In her first few months on the job she traveled from site to site, Akron and Youngstown, Ohio, Alexandria, Virginia, Denver, Chicago, Baltimore, East St. Louis, talking with household workers. A small group of household workers in Auburn, Alabama, for example, had been meeting regularly since 1969. In early 1971, they contacted NCHE, which sent organizing materials and arranged a visit by Hulett. This proved transformative. The small informal group formed a functioning organization and sent five representatives to the first national household-workers conference in Washington.[51] Personal outreach and Hulett's ability to inspire other household workers became the hallmark of her leadership. She recognized their "need to feel that someone can say it like it is." As she explained it, her firsthand experience with domestic work is what made her an effective leader: "I have to . . . really say what my life has been like . . . so that other women who are household workers may be able to connect with my story, and see what we can do together to change our lives."[52] Hulett's story included a growing awareness of the need to assert her rights. It reflected her belief that political engagement by domestic workers was key to achieving reforms. "When I visit with them," she observed, "they become highly motivated and dedicated to the cause." Hulett encouraged the women she met to take action and be a part of the larger movement of household workers.[53]

PAY, PROTECTION, AND PROFESSIONALISM

Dorothy Bolden and Geraldine Roberts were two of the women Josephine Hulett and Edith Sloan brought together in July 1971 at the first convention of domestic workers, which eventually became the

Household Technicians of America (HTA). Household workers traveling to Washington, DC, included Mary McClendon and Bernice Thompson of the Household Workers Organization in Detroit and Geraldine Miller from New York City.[54] They came together for what they called the three P's: pay, protection, and professionalism. All together six hundred household workers from thirty cities participated in a weekend filled with festivities—dignitaries, dinners, and testimonials.[55]

The gathering at the Twin Bridges Marriott was inspiring. Edith Sloan, in her keynote address, told the gathering: "I know you don't need to hear the reasons why we are here . . . Your memories and aching bodies and tired bones give you all the answers necessary." Speaking to the power of the gathering, she claimed: "Unless there are some changes made, 'Madame' is going to have to clean her own house, and cook and serve her own meals, because *everyone* is going to quit."[56] Hulett urged the women to speak out: "We're women, and we've got big mouths. But you ain't afraid of your big man—now are you gonna be afraid of Miss Jane?"[57] One reporter called the gathering "an odd blend of religious fervor, black militancy, women's liberation and union solidarity."[58] Representative John Conyers declared that "the day for exploiting the domestic worker is over."[59] According to one report, Walter Fauntroy, pastor at New Bethel Baptist Church and congressional representative for Washington, DC, "thrilled the Saturday evening banquet audience" by singing "The Impossible Dream."[60] Esther Peterson attended, as did Shirley Chisholm, the first black woman in Congress, who told the enthusiastic crowd: "We want our piece of the American Dream."[61]

Becky Esquivias of Oklahoma City, one of four Native American domestic workers at the conference, shared her story of being expected to wash, cook, plan meals, and clean, although she was hired as a practical nurse.[62] Wilhelmina Adams, a mother of three from Charlotte, North Carolina, had worked as a domestic for decades and was involved in several community organizations including her church and the PTA. In the 1960s she became president of the board of Domestics United Incorporated and a paid staff member responsible for training, placing domestic workers in jobs, as well as setting employment standards, such as the refusal to wash windows.[63] Domestics United, supported by the Charlotte Area Fund, was formed in 1966 when African American household workers reached out to the Westside Neighborhood Service Center for help with problems of low wages and long hours. By the late 1960s, there were six chapters in the Charlotte area and an estimated two hundred people involved.[64] The domestic workers' conference was a forum to discuss how to organize and build support. The women who gathered in Washington usually knew little about other domestic-worker activism prior to this meeting. Their impetus to organize was rooted in their day-to-day lives and the communities in which they resided. So the gathering provided an opportunity to meet and connect with other domestic-worker organizers. As an attendee from North Carolina said, "Now I know I'm not alone."[65] In that regard the HTA was less an architect of domestic-worker organizing than a conduit linking together the disparate local struggles.

Two weeks after the national gathering, a committee elected at the conference met at the Washington, DC, Statler Hilton Hotel to hammer out the details of the new organization. The planning meeting was a multiracial group of women—black, white, Native American, and Chicana. The Chicana and Native American domestic workers dropped out shortly, and although NCHE attempted to replace them, the organization was never able to build a truly multiracial movement.[66] Committee members decided to call the new organization the Household Technicians of America (HTA) and intended "to work with and for workers of all races and ethnic groups."[67] The HTA was composed of elected representatives of local groups of workers and a board of directors, and instituted a dues system to enable the organization to be self-supporting. Geneva Reid of Warren, Ohio, was named the first president. NCHE promised to help advise and fund the organization for one year, then expected it to be independent. Eventually, HTA came to represent over three dozen groups, had a full-time staff, and a membership of some twenty-five thousand, from diverse places like San Francisco, Sacramento, Tulsa, Detroit, Atlanta, Cleveland, and Dallas. The hope was that the HTA would remain independent, but the organization struggled financially and the institutional history of the NCHE and the HTA overlapped, as did the membership. So, in addition to the HTA, the NCHE increasingly came to represent the voices of household workers.

The NCHE's commitment to organize local domestic workers' rights groups and form an organization "which would become the national voice of the workers and their instrument for change" was a watershed moment for household workers. Many of the reformers who had been involved with NCHE in its early years, including Dorothy Height, Frieda Miller, and Esther Peterson, were ecstatic about the new organization. Even if they didn't initially make this a priority in their reform efforts, they were aware of the significance in this turn in direction. Although Frieda Miller died in 1973 shortly after HTA's formation, Esther Peterson was connected to household-worker organizing until the late 1970s and attended several of its national conferences. And Dorothy Height similarly remained a stalwart supporter. After generations of silent struggle or quiet endurance, of feeling that there simply were no options, domestic workers had begun to come out of the shadows and emerge from behind closed doors.[68] The decision to bring together the disparate local groups to work collaboratively to build local organizations and push a national agenda transformed what had been individualized resistance, or informal community organizing, as was the case in Montgomery, into a visible political movement.[69]

With a cadre of women such as Josephine Hulett in leadership, HTA launched its program of "giving voice" to domestic workers, and as a result, workers' voices came to play a prominent role in domestic-worker activism. The stories of mothers and grandmothers, of aunts and sisters, and of workers themselves recounted decades of hardship, few rewards, limited opportunities, and, for black women, a history of slavery and servitude. Edith Sloan's story of Aunt Rie was one such example. It was a way for her to connect with household workers and to make a claim for why reform of the occupation was so urgently needed. Both the stories and this first national gathering of domestic workers proved to be pivotal in the construction of these women's identity as domestic workers—that they had a set of common interests and could mobilize around a political platform for change.

For household workers, storytelling highlighted their relationship to domestic work, linked past and present, and was a means to achieve dignity and self-empowerment. Storytelling served as a base-building tool, gave legitimacy and authority to those speaking on behalf of domestic workers, and helped craft their identity. They learned about the experiences of other domestic workers and empathized about the common patterns of mistreatment. Moreover, their stories enabled women from vastly different backgrounds to develop a thread of connection that would be the basis of their collective mobilization. By speaking about their lives, their hardship, and love of their work, they hoped to bring dignity and value to household labor.

CHAPTER 4

INTIMACY, LABOR, AND PROFESSIONALIZATION

I have completed my training as a household technician and know that I don't have to scrub floors down on all fours anymore.

—A GRADUATE OF NDWUA'S HOUSEHOLD
MANAGEMENT TECHNICIANS PROGRAM

In 1970 Dorothy Bolden and the NDWUA in Atlanta established Maids' Honor Day to recognize the contributions of domestic workers. Employers were asked to submit letters of nomination explaining why their maid should be named "Maid of the Year." "The purpose of this event," the NDWUA announced, "is to recognize and honor outstanding women in the field of domestic labor, for their courage and stability, and the remarkable ability of being able to take care of two households at one time."[1] The Maids' Honor Day banquet was held annually in May; the celebration included distinguished speakers, citations, awards, and a benediction.

Maids' Honor Day, which sought to bring respect and recognition to an occupation both undervalued and underpaid, was part of a broader campaign to improve working conditions for domestic laborers. The struggle for dignity was part and parcel of the struggle for rights. For poor black women who scrubbed other people's floors, the banquet was a rare opportunity to dress up in their finest attire, enjoy a lavish dinner, and publicly take pride in who they were. Even workers who did not win the honor of Maid of the Year undoubtedly benefited from basking in the praise of their employers.

Bolden's was not an isolated effort. Across the country, domestic-worker-appreciation events sought to recognize the contributions of domestic workers. Some "honor days" were established and run by domestic workers themselves. In other cases, states issued formal proclamations in response to activists' campaigns. In Michigan, Governor William Milliken declared a Household Workers Week in April 1972. Governor John J. Gilligan of Ohio, in announcing an annual Household Employees Week, described domestic labor as "an honorable and indispensable profession which requires a high degree of skill and expertise," and hoped to "pay just and proper tribute to the domestic specialists and technicians."[2] When Governor Jimmy Carter signed an executive order to proclaim Maids' Honor Day in Georgia in April 1972, he was flanked by Dorothy Bolden and other household-worker activists.

Implicit in these efforts to honor household workers was the acknowledgment that household labor is different from other kinds of labor, by virtue of its taking place in the domestic sphere. The home as workspace fostered a perception that domestic workers did what they did

Jimmy Carter signs the Maids' Honor Day proclamation in 1972. Dorothy Bolden is on the right. (Special Collections and Archives, Georgia State University Library)

out of love and loyalty; in this sense, the work was equated to the unpaid labor of housewives. One employer nominating her maid wrote, "This letter is a love story." Another said of her employee, "She is more than a maid (just as a wife is more than just a housewife). She is a very dear part of us."[3] Another claimed she is "my very dearest friend." Employers' framing of the labor as "care work" reinforced the notion that this was labor emanating from and centering on an emotional connection. In contrast, household workers in the 1970s rarely used the framework of care to talk about their work. They preferred a "labor" construct over a "care" construct—a focus on rights rather than emotion. At the same time, employers maintained a strict separation between family members and women working in their homes to justify unequal treatment. Thus, proximity and distance, familiarity and difference, characterized household labor.[4]

Domestic workers had complicated relations with their employers because of the personal nature of the work and the fact that their workplace was a private household. Their jobs brought them in intimate contact with members of the household, and the "housework" they performed tended to be devalued. Household workers often expressed a love for their work and felt that maintaining a close, cordial relationship with their employers was necessary. But they also rejected the culture of servitude that had produced the mammy stereotype and wanted to be seen in a professional context. As Josephine Hulett explained: "I have found that a major problem is to break down the maid/domestic/servant images, and the misunderstandings and prejudices that go with these images. Since people think that household work is inferior, they are prone to think that the people that perform this work are inferior."[5]

At the core, domestic-worker activists advocated recognition of their labor as work and the same protections afforded to other workers. They sought control over the work process and wanted to determine for themselves the standards and expectations of the occupation. They rejected employer-initiated training programs and created their own programs and uniform codes of job standards. They asserted their rights as workers by insisting on basic rights and protections. They hoped to professionalize the occupation and raise wages to enhance the power of workers and transform the employer/employee relationship. In short, they wanted to reshape the contours of the occupation and reestablish it as one of dignity, respect, and professionalism.

THE DOMESTIC SPHERE

Alice Childress used the phrase "one of the family" to describe a central reality of domestic labor: individuals laboring in the home with little public recognition of their status as workers.[6] The location of the work fostered an environment where the boundary between being a worker with specific responsibilities and acting as a personal attendant was fuzzy, even for household cleaners who theoretically were not caretakers.[7] Workers were often expected to be at the beck and call of their employers rather than having a clearly defined set of responsibilities.[8] The confusion extended beyond assigned tasks and blurred the distinction between employee and household resident. The fiction of familiarity was used to extract additional labor from workers and make leftovers and hand-me-downs acceptable forms of remuneration.

Testimony from employers during Atlanta's Maids' Honor Day illustrates how employers viewed their domestic help and the roles they played in the household. The nomination letters included numerous accounts of household workers simultaneously cleaning, cooking, caring for children, helping neighbors and other family members with chores, and taking care of the disabled, ill, and dying. A worker's commitment to the household, often at the expense of her own family and personal well-being, was an ever-present theme. Household worker Leola King, for example, stayed at her employer's house over the Easter weekend because the family was out of town and someone needed to "take care of things" and look in on the employer's sister, who was in a nursing home. When the woman became ill, Leola had to find care for her own grandson, whom she was caring for, as well as contact the woman's doctor and go to the hospital, missing "the only thing she wanted," which was to attend evening service on Easter Sunday.[9] Mrs. Toon, another employer, testified about Jeanette Everhart: "Numerous times, she has neglected family and come to my rescue."[10] One employer nominated her domestic worker because she was "the epitome of quiet, gentle strength."[11] Mrs. James Coody explained that Sophie, even though she had her own family, worked for thirty years for her employers, acting as "pediatrician, psychologist, advisor, counselor, confidant, companion and contributor to spoiling our son."[12] Anne Winston explained that her domestic worker, Rosie Powell, "swooped in like Mary Poppins" and saved the family from being broken apart, while accepting a "very low salary." Moreover, Rosie "sustained third-degree burns of her forearm when she risked her life to put out a kitchen fire which endangered my baby. When she returned from the hospital with her arm wrapped in bandages, she insisted on serving supper to the family rather than leaving the chores to me after I had been at school all day."[13] Maids' Honor Day provides a window into employer perceptions about household workers—the affection they felt for their employees, how they depended upon them, and their expectations of what defined a good household worker. Many employers believed they simply could not survive without the help of their workers.

Employer testimony sometimes invoked the stereotypical mammy figure. Betty Talmadge of Lovejoy, Georgia, wrote about the family's maid, Lucille, whose mother also worked for the family. The women lived on the family farm, and Lucille not only tended to her employer's children, grandchildren, and dying mother, but also cooked, cleaned house for her employer, and worked in the employer's ham processing plant. The multigenerational family ties and claims of loyalty seemed to harken back to an earlier era.[14] Another employer submitted, as part of the Maids' Honor Day nomination, her fourteen-year-old daughter's school essay on her "most favorite character," with the title "Rustin's Mary." After detailing Mary's multiple roles in the household, the daughter wrote, "Many people ask us if we 'own' her, but the truth is, Mary actually 'owns' us . . . [because] Mary told everyone what to do and when to do it."[15] The essay reveals how the slave past continued to inform notions of household labor and how the mammy stereotype persisted within the white household, with the image of the unswervingly loyal black maid as central to family life.

Employer stories became part of the narrative of the struggle for domestic-worker rights and were the basis for honoring particular maids because they conveyed a sense of the value and importance of this labor. Employers repeatedly testified about the indispensability of their household workers. As one explained, "I don't know what I would do without her"; another asserted, "She is a stand-in mother to my babies while I work."[16] These stories also reinforced the power of employers to define the terms of employment and determine what distinguished a "good" from a "bad" worker. Clearly, these employers lauded the values of deference, loyalty, and self-sacrifice (even to the point of a maid putting her own life in jeopardy)—the very aspects of the occupation that domestic-worker rights activists found intolerable. Johnnie Saulsberry, the 1976 "Maid of the Year," deserved the honor, her employer wrote, because she bathes and cares for the employer's seventy-five-year-old mother, entertains her mother's friends for afternoon tea, takes care of a dog, cleans a ten-room house, does the laundry, tends to fifty plants, cooks fabulous meals, never complains about unexpectedly having three or four guests or large numbers of extended family for dinner, and often stays late if her employer is delayed returning home. Another supporter wrote that Johnnie was "cheerful, bright eyed, and remarkably pleasant." Another letter writer for Johnnie wrote that she was "unselfish" in giving extra time, underscoring the way the labor was perceived as caring work and that refusing to give extra time may have been viewed as selfish. Johnnie's own status as a mother was mentioned, but as a footnote in her list of attributes.[17] Rather than scrutinizing the unrealistic demands of employers or the standards of employment, Maids' Honor Day redirected attention to how well employees conducted themselves and whether or not they fulfilled the expectations of their bosses. Maids' Honor Day revealed how many employers depended on their workers, and how this dependence sometimes came at the expense of domestic workers' basic rights.

As "one of the family," domestic workers had to ensure that household members were taken care of and tasks completed, even if doing so meant longer hours and no additional pay, since household members—especially women—routinely engage in caretaking out of love or responsibility, without compensation. Indeed, Jewel Adams's employer called her "our friend and part of the family."[18] The metaphor of family suggested an emotional bond, mutual obligations, and a relationship separate from the marketplace, obscuring what was in fact a market relationship. Characterizing domestic workers as "family" and constructing their work in terms of "care" enabled employers to flout the law and create informal and unpredictable work situations. Employers were entrusting their home and their children to another individual. And in order for that situation to be viable, they had to believe that care and love were central components of the occupation.

Many household workers were devoted to the people they worked for and took pride in what they did. NDWUA established Maids' Honor Day in part to express "love for our labor" and the ways in which workers exhibit "voluntary love with an aim for service to others."[19] This sentiment was an important theme in household workers' campaigns and emerges again and again in their testimonies. Many household workers became emotionally intertwined with the families they worked for. Geraldine Miller described grieving over the loss of someone in one family and worrying about an illness in another family.[20] Household workers valued and recognized the work they did and they genuinely enjoyed it. But even though household workers expressed love of their labor, they did not see their work as a labor of love. Mable Franklin, a member of the Dallas Committee on Household Employment, grew to love the family she worked for: "The love and joy I have known for doing my best is something nobody can take from me. The loving and caring goes two ways and most people have it—at least some of it—with the people they work for. But love won't pay their grocery bills."[21]

Employer claims to kinship were rarely genuine, and in any case were not reciprocal. Although domestic workers were expected to carry out familial responsibilities, they were rarely accorded familial rights such as using the front door, sitting at the dinner table, or being properly fed. The question of food was a recurring one. Food served to workers was often poor quality, leftover, or simply not enough. Geraldine Miller recalled being offered food that was inedible: "I've had sandwiches where the cheese was so hard I could throw it and hit you in the head and hurt you."[22] Moreover, domestics were not interested in building these sorts of familial relationships. Bolden and others wanted to be treated as workers. They saw their work as rooted in a labor-market transaction, not an emotional connection. For household workers, the language of care and kin masked their central concerns of rights and responsibilities. As Carolyn Reed, who became a national leader in the movement, put it, "I don't need a family. I only want a job."[23]

The location of the work tied it closely to unpaid labor in the household and what traditionally has been considered "women's work." The association contributed to its degradation because it was often not considered "real" work.[24] Household work as nonproductive labor is a modern construction. For centuries, the home was the core of the economy, the center of both production and consumption. Or to put it another way, as Charlotte Perkins Gilman asserted in 1903, all "industry began at home." Since the nineteenth century, with the rise of a "separate spheres" ideology, home and work were constructed as distinct places—making it hard to recognize the work that takes place in the home, whether paid or unpaid.[25]

Although the home has been artificially cast as a private space—a space of nurturance and love—the kitchen, the dining room, the bedroom, and the bathroom were locations where hierarchies of difference were created and re-created through the practices and policies that governed domestic work. The widely accepted customs of having household workers enter through the back door, use separate rest rooms, and eat leftover food was how race was remade on a daily basis in private spaces. The racial boundaries established by employers constructed a politics of inhumanity and invisibility that domestic workers encountered in their places of employment.

In an oral history in the late 1970s, Geraldine Roberts recounted a degrading job-interview experience. After examining Roberts's teeth, a prospective employer told her: "Any girl . . . with a mouth this clean and pretty clean teeth was a pretty clean gal 'cause I don't like dirty help in the house."[26] This illustrates the employer's orientation as a prospective "owner" of the employee. The story conjures up images of the slave auction block where slaves' physical health, including their teeth, was closely examined by potential slave buyers and was emblematic of the way in which the bodies of domestic workers were scrutinized and subject to regulation. The connection between domestic work and slavery was reinforced by Josephine Hulett. In a 1973 workshop of about fifty household workers in Miami, she gave a talk titled "Are You a Household Slave?" claiming, "We are not the old stereotype, you know, fat, black, and with a rag tied around our heads."[27]

Roberts's experience illustrates how the intimate nature of the work subjected domestic workers to a degree of monitoring and regulation rarely experienced by other workers. Domestics worked, and sometimes lived, in close physical proximity to employers and engaged in food preparation, washed the family's laundry, spent time in bedrooms and bathrooms, and physically cared for the young, elderly, and sick. This intimacy often became a justification for queries about health, demands for medical documentation, or degrading personal examinations.

Employers had long been concerned about domestic workers' exposure to disease and were fearful, especially in the early twentieth century, that domestic workers were infected with tuberculosis or syphilis. Employers and public health officials believed the occupation required a degree of control that included government regulation of the bodies of household workers. States and municipalities passed laws requiring domestic workers to submit to medical tests and obtain doctors' certificates, and employers sometimes expected their help to carry cards verifying their health status. While purportedly about safeguarding the well-being of middle-class families, such attitudes served to reinforce control and bodily ownership of domestics by their employers.[28] Employers wielded enormous power to monitor their workers and enforce arbitrary standards, which served in part to structure hierarchy between employer and employee. Yet the concerns about disease offered little regard for the health of domestic workers.

In *Like One of the Family*, Alice Childress, in an account titled "The Health Card," conveyed the sentiments of many household workers. Mildred's employer, after inquiring if she lived in Harlem, asked her if she had a health card. Mildred told her that she did indeed and would bring it the next day. Her relieved employer responded that she didn't mean any offense, but "one must be careful." Mildred agreed fully and explained: "Indeed *one* must and I am glad you are so understandin' 'cause I was just worryin' and studyin' on how I was goin' to ask you for yours, and of course you'll let me see one from your husband and one for each of the three children. Since I have to handle laundry and make beds, you know . . ."[29] This exchange colorfully illustrates the double standard that household workers were subject to, as members of the household and yet other.

Many employers acted in the belief that they were not simply purchasing the skills of a domestic worker but their physical presence. Domestic workers were expected to invest their household tasks with positive emotional energy. One employer singled out her maid as someone who "scatters sunshine with her cheerfulness." Another adored her maid because "she has not complained once in nine years."[30] Unlike other forms of labor, where employees sold their time or a service, domestic workers' bodies were considered commodities. This fostered a work environment where employees' character, not only their ability to complete specified chores, became a measure of one's job performance. One employer appreciated her maid because "she always answers in a pleasant 'yes, Ma'am.'"[31] Domestic workers were often, especially in the 1960s, hired and fired because of particular personality traits rather than their occupational skills. As Carolyn Reed put it, "Household workers have not been selling their services; they have been selling their souls."[32] The intimate nature of the work made it different from other unskilled labor that was filled by bodies believed to be easily replaceable and interchangeable. Domestic workers were evaluated by their ability to be cheerful, caring, and compassionate. They were expected to listen to and comfort employers, nurture children, and project an upbeat yet deferential personality. The occupation required employees to engage in the physical labor of cooking, cleaning, and household maintenance, as well as, to use sociologist Arlie Hochschild's term, emotional labor.[33] Geraldine Roberts explained her dissatisfaction with the emotional labor expected of her: "We were *not* satisfied; we were afraid we may not have the job—that we might get fired. So we was submissive to the boss lady to some degree; as we were to our mistresses in slavery time: the fear of the employer, the fear of not being able to get another job, no references being given if she got angry. We had to pretend and smile when we didn't want to smile and show our teeth and laugh loud and [act] stupid to make her feel that we were quite humble to her."[34]

Roberts's reference to slavery and performative behavior is significant because it suggests that despite outward appearances, domestic workers were deeply unhappy with the expectations of their work and that a degree of coercion shaped their behavior. She suggests that the act of smiling and laughing was often for the benefit of the employer and didn't reflect how employees actually felt. In her history of African American women and rape, Darlene Clark Hine identifies a "culture of dissemblance"—in which African American women created an appearance of openness while in reality shielding their inner selves. In their employment relationships, household workers developed a similar culture of dissemblance, shielding their true feelings from employers. So, household labor was embodied labor in which not only the body, but the mind and the heart, as well, were seen as determining the quality of the work. Workers were expected to lift, bend, climb, carry, scrub, protect, sooth, smile, and love. They were evaluated by their personality, demeanor, hygiene, character, as well as their set of acquired skills. Patterns of deference enabled white employers to wield power over women of color, fostering a relationship that was both personal and paternalistic.[35]

Although household workers' bodies were hypermonitored, domestics were simultaneously deemed invisible, as if they were not present in the workspaces they inhabited. Consequently, domestic workers were privy to personal information about the family. Josephine Hulett explained how domestic workers often overheard conversations not meant for their ears: "Some employers will discuss your most intimate affairs over the dinner table. They will discuss *their* most intimate affairs around you, too, but you're not supposed to have ears, or to understand. Or they'll discuss racial issues, talking about how 'they' are trying to move into their neighborhood. You're not supposed to hear that, either."[36] This assumption that topics could be discussed or workers could be a subject of conversation and that, despite their presence, they somehow wouldn't hear is further evidence of dehumanization and domestic workers' treatment as nonpersons.

Carolyn Reed experienced this as well. When Reed took a live-in job for a wealthy family in Scarsdale, New York, she was welcomed as "one of the family." That meant working from seven in the morning until midnight. In five years, Reed never got a raise, received Social Security, or had a vacation. "Then one night, the woman of the house—who had been having an affair and was very, very nervous—began to scream at me for not having done something she thought I should have done. . . . As she screamed I realized I wasn't real to her. I mean, I wasn't a *person* to her. . . . She had no respect for me, for what I did. . . . I was a *servant* to her, maybe even a slave. I remember while she was screaming I began saying 'I don't work for you anymore.' . . . And that was it. I packed my bags in the middle of the night; my husband, who was then my boyfriend, came and got me, and we took off."[37]

These practices of bodily control, emotional demands, and invisibility illustrate core features of household labor. Race, class, gender, sexuality, and unequal power relations were constructed, articulated, and experienced within the home. In that regard, the processes constituted—and resisted—in the so-called private sphere were a reflection of larger political and economic structures.

Dignity: What's in a Name?

Domestic workers engaged in multiple strategies to reclaim their labor as legitimate work and challenge the unequal power structure that characterized their employment. They tackled the problem of lack of recognition in part by thinking about naming and forms of address as a way to remake their identity and subjectivity. Naming reflected status and identity.[38] Household workers were expected to engage in deference rituals—to refer to their bosses as Miss or Mrs.—yet they were often called by their first names, or even more offensively as "girl." Employers' reference to their workers by their first names indicated a degree of personalism and informality that didn't accurately reflect how domestics felt about the relationship—nor how they believed their employers felt about the relationship. Geraldine Roberts expressed her disapproval of employers calling their workers "girl" with a rhetorical question: "Was she twelve, or was she ten, or was she twenty-one, or is she fifty?" A typical employer response, according to Roberts: "Well, I call my best girlfriends . . . girls." Roberts retorted: "Well, she's not your best girlfriend. She's your employee."[39] When household workers gathered for their first national convention in 1971, the question of respectful form of address was a key one. Edith Sloan urged the women in attendance: "The next time someone calls you Sally or John, you tell them that you are Free, Black, Brown, Red or White and 21 and that your name is MISS Sally or MR. John. And if someone calls you AUNTIE, as Mary McLeod Bethune once answered, you ask them 'and which one of my sisters' children are you?'"[40]

Roberts elaborated on how changing perceptions and forms of address led to a shift in the status of the occupation: "We've changed some of that, attitudes towards you. Mainly the middle class looked down upon their servant help in such a very unpleasant way, a possessive sort of thing that they owned and we were their things. It was 'my Mary' and 'my Annie' and 'my Gerry' and we were a part of the family . . . but nevertheless, I was not in the family will or if there was any illness and I could no longer work all at once I was not a part of that family any more."[41] "Now we meet our new employer and we are respected as Mrs. Roberts, Mrs. Thomas." Being addressed as Miss or Mrs. was a sign of respect and recognition of professionalism and independence that many domestics insisted upon.

The shift in terminology also extended to the category of work, and activists were eager to put forward more empowering names for their labor. Although Bolden used the term "maid," most household workers were moving away from that word as a term that signified subservience. By the mid-1970s, Bolden was also using the designation "household technician." Irene Lloyd, who headed the Nassau-Suffolk Household Technicians in Long Island, explained, "The word 'maid' makes me a slave, and I am not a slave."[42] As Carolyn Reed explained: "When I think of *domestic*, I immediately think of a very tame animal—a cat or dog or something. I am not a tame person, I am not a domesticated person. *Servant* to me goes back to the days of slavery."[43]

The term "household technician" was a deliberate choice on the part of domestic-worker organizers, who sought to convey a degree of professionalization. They wanted to be acknowledged, not as maids or servants, which had connotations of subservience, but as skilled workers. Geraldine Miller, a New York City–based activist, explained: "We took the name of Household Technicians because we feel that we were able to do anything with little or no supervision."[44] A graduate of one of NDWUA's training programs in Atlanta testified that when her employer demanded that she scrub the floor on her hands and knees, she responded: "I have completed my training as a household technician and know that I don't have to scrub floors down on all fours anymore."[45] For this worker, the designation "household technician" defined the type of labor that could be expected of her.

Domestic workers were convinced that the degradation of domestic work hinged in part on public perceptions and lack of value attached to their labor. If those could be remedied, they believed the status of the occupation could be transformed. Josephine Hulett observed, "Isn't it funny how garbage collection was a dirty job until they changed the name to sanitation engineers and raised the salaries to $12,000 a year and up?"[46] So, professionalism, along with pay and dignity, was a rallying cry of the movement. As Geraldine Roberts explained, "I considered myself a professional and I said, other domestics, look upon yourselves as professional technicians."[47] The naming and renaming associated with household labor, much like the stories that domestic workers shared with each other, was part of the process of establishing a new identity for domestic workers.

Professionalization and Training

Household workers also reframed the character of their labor through professionalization and training programs. For domestic workers, personalism, intimacy, and the location of their work led to battles with their employers over control of the work process.[48] The unregulated nature of domestic work gave employers an enormous amount of power to determine tasks and assign chores arbitrarily. Domestic workers defined the expectations of their labor and established the boundaries of acceptable work through uniform codes and standards. A booklet published by one local group delineated chores that domestic workers wouldn't do, including climbing ladders, washing windows, cleaning walls out of reach, and scrubbing floors on their knees.[49] Model contracts and codes of standards outlined benefits and specified work expectations, which enabled workers to be autonomous rather than subject to minute-by-minute supervision by employers.[50] When expectations were explicitly detailed and previously agreed upon, employers wielded less authority to make unusual or unexpected demands on workers. And employees would have a clear sense of how to accomplish their specific tasks. According to Edith Sloan, "Through implementation of the code, and organization of activities and programs, NCHE seeks to end the master-servant relationship and to render private household employment a respectable, well-paid occupation."[51] DC Household Technicians also prepared "A Code of Standards" detailing minimum wages and hours, and declaring that "clothing and/or food should not be considered part of payment." They insisted on time-and-a-half for work over forty hours a week and double time for more than forty-eight hours a week. They suggested: "A written agreement between employer and employee should clearly define the duties of the position, including specific tasks, how often they must be performed and the desired standards." The contract outlined specifics such as: "Schedules with provisions for rest period, meal times, telephone privileges and time out for private activities (such as church attendance for live-in employees) should be agreed upon in advance of employment." And they insisted that "a professional working relationship should be maintained," which "includes proper forms of address for both employee and employer and their respective families."[52] By standardizing the labor process and trying to professionalize their work, private household workers eroded some of the racial and class power that employers wielded and challenged the disciplinary practices that were designed to disempower and create a more compliant and controllable workforce.

Domestic workers also established training programs to professionalize the occupation. The perception of domestic work as unskilled labor was one reason for the occupation's low status. Yet most household workers were aware that their jobs were not ones that just anyone could step into, but required a certain kind of skill: "We were well educated with a PhD in common sense," explained Dorothy Bolden.[53] Despite the substantial knowledge necessary to care for small children and maintain a household, domestic work was considered a job that didn't require a formal education or specialized training. This assumption—that employees had few marketable skills and employers could offer the necessary guidance—contributed to the power imbalance between worker and boss. It divested workers of control over the work process and invested their employers with the power to determine how work would be completed. Much like deskilled manufacturing workers in the early twentieth century, domestic workers found that as "unskilled laborers" their leverage as workers was diminished.

Geraldine Roberts believed that the perceived unskilled nature of the work offered limited occupational advancement and left black women stuck in the same position decade after decade. "There isn't any advancement. For thirty years a domestic worker's still the same cook in the kitchen. For thirty years she's still the same lady who runs the vacuum cleaner and for thirty years she's the same laundry woman. The first chore she had upon acceptin' that job thirty years before usually is her same task thirty years later and, in most cases, not very much advancement in pay, no promotions, no scholarships offered, no fringe benefits."[54] In response, Roberts organized programs to give women the skills and training to leave domestic work. In Cleveland, she developed a collaborative relationship with a Cuyahoga community college and encouraged domestics to pursue their education to learn skills and move up the economic ladder: "We feel that the domestic worker must look further ahead especially if she's a younger person that house cleaning should not be her goals for her life. That she should seek educational programs, scholarships and ways and means to improve and bring pride and dignity to her life."[55]

Most training programs, however, aimed to elevate the status of domestic work, rather than enable them to leave the occupation. They advocated specialization of their work, where employees were responsible for a clear set of tasks that may include cooking or cleaning or child care—but certainly not all. Geraldine Miller explained how at one time, household labor was more specialized, with laundresses, cooks, and chauffeurs, but now, "They lumped it all up into one. Your housekeeper now is doing at least three to four or five, six jobs."[56] A number of local groups offered courses, prepared workers for the job market, and placed them in employment positions. NDWUA's training programs enabled domestic workers to acquire "specialized and technical training to provide better services in the field of Household Management."[57] Trainees engaged in comparison-price shopping, cooking lessons, driver education, child care, elder care, and first aid. They learned how to dress appropriately, answer the telephone, and set the table. Upon completion of the course, they participated in a ceremony, received a certificate, and, according to Bolden, became "professional women." Training reinforced the idea that household work was skilled labor and required both a level of knowledge and a measure of instruction.[58] It also placed household workers in positions of expertise, since they ran the programs. As NDWUA outlined in its training proposal: "It was determined by the members of the union that the best teachers in any training program would be the domestics themselves."[59]

Mary McClendon, a household worker in Detroit, was one of the foremost advocates of training and professionalization for domestic workers. McClendon founded and led the Household Workers Organization (HWO) in Detroit, which held its first meeting on September 4, 1969, at the offices of the Civil Rights Commission.[60] McClendon was the most active and passionate member and the force behind the organization. She was born on October 3, 1922, in Andalusia, a small town in Alabama about an hour and a half south of Montgomery. She was one of six children and graduated in 1944 from the Covington County Training High School.[61] Both her mother and grandmother, who was a slave, did domestic work. Like so many other black women, McClendon began domestic work at a young age, when she went to work with her mother. She moved to Detroit in 1955 to join her cousin, who was a doctor. In some ways things were quite different in the North. McClendon voted for the first time in her life, which she described as "like a flash of freedom."[62] Her experiences as a household worker, however, were not all that different in the North, and the slavery metaphor was one that seemed to apply to her new setting, as she explained after she began to organize, sounding very much like Ella Baker and Marvel Cooke in their description of the slave markets: "Slavery is alive and well and living in Detroit. Each day hundreds of women—predominantly Black and poor—are taken to the suburbs to clean house. In exchange for their back-breaking labor, they earn nine to eleven dollars from which social security is deducted. The workers earn no sick or vacation pay; they are not entitled to Workman's Compensation; they have no say about working conditions, hours or fringe benefits; there is no grievance machinery to handle their complaints against the employer. After a nine or ten hour day, spent cleaning two or three large suburban houses, the workers return to Detroit with often no more than nine dollars in their pocket, and no assurance that they will have a job tomorrow."[63] These observations were compounded by her own personal experience: "I never shall forget I was working for one woman and she told me to eat my food in the room where the dog was, not in the room with the family. Some of these people were treating their dogs and cats better than we were treated."[64] By the time she became involved in the domestic workers' rights movement, her husband, Benjamin McClendon, passed away and she was a single mother raising her son alone. HWO had no office, limited funds, and operated out of McClendon's home. In 1969, after nearly forty years as a domestic worker, McClendon started working full-time for the HWO, and within a couple of years it had about 150 mostly black and Latino members. McClendon also connected with HTA through Josephine Hulett and Edith Sloan, who went to Detroit several times to offer their support.[65]

HWO engaged in a range of activities, including offering an employment service that guaranteed employees a minimum wage and lunch and rest breaks, and promised employers a "neat, punctual, honest worker."[66] It also advocated on behalf of individual workers who were having problems with employers. McClendon shared the typical example of an employer who promised to make Social Security payments. She inquired with the Social Security office. If no payments were made,

HWO needed to prove that the worker was employed by that individual. It sent the employee to a department store to apply for a credit card, using the employer as a reference. When the employer verified that the individual worked for them, the organization had a case.[67]

The center of McClendon's work in Detroit was the training programs. She, like other domestic workers, believed that the category of "household labor" was a catch-all label that masked domestic workers' many roles. She insisted on spelling out the multiple kinds of household tasks and the expertise necessary for each. In a training manual, McClendon delineated the following areas of specialization: "General Housekeeping Technician, Kitchen Manager, Child Supervisor, Home Geriatric Aide, Party Aide, Party Supervisor, and Household Manager."[68] She developed nine different courses, one in "Job Readiness" which taught basic remedial skills, attitude, rights and benefits, as well as grooming and personal appearance; "Home Safety and Sanitation" included first aid, accident prevention, insect and pest control, and handling food and toxic materials. The course on "Home Geriatrics" covered psychology of the elderly, home nursing, and recreational therapy.[69] McClendon defined a household technician as "a person with college-level vocational training for employment in private households."[70] She also counseled domestic workers to set boundaries on what they would do. Household work that included picking up toys off the floor, cleaning cobwebs, mopping, dusting, and polishing were all acceptable. "But we tell them not to pick up personal underwear."[71]

McClendon also made a point of educating employers. Most household workers believed that unless employers saw their jobs as professional and came to think of the work differently, little headway would be made in transforming the occupation. So employer training was part of their agenda. In 1971 McClendon worked with the Grosse Pointe Human Relations Council, an organization that included many employers, to publish a pamphlet entitled *You and Your Household Help* that aimed to teach employers "the art of finding good help and maintaining a good business relationship." It suggested paying employees fifteen dollars a day plus carfare, and live-in employees seventy-five dollars a week, with all meals, "a pleasant private room and bath," and two days off each week. Paid sick leave after three months of employment, paid vacations, overtime pay, paid national holidays, Social Security, a clear definition of household responsibilities, regular breaks—a half-hour lunch plus two fifteen-minute breaks for an eight-hour day—and two weeks' termination notice should all be considered standard. "The employee should be referred to as 'housekeeper,' not 'maid,' as a 'woman,' not a 'girl,' and never should be referred to as 'part of the family.' The master-servant attitude is out of date."[72] While some employers, such as those affiliated with the Grosse Pointe Human Relations Council, were supportive, others were not. After a local television appearance in 1973, McClendon received hate mail. One individual, after racist and vitriolic insults, wrote, "What really got me upset, was your dumb statement that unskilled workers should get as much pay as SKILLED WORKERS, on account of their expenses being as big! . . . Domestic workers are at the bottom of the totem poll [sic], just exactly where they belong. They aren't educated sufficiently (neither are *you*) to do any other kind of work, so it isn't anybody's fault but their own."[73] This sentiment was indicative of some of the barriers household workers faced.

Through professionalization and training, women like Mary McClendon worked to transform the occupation in which generations of African American women and other poor women had long been engaged. She argued, "We would also like to see a curriculum for household workers in the schools—just like home economics—so that it will become an occupation, like nursing. . . . What's a dirtier job than nursing? Yet there is dignity attached to it."[74] Employers and employers' associations had for generations established training programs, usually to mold women into their ideal workers. Training programs implemented by women like McClendon were designed to upgrade the skills and pay of workers even as they set employment standards. The question of who ran the training programs distinguished HTA's programs from those initiated by employers. Workers were wary of programs not run by workers. One member of the executive board of the HTA suggested that certain training programs exploited women. "These pilot programs get the women's hopes up and then leave them. Zora Gardner told of a training program in which she was trained as a medical technician and upon completion of the course she was asked to be a nurse's aide. She told them that this was not what she was trained for, and she then refused the job. This was an example of those government programs which just pacify the public."[75] Josephine Hulett experienced something similar when she enrolled in a practical nursing correspondence course, which she later learned was not accredited and wouldn't enable her to move out of domestic labor. Whether or not it was always successful, training, especially training programs organized by domestic workers, became one avenue to regain control of the work process.

Domestic workers' campaigns for training, professionalization, and recognition of their work were designed to reorder household arrangements and redefine the boundaries that shaped domestic work. Domestic-worker activists boldly challenged the social scripts of deference, which suggested that domestic workers remain passive and silent, but smile on demand. They questioned the assumptions that domestic workers should take hand-me-downs and do any and everything asked of them. They analyzed the cultural production of their labor—its roots in slavery and servitude and the daily practices of their employment—and objected most strenuously to the ideological construction of domestic workers as servants. They addressed the degradation of their labor and worked to establish a new level of respect for the occupation.[76] In the mid-1970s Dorothy Bolden reflected on shifts in the occupation: "In the past seven years there's been a great deal of change. These women used to be embarrassed about saying they were maids. You had to take such hardships that you didn't want nobody to know you were. Now it's different. You can't tell a maid from a secretary anymore. In the past, if a black woman was a maid you could tell by the way she dressed. Now they don't carry the shopping bags as much, they go neater, and they look more lively and intelligent."[77]

Jessie Williams of the Household Technicians of Auburn, Alabama, similarly declared: "We won't go in the back door any more. We won't be told to eat scraps in the kitchen and stay out of the living room, except when we are sweeping. We feel domestic work is just as professional as any other job. If people go on making it degrading, there won't be any workers doing it much longer."[78]

The connections and political alliances that domestic workers made with one another both in their local groups and through the national HTA offered a space and opportunity for them to tell their stories—stories that all too frequently revolved around exploitation and lack of respect. The stories wove together the shame and degradation of the labor with love, empowerment, and aspirations. Although these were individual stories, collectively they created a common narrative of domestic work that included the history of racism, sexism, and a struggle for rights and dignity. The public testimonials and stories helped construct an identity among domestic workers and erased some of the shame publicly associated with domestic service.[79] The stories served as a tool to build solidarity among household employees and laid the groundwork for some of the critical themes the movement would address.

Domestic-worker narratives about bodily control, about working in the intimate space of the home, about contested notions of family and "care" work, disrupted employer narratives about the meaning of domestic labor. Yet they also relied on employer narratives to bring value and recognition to their work—a strategy they would use again when they pushed for federal minimum wage coverage. They asserted that household labor—both paid and unpaid—was work and ought to be treated as such. Through their narratives domestic workers challenged the racial and class differences that others had attached to the labor. Their campaign illuminated the links between home, market, and state and highlighted the ostensibly private domestic sphere as a site of labor where hierarchy and inequality were created through daily ritualistic practices. Household workers claimed dignity and respect and sought to put employers and employees on a more equal footing and erase the vestiges of racial servitude that were so closely tied to domestic service. As Geraldine Roberts explained: "Our pride, dignity, and respect has meant a lot to household workers. . . . Human dignity is one's total pride of life. Without dignity, one is nothing."[80]

CHAPTER 5

SPACE, PLACE, AND NEW MODELS OF LABOR ORGANIZING

Labor has to recognize us as a force. And how do you do that?
Maybe it's developing a union of our own.

—CAROLYN REED

In 1971 Geraldine Miller, a household worker, was riding the train to work in Westchester County in suburban New York City when she struck up a conversation with a woman who began to talk about "fringe benefits" for household workers and informed her about the Urban League's organizing efforts.[1] The idea of better working conditions for household workers immediately caught Miller's attention. "I wanted it, and I wanted it with a passion."[2] She attended a meeting of the Professional Household Workers Union, a New York City group initiated and led by Benjamin McLaurin of the Urban League, and learned about the work of the NCHE and the upcoming national conference of domestic workers. Miller arranged for league sponsorship of a bus for a group of workers to travel to the meeting in Washington, DC. To recruit workers, she created a leaflet that read: "Stop, Look, and Listen. Become Aware of Your Rights as a Household Worker." She recalled: "I went out on street corners especially near the trains and I gave them out to all the people that rode on my train. Days that I didn't work, I would catch a corner where [there was] a bus stop . . . we stood outside a couple of the unemployment offices and gave them out." Some women needed an incentive to get involved. "They said we'll come if you cook and take something," Miller, known for her culinary talents, explained. "I said okay, I'll cook. So I took a certain amount of my money and I gave them what they wanted. They wanted food that I had cooked and they got it." Through her organizing and culinary enticements, Miller mobilized thirty-three women to attend the national conference. Although she had no prior political experience, after returning home from the conference, Miller formed the Bronx Household Technicians and the New York State Household Technicians, eventually becoming a prominent organizer and leader in the Household Technicians of America.[3]

Domestic-worker activists, like Miller, were labor organizers attempting to build a movement to transform the conditions of their work. They were continuing a long history of domestic-worker organizing. From the washerwomen's strike in Atlanta in the 1880s to the upsurge of activism in the 1930s, household workers had repeatedly demonstrated not only their ability to resist and control the work process, but to organize collectively and make demands on their employers and the state. Workers in the 1960s and 1970s received little support from mainstream unions and maintained their autonomy from traditional labor leaders. Because they were not subject to union procedures or National Labor Relations Board rules, they were free to chart an independent course. Their marginalization from the labor movement as well as the distinctiveness of their labor made it necessary for them to develop new and untested patterns of labor organizing. They were isolated workers working in the privacy of the home, typically as an employer's sole employee. This demanded a more nuanced approach to labor organizing, departing from the confrontational, zero-sum model guiding traditional labor organizing. More often than other labor activists, domestic workers attempted to cultivate support from employers. Workers sometimes used their importance to the household, and their intimate association with family life, as leverage in their negotiations. In addition, they sought state-based protections, such as minimum wage, that applied to all household workers, not only those who were formally organized. They utilized social movement strategies and advocated more egalitarian approaches to labor organizing. Their strategies were often community based, since reaching out to workers in their places of employment was often difficult. So neighborhood associations, public places, and city buses became centers of domestic-worker activity. Activists tailored their tactics to the contours of the occupa-tion. Because of this they broke new ground in worker resistance—mobilizing poor domestic workers, primarily women of color—and expanded the history of American labor activism.[4]

NEW APPROACHES TO ORGANIZING

Miller's commitment to organizing household workers was seeded dur-ing her forty-plus years of experience as a domestic worker. She was born in Sabetha, Kansas, in 1920, in her words, "the same year that women got the vote," and came from a family with a long history of domestic work, and seemingly few escape routes.[5] "Well, housework is something that's been here for ages and it's gonna be here after I'm gone if they have houses. It's something that the average woman does. And that was my one reason for putting the Household Technicians together, was that . . . all the family that I knew . . . did housework. So that meant they was working for peanuts."[6] When her family moved to Atchison, Kansas, her grandmother, mother, and her aunt Retta all worked in the Burns Hotel, washing sheets and dishes, floors and win-dows. When she was still in preschool her mother started taking her to work, and at the age of six, she was sent to the kitchen to help out. By the time she was twelve, she was fully schooled in housecleaning and worked on weekends and evenings. "Aunt Retta gave me a sense of dig-nity about the profession," she said. "She was very particular about what you should do in a home; how the home should look."[7]

Her aunt saved money to put Geraldine through college. But when Geraldine was seventeen, her mother was murdered, and Geraldine, distraught, refused to go to college. "I was really interested in doing whatever it was that dulled the pain."[8] After finishing high school she decided to follow her lifelong dream of becoming a dancer, and joined a traveling show that took her throughout the South. "It was my fault that [college] didn't happen. My idea back then was to run down the road and dance."[9] She married at the age of twenty-one, but her husband was a "womanizer" and within two years she'd left him.[10] During and after World War II, Miller held a number of jobs in addition to dancing and household labor—she worked in stores, hotels, and on an assembly line in a chicken-processing plant.

Searching for something better, in 1954 Miller relocated to New York City, where she ended up doing mainly domestic work and living in the Bronx on Morris Avenue, a short distance from the site of the most notorious "slave markets" of the Depression. She recounted hearing stories from women who stood on Burnside Avenue, waiting to be selected for cleaning jobs. "Sometimes they'd ask to see your knees and the women with the worst-scarred knees were hired first because they looked like they worked the hardest."[11] Hearing these stories was transformative for Miller: "This is just one of the things that kind of woke me up."[12] But scrubbing floors on her knees was not Miller's preferred chore. She prided herself on her cooking ability, a skill she'd cultivated over the years. "Whatever I did, I would try to make it better the next time. You know, if it was cooking, find out more, do what you can, and I did—served on all the Jewish holidays. I've had people who would call me back each time. And each time, it was sometimes more money because they would like the way I do things."[13] Geraldine never had children of her own, but she took care of plenty. "I wished I had a dime for every time I helped somebody with a baby, you know, because I love children."[14] Despite Miller's love for what she did, she recognized it as work and was convinced "that we were a labor group."[15] Miller had previously not been involved in politics. But she did attend the 1963 March on Washington at the urging of her employer. She didn't know a soul there and didn't fully understand—until much later—the significance of King's "I Have a Dream" speech. She was nevertheless moved, because "he was a symbol for us . . . the little people he probably didn't even know about."[16] After learning of the incipient movement of household workers, she dedicated herself to fighting for the rights of those "little people" who she soon realized were not that little after all.

Joining hundreds of other household workers at the first national gathering of the HTA in 1971 thrilled Miller. It was unlike anything she had ever seen before: "Over 500 black women who were household workers, who looked like they was Miss Ann herself—not Miss Ann's maids, but Miss Ann." She explained: "When you say, 'Miss Ann,' you're talking about that person you worked for, who had the money, who was able to buy the clothes and think nothing of it."[17] Miller attended the Saturday-night banquet, toured the White House, and listened to Shirley Chisholm and Josephine Hulett. "That was the thrill of my life, to see that many women and listen to their stories and how hard it was for some of them."[18] When household workers gathered in the nation's capital, they shared their experiences as workers and also discussed how they could wield power.

Like other workers, household workers attempted to negotiate with their employers for higher wages and better working conditions. But they could not do so as a unit, as was the case for workers who had union representatives and bargaining agents and could use the threat of a strike as leverage. The employer-employee relationship in household work was distinct from that of other occupations because of its personal nature and the ways in which employers could easily let workers go. Miller was deeply aware of how the one-on-one relationship structured employer-employee negotiation. After working for one woman for eight years, Miller was let go because her employer thought she was getting too old. "She fired me. She didn't think it was going to work out. In housework you don't have any recourse. If a person decides you're getting too old and you're not capable of doing the work instead of sitting down and discussing it with you and letting you know that there's something amiss here." Miller was deeply troubled by her treatment and wished that her employer had engaged her in a respectful discourse about her expectations. A better model, she suggested, would be to "let the woman know that you cannot do this type of work. . . . You sit down and you talk about your duties" rather than simply disposing of one person and replacing them with another.[19] The intimate nature of domestic labor necessitated that positive personal interactions be maintained. Most household workers valued cordial relationships and open lines of communication with their employers. Josephine Hulett said of one employer: "We did . . . learn to communicate, which was an advantage to both of us."[20]

Domestic workers had historically used quitting as a form of resistance. Quitting was the primary way of wielding power for individual workers who had few other avenues of resistance. Carolyn Reed learned through her organizing that it might not be the best, or the only, strategy: "Whenever I got tired of a job, I'd just walk away from it. It's the very things that I tell some of our women *not* to do today. If there's something that's wrong, I should be able to talk to you about it."[21] So, while employers were the source of low pay and poor working conditions, workers navigated the relationship carefully—striking a balance between persuading and educating employers, while also asserting their rights.

The personal relationship that made this job so capricious and unpredictable could also be a source of power for domestic workers. Families became dependent upon individual workers because of the emotional ties and bonds of trust that had been forged, and because their personality seemed well suited for the job. Some children saw caretakers as "second mothers," and some employers relied on housekeepers to ensure the smooth functioning of the home. One employer referred to her worker as a "security blanket, always there to help me."[22] Domestic workers—in many cases considered essential to the management of the household—used this power of loyalty to win demands from their employers. "Maids was very valuable to a household," observed Dorothy Bolden.[23] When Geraldine Roberts became aware of how indispensable she was to her employer, she was emboldened: "Many of us learned that we were important to them, which was amazing and surprising to us, and that's when we began to feel we didn't have to say 'yes ma'am' anymore."[24] The reliance of the family on specific domestic workers enabled employees to use this leverage to their advantage. Bolden explained: "I always understood that the employer was a human being too. You have to learn how to sit down and relax and talk to her."[25] Many domestic workers were able to negotiate higher salaries and better working conditions precisely because employers could not imagine life without "their girl."

Household workers' method of negotiating is instructive as a model for contemporary labor organizers. Because each employer—in the vast majority of cases—had only one employee, and because employees were isolated from one another, they engaged in one-on-one bargaining. A lone domestic worker could not be represented by others and had to act as her own bargaining agent. So instead of relying on a union hierarchy to speak for them, domestic workers were individually empowered. As a result, the ability of individual domestic workers to establish ground rules for employment and wield power within the relationship was critical. According to Bolden, the organization "can't negotiate with private employers, private homes. You have to teach each maid how to negotiate. And this is the most important thing—communicating. I would tell them it was up to them to communicate. If I wanted a raise from you I wouldn't come in and hit you over your head and demand a raise—I would set out and talk to you and let you know how the living costs have gone up."[26] In this spirit, NDWUA offered mediation for employer-employee disputes to reach fair and just solutions. Rather than placing their fate with union leaders who they may or may not have voted for and who may not effectively represent their interests, activists' approach put the power in the hands of individual workers who could decide for themselves their priorities and under what circumstances they would work.

Although domestic workers used personal leverage and negotiation, they could not always rely on employers' goodwill. Even though individuals negotiated by themselves, collective demands and mobilization were central to the movement. And domestic workers routinely relied on other workers as a source of support. They shared grievances and came up with common solutions that strengthened their individual bargaining positions. As household workers reached out to other workers, their stories became a way to convey acceptable and unacceptable standards of employment—including wages and benefits. This kind of informal education was critical for shifting expectations. The stories of scarred knees, for example, became emblematic of what domestic workers would not do. And after that story was told, few wanted to ever scrub floors on their knees again. The formation of community and common standards, even if not a union, was seen as a way to shape labor relations and establish a level of job control.

Unlike more traditional forms of labor organizing that recruited workers employed by a single company or individual, household workers mobilized workers regardless of their employer. But multiple employers meant that strikes were difficult to organize among household workers. When she first began to organize in Cleveland, Geraldine Roberts planned a one-day strike with the goal of having workers attend a daylong seminar. The loss of a day's wages was significant for household workers, however, so Roberts called for community donations to cover workers' wages. But little came of this. In addition, many employers threatened to fire their workers if they participated in a walkout. The strike was called off.[27] Due to their financial dependency, and because they were dealing with multiple employers rather than a single company, workers instead sought state-based legislative protections such as minimum wage that would apply to all household workers, not only those who were organized or had more enlightened employers. But this also required mass mobilization.

CAROLYN REED: "NATURAL ORGANIZER AT LARGE"

Household employees worked extended hours in the ostensibly private space of the home, isolated from other workers, sweeping, dusting, scrubbing floors, washing windows, doing laundry, preparing food, and caring for children. During working hours they had almost no contact with anyone other than their employers. It was difficult for organizers to determine which households employed domestics and it was nearly impossible to contact these workers on their worksites. It was an atomized occupation, with an estimated 1.1 million workers in 1970.[28] Since many domestics worked for more than one family, there may have been close to three million employers. Given the difficulty of organizing in the home, public spaces became a central site of these efforts. In New York, Geraldine Miller built a political base by painstakingly recruiting private household workers in housing projects as well as other public venues: "We put notices in the washrooms, you know, the laundry rooms, and we would talk to each other—if I could find someone to talk to, as you come in and out of the place where you worked, you'd talk to any of the other maids you'd see and tell them what you were doing and why you were doing it."[29] But she was not the only one. Another New York City domestic worker, Carolyn Reed, also became deeply involved in household-worker organizing and committed to building an alternative labor movement.

Carolyn Reed learned about household-worker organizing after she read an announcement in the *Amsterdam News* about a meeting for domestic workers in a Harlem church in October 1971. At that meeting she met Josephine Hulett and Edith Barksdale Sloan, and was moved by what she heard: "I identified very much with Josephine Hulett, because . . . she had been a household worker. . . . And it was really Josephine's whole speech, whole thing, that really got me involved in that."[30] A few months after Geraldine Miller had started the Bronx Household Technicians, Reed joined the organization. And much to Miller's consternation, other members selected Reed to assume leadership.[31] Reed recounted: "I went to this meeting in a woman's house in the Bronx. And at the first meeting, I became the Financial Secretary. . . . I kind of saw that as a thing of trust."[32] Reed eventually became the head of the National Committee on Household Employment.

Reed connected with Hulett in part because of their shared experience and understanding of domestic work. Like Hulett, Reed had worked as a domestic since she was a teenager and was deeply troubled by the stigma of household work, its culture of servitude and intimate nature. Her early experiences also instilled in her an independent streak and a feminist sensibility. Reed was born on November 25, 1939, in Rockaway, New York. Her mother, who got pregnant as a college student in South Carolina, went to New York to have the baby, then disappeared.[33] Reed initially resided with her aunt in New York, who sent her at the age of seven to live with a family friend in Orangeburg, South Carolina. Her adopted family in South Carolina had a vegetable farm, but the mother also worked as a domestic three days a week to supplement the family income.[34] Reed described her childhood as "painful." She was not physically hurt, but felt "mentally abused with [my adopted parents] always instilling in me that my parents did not want me."[35] At the age of sixteen, after finishing high school, she returned to her aunt's place in Brooklyn and soon began live-in household work. Several years later, when she was around twenty, she saved up some money and sent a check to her adoptive parents to repay them for taking her in. For Reed, the check was a final good-bye. She no longer felt indebted to them or any responsibility to stay in touch. She got an unlisted number and when asked about her family told people they were dead.[36]

Part of what Reed cherished as an employed teenager was her new-found independence. "I knew at my aunt's that I didn't have my own room, and I had to share it and everything, so this was kind of my own—even though I could have left [my job] and gone back any day. It was just that whole matter of being in control."[37] After being shunted from place to place throughout her childhood, Reed sought stability and control over her life, and gained a certain satisfaction from being able to take care of herself. "I am on my own. I'm doing what I want to do. And so there was that freedom that I had." Reed also appreciated her autonomy as a household worker. "Most household workers are their own bosses. And I think that that's probably what I liked most. . . . There was no one in a factory telling me—because I could have gone to work in a factory on an assembly line to do something to make money to go to school. But I chose this instead."[38]

Reed did not see herself doing domestic work for the rest of her life; she planned to return to the South and attend the historically black South Carolina State University.[39] "I used to fantasize at being a doctor. And . . . whenever I cleaned the fish, that was my surgical table, and I was dissecting. . . . But I just never thought that I would grow up to be a household worker."[40] Indeed, when she was a child, she hoped to someday become president of the United States. "I had teachers that said you could be anything that you wanted to be. What they never told me about was racism and sexism in this country, and that women did not aspire to be president."[41] Although she couldn't achieve her dreams, in her words, she ended up doing "the next best thing": household work.[42]

When she arrived in New York in the mid-1950s, Reed perused the newspaper ads and found a live-in position in East Meadow, Long Island, working from 7:30 a.m. until 9:00 p.m. for fifteen dollars a week. The family had two children who were so unruly they turned Reed off motherhood: "I've never seen brats like that in my life. Maybe that's when I made the conscious decision not to have children."[43] The family was "kind and everything, but, you know, they worked the shit out of me."[44] Although she was hired to take care of the children, she ended up also doing the washing, cooking, and cleaning. Reed's "room" was a tiny space in the basement near the furnace. "That's when I realized that we were supposed to be poor . . . and I was really upset for the first couple of nights, having to be there." The cramped quarters were compounded by isolation. As she explained, "I was very lonely."[45] Reed worked for the family for two years. "One day, I brought the children home from school, and I walked out of that house, and I never went back. I never said a word to anyone. I just left. I've learned a lot in these 20 years. And . . . what I've learned most is: we've got to organize." One journalist wrote of Reed that her "passion is the ultimate organization of her sister workers into the mainstream of American labor."[46]

The longer she labored as a domestic, the more critical Reed was of the occupation. "I became acutely aware of the differences in the people who were doing [domestic work] . . . and the stigma that was attached to it."[47] In addition, her employers wielded a great deal of control over her life, leaving her few opportunities to learn of her rights, let alone assert them. The first family she worked for warned her not to "mix with the people in the neighborhood." Her employers, she believed, were afraid she would "find out that those people were making fifty dollars as opposed to my fifteen dollars."[48] Her employer promised to "save" her money for her, although when she tried to collect it, there was disagreement about how much she was owed. According to Reed, employers defined a good worker as deferential and submissive. She explained, "The trouble is, people regard their homes as their empires. I say that you have no more right to exploit me in your home than you do to exploit me in your office. The good household worker is usually a slave. She doesn't complain, she doesn't know her rights, she doesn't ask for paid holiday or pay increases. She is indeed a gem. I was known as a good household worker. For five years I worked without a holiday. Sometimes I worked from 7 a.m. to 10 p.m."[49] Despite the difficulties she encountered, Reed spoke positively about the work she did. "I really love the work, and that's why I chose to organize the work—because I love what I chose to do as a profession."[50]

Reed dates her political awakening to the 1963 March on Washington, which she saw as historic, a cathartic moment that would bring the racial injustice she had endured into the national spotlight. Ironically, it was precisely the racial politics of household labor that prevented her from joining the 250,000 people who gathered at the Lincoln Memorial that day. Reed wanted to attend the march, but her employer insisted that she serve at a dinner party instead. Perhaps it was the disjuncture between the massive mobilization for black freedom and the ways in which the occupation inhibited her participation that fueled her commitment to reform. As she explained it, "I was just grouchy, really grouchy all day long, because I knew I was supposed to be in Washington. I would have gone—no doubt about it." As Reed was serving the meal that evening, the news footage of the march played in the background. One dinner guest commented: "I wonder what *they* want. . . . What *they* need is an education." Furious, Reed "accidentally" dumped a tray of green beans on the guest's lap, exclaiming: "Gee, I am so sorry. I really have to be educated as to how to serve beans."[51]

The stigma and exploitation Reed experienced, and her incipient feminism, convinced her that she needed to get involved. She "began thinking over my own life and trying to figure out how all those horrible things had happened to me in those houses I worked in. . . . And I began to think of the thousands, the millions of women just like myself who were working like slaves. . . . I thought, I've got to do *something*. So, then I heard about Dorothy Bolden who was organizing household workers in Atlanta, and then I made contact with the Women's Political Caucus and they put me in touch with the Household Technicians of America here in New York."[52] After her initial contact with the Bronx Household Technicians, founded and led by Geraldine Miller, Reed went on to form the Progressive Household Technicians and the New York State Coalition of Household Technicians. Despite some initial tension between Miller and Reed for control of the local chapter, the two were deeply committed to upgrading the occupation and organizing private household workers and found ways to work together.

Just as Dorothy Bolden organized on city buses, Reed traversed communal spaces in New York in search of household workers who would be receptive to her recruitment message. In the mid-1970s Reed worked for a family on Manhattan's Upper East Side from 7:30 a.m. until 1:30 p.m. and then returned at 5:30 to prepare dinner. Carolyn had a very close relationship with her employer, Mrs. Clayburgh, the mother of actress Jill Clayburgh. "She was wonderful. She was marvelous. . . . There was just general respect for what I did."[53] Mrs. Clayburgh encouraged Reed to become involved in the household technician movement, worked out a schedule to accommodate her activism, and even attended organizational meetings with her. She offered her a written contract, and always paid her on time. When Reed first applied for the job as a live-in housekeeper, she and her husband were warmly greeted at the door as "Mr. and Mrs. Reed." She took the job for $125 a week plus food and lodging. She and her husband, who was an accounting clerk at Columbia University, moved into the basement apartment of her employer's brownstone.

Reed devoted her afternoon break to organizing for the HTA. She entered the laundry rooms of apartment buildings: "The first rule of thumb is to get friendly with the doorman." Everyone in the neighborhood, not only the doormen, knew Reed. She also recruited at bus stops, service entrances, and neighborhood gourmet shops. Shopkeepers on Lexington Avenue regularly sent household workers her way. The *Village Voice* called her a "natural organizer at large."[54] There were no clear geographical boundaries for household-worker organizing, especially as the workplace was often off-limits for outreach efforts. Reed firmly believed that household workers had power, which she suggested may take the form of a strike with the support of other service workers. One reporter explained Reed's position this way: "The idea of striking entire residential streets of Manhattan with delivery and repairmen honoring the picket lines doesn't faze Reed in the least."[55] Her sense of the potential to strike came from her view of the fundamentally indispensable labor power of household workers: "The houses could not be run. You could never know how helpless people can be—especially wealthy people—until you've worked in their homes. Just one day of true hardship or true inconvenience and they'd want to bargain."[56] Only through this kind of collective power, she argued, could wages be raised and working conditions improved. For Reed, "Housekeepers, mostly black women, are the last frontier of labor organizing."[57]

Household Labor and Unionization

As Miller and Reed embarked on building a labor movement of household workers, their uneasy relationship with mainstream labor unions became clear. The largest and most influential unions had created a male-centered mass-production manufacturing model that has dominated US labor history. Since the early twentieth century, steelworkers, autoworkers, and mine workers, among others, initiated walkouts or sit-down strikes that very often stopped the wheels of production, forcing employers to recognize the union and meet their wage and benefit demands. The power of these workers stemmed from their large-scale workplaces. Coworkers could conspire on the production line, share grievances, and congregate and strategize in the break rooms and bathrooms. Utilizing mass power, they organized slowdowns and strikes that effectively shut down the factory.[58] In the 1960s service-sector workers—teachers, social workers, postal workers, clerical workers, healthcare workers—shifted the focus to the service counter.[59] This wave of service-sector organizing was an important turning point for the labor movement and brought more women and people of color into the fold. But like manufacturing employees, these new union members also worked in collective spaces. As powerful as these models were, domestic workers could not easily replicate them.

In addition to the circumscribed history of the union movement, the unequal development of social policy ensured the marginalization of household workers. The exclusion of domestic workers from key labor rights, such as minimum wage and the right to organize and bargain collectively, placed domestic workers outside the category of labor in the eyes of many people. Domestic work was one of the occupations that was not granted the protections extended to other workers with the passage of New Deal legislation in the 1930s because of racial politics as well as assumptions about what constituted work. The 1935 National Labor Relations Act that set up the National Labor Relations Board to facilitate collective bargaining between labor and management and guaranteed workers the right to form a union and negotiate with employers, for example, did not apply to household workers. The way both the union movement and social policy unfolded generated a perception that domestic workers were "unorganizable."[60] But the long history of household-worker activism belies this assumption. The view that domestic workers are unorganizable stems from cultural and legal constructions of "work" generated through law and patterns of mainstream labor organizing, rather than some inherent characteristic of household labor. That is, labor law in the 1930s, by creating distinctions among different kinds of work, as well as labor organizing that focused attention on the manufacturing sector, fostered a perception that household workers could not be organized. Certain categories of work were privileged as work and given the right to organize, while occupations such as domestic work were not.

Unions, because they established boundaries of privilege around their members, contributed to the marginalization of household workers. Most US unions didn't develop a commitment to a broad working-class politics. They pursued what historians have referred to as "bread and butter" politics—ensuring the economic well-being and advancement of their members, sometimes at the expense of other workers. Perhaps the most notorious example is the Cigar Makers Association in California at the end of the nineteenth century. It opposed the hiring of Chinese workers, denied them union membership, and affixed a union label verifying cigars had been made by white men to encourage consumers to buy only cigars made by white labor. Even when exclusions were not so blatant, unions had rarely organized workers who seemed to be on the margins of the American workforce.[61]

Because of this history, household workers had a degree of ambivalence and outright distrust of unions. Geraldine Roberts viewed organized labor as largely white and male with little interest in either women or workers of color. "I think that only males have control of organized labor." As Dorothy Bolden explained: "A lot of the maids were afraid to join. They were skeptical because they knew what unions had done in the past. . . . I don't think we realized how much 'union' frightens people."[62] In fact, Bolden, who had originally named her organization the National Domestic Workers Union of America changed it to the National Domestic Workers of America. Many of these women reached out to the labor community but found little support for their grass-roots organizing. Roberts lamented the disregard for her own work: "I haven't had very much support at all from the labor unions."[63]

Despite the checkered history of the mainstream labor movement, Carolyn Reed had a clear sense of the importance of class-based politics and the role of unions in shaping and redirecting political debate. Skeptics of unions, she argued, only looked at the negative: "What people see are the Teamsters' Union, or . . . they see the rip-off. They don't see the positive things that unions did."[64] Reed believed unions minimized class differences and created greater equality among Americans: "If it had not been for unionizing in this country, we would have a royal class."[65] Her vision was to create union-like structures and collective formations for domestic workers that could similarly reshape the political landscape. This could only be done effectively, however, if household workers had autonomy. Reed didn't want outside forces in control. "What I'd like to see is a strong union of household workers. . . . I think it has to be on our terms, not on the terms of some union organizers who see it as another membership—as another fee. I would never sell my household workers out to a union on that level."[66] Household workers could be much more effective organizing one another because they understood the occupation better. "I listen and I try to speak to the needs that they want," Reed explained.[67] "Unions . . . are run by men. I want the household workers union to be run by women."[68] Like Reed, most household technicians insisted on female control of organizations seeking to represent them.

Although most household-worker organizations were activist-type community-based groups, there were a few attempts by domestic workers and their allies to form labor unions. Notably, Mary McClendon, based in the union-stronghold city of Detroit, was closely allied with the labor movement. Lillian Hatcher of the UAW spoke at the founding meeting of the HWO. McClendon had considered the possibility of HWO joining the radical black auto union the Dodge Revolutionary Union Movement, which had organized in 1968 to obtain concessions from Chrysler and challenge racial inequality in the United Auto Workers local. She also launched a drive to unionize workers in the cleaning firm Dial-A-Maid with the goal of "building consciousness among the workers, informing them of the advantages of collective bargaining." McClendon joined Dial-A-Maid in 1972 to learn about the working conditions. Teams of two workers cleaned two houses a day earning $11 each. Workers received no benefits and only about 50 percent of the fee that the company charged the householder. McClendon persuaded enough Dial-A-Maid workers to sign authorization cards to hold a vote about whether to unionize in November 1972. But the day before the election, the company unexpectedly paid an additional bonus to its employees, who subsequently voted against unionization.[69]

In New York, longtime African American labor leader Benjamin McLaurin of the National Urban League and the Brotherhood of Sleeping Car Porters organized the Professional Household Workers Union with chapters in New York City and Westchester County.[70] Born in Jacksonville, Florida, McLaurin joined the International Brotherhood of Sleeping Car Porters in 1926. He worked with the union through the 1930s, serving as vice president and national secretary. McLaurin was broadly concerned with working-class and civil rights issues and was a key organizer, along with A. Philip Randolph, of the planned but not executed 1941 March on Washington, designed to pressure President Roosevelt to desegregate the defense industry and the armed forces. McLaurin also chaired the Mayor's Committee on Exploitation of Workers under New York mayor John Lindsay. As head of that body he drew attention to the plight of private household workers. This history and political commitment, as well as his hope to revitalize the Brotherhood, prompted McLaurin in the early 1970s to organize household workers.[71]

The Professional Household Workers Union, chartered in 1971 as Locals 1 and 2 by the International Brotherhood of Sleeping Car Porters, claimed a membership of two hundred to three hundred.[72] It called for a minimum wage of three dollars an hour, Social Security protections, and a standard contract, and ran a benefits and training program to upgrade the occupation.[73] It was the Professional Household Workers

Union that Geraldine Miller first came in contact with when she began to organize. Although the union and McLaurin helped organize the trip to the NCHE conference for several dozen household workers at Miller's urging, she was not impressed by the organization. Few domestic workers attended the meeting, and middle-class supporters crafted the agenda and set priorities. Needless to say, Miller was turned off. "I don't think that someone else can tell me as a person what it is that I need if I'm a household worker." Miller valued household worker autonomy and decided not to join the union or any organization run by McLaurin. "He did not strike me as being the person that I wanted to be under and I'd found out through NCHE that I could . . . get my own group together and it could be woman-run."[74] Miller, like other household workers, eagerly embraced the idea of establishing a labor organization of household workers but she staunchly resisted control and domination by individuals outside the occupation.

Although the Professional Household Workers could not sustain itself, established unions soon came to see the value of organizing women who worked in the home. In the late 1970s and early 1980s, several unions took up the task of organizing women employed by cleaning companies or state agencies as home-care workers. In 1977 New York State, with the support of Bronx state assemblyman Seymour Posner and local activists such as Carolyn Reed, gave domestic workers the legal right to organize and bargain collectively. Household workers in New York mobilized in support of the legislation. They took time off work on Tuesdays and traveled to Albany to speak on behalf of the bill. The original bill, which included all household workers, encountered opposition in the state senate and was whittled down to apply only to workers employed by cleaning firms and employment agencies. In the end, the legislation didn't affect the vast majority of private household workers. Many workers were critical of their lack of autonomy when employed by private firms and chose to work independently. As Carolyn Reed explained: The employment contracts with private firms are "like something out of the 19th century. Those agencies are run strictly for the protection of the employer. I'd like to see them all closed up tomorrow. No, we must have a union, and it must be our own union."[75]

Nevertheless, activists who supported the legislation saw it as a first step, as a tool to bolster their own organizing campaigns that established an important precedent.[76]

Home-care workers, who were paid by the state but hired by private individuals who needed home-care assistance, had many more organizing victories. The Service Employees International Union (SEIU) started a Household Workers Organizing Committee in New York City, which unionized workers in the housekeeping programs of charitable agencies as well as the city's Division of Home Attendants. By 1982, SEIU represented fourteen thousand workers in their home-care division in New York City. On the West Coast, the California Homemakers Association engaged in collective bargaining on behalf of home attendants. The organizing of home-care workers was effective because multiple employees worked for and were paid by a single agency, so even though the work was isolated, they were able to use collective pressure to secure concessions.[77] This new phase of organizing represented important shifts in the labor market because of how the labor of care and cleaning was increasingly paid for by third parties when it was done in the home. Still, it didn't address the problems of private household workers paid by individuals.

The particular character of private household work, the long-standing distrust of unions, and the inapplicability of traditional organizing models fostered distinctive strategies for domestic workers. They relied on nonhierarchical approaches to movement building, empowered domestic workers to negotiate individually with employers, and lobbied for legislative and state-based protections. They utilized the personal nature of the relationship to their advantage as well as collective demands to empower workers and claim control over the work process. Domestic-worker organizations were never able to achieve the same kind of institutional standing as other labor formations. Nevertheless, household workers embraced their status as labor activists and this became an integral component of their identity. As a category of workers not protected by—or subject to—NLRB rules, domestic workers were able to develop different kinds of mobilization methods and, in some cases, a more democratic process. Out of necessity and with an arsenal of creativity and imagination, these poor women of color developed alternative approaches to labor organizing in the 1960s and 1970s.[78]

African American women brought visibility to the domestic workplace, turned public spaces into organizing sites, made claims for social and economic rights, and worked to raise the status of their employment. They offered new narratives about the sense of themselves as workers who deserved rights and in that process shifted conversations about the meaning of labor organizing.

CHAPTER 6

Social Rights, Feminist Solidarity, and the FLSA

Until they recognize the unpaid labor in the home,
they won't recognize paid labor.

—CAROLYN REED

In the early 1970s, Gloria Steinem, prominent feminist, journalist, and supporter of NCHE, held a fund-raiser in New York City, hiring members of the Household Technicians to cater it. Some guests were appalled by the image of black women in uniforms serving the crowd of largely white women. HTA member Carolyn Reed served at the gathering that evening but perceived the situation very differently. She lectured the attendees of the fund-raiser: "I don't like you to think we're *maids*—we are household technicians; we're experienced; we are professionals. And we're being paid—that's very important . . . so you have to get it out of your head that this is a demeaning job. If you don't want to do it, I'm glad you don't want to, because we will gladly do it for you—but for a salary, and with respect."[1] Reed recounted this incident in many public venues, using it to illustrate her fundamental commitment to the professionalization of household labor. When she was invited to the White House a few years later and observed black men, and only black men, in white gloves serving tea and coffee, she expressed a different view of the racial divide: "What I saw in the White House was very disturbing to me, because it certainly reminded me of plantation days."[2] In the case of the Steinem fund-raiser, Reed seems to have been restricting her critique to a feminist devaluation of household labor that existed in the 1970s. Reed's insistence in this feminist gathering on the value of household labor and the need for adequate pay reflected the domestic workers' campaign in the early 1970s to build a feminist alliance to support the passage of minimum wage legislation for domestic workers.

The minimum wage campaign was part of domestic workers' claim to social citizenship—the economic security that was increasingly guaranteed for workers by the state.[3] Domestic workers, who up to that time were excluded from most labor laws, lobbied for and won amendments to the Fair Labor Standards Act in 1974, which granted them a federal minimum wage. Household workers testified about the value of this work and its need for recognition and legal protection, countering racial and gender assumptions that undergirded congressional debate on the amendments.[4] Domestic workers' views dovetailed with those of some feminists who felt stifled and burdened by their roles as housewives and sought to draw attention to unpaid household labor. Despite what seemed like a conflict of interest between middle-class feminists, who were sometimes employers, and household workers, they developed a strategic alliance to push for federal labor protection, both having experienced the consequences of the degradation of household labor. The HTA's coalition building and lobbying relied on feminist labor activism and cross-class alliances among women.[5]

The passage of the amendments, however, was a bittersweet victory. It reversed a historic exclusion of domestic workers from basic labor protections and won legal recognition of their work. But the legislation also created a new stratification among domestic workers, some of whom—such as home-health-care aides employed by an agency and live-in workers—were explicitly excluded from the legislation. The campaign for minimum wage was historic nonetheless—it expanded the definition of "worker," which had been circumscribed in the 1930s. If the struggle for civil rights was intended to deracialize American political citizenship, then the domestic workers' rights movement aimed to deracialize and degender the concept of work as embedded in American social policy.

DOMESTIC WORK, RACE, AND RIGHTS

For decades, household work was traditionally outside the boundaries of US labor law. Legislation passed in the 1930s as part of the New

Deal became the key marker of social citizenship. It assured much of the working class the economic and political benefits of American national belonging. Through guarantees of a minimum wage, unemployment compensation, and Social Security, as well as the right to organize and bargain collectively. But because these rights were not universal, the New Deal fostered inequality. By linking the benefits of social citizenship to contributions made through employment and excluding certain types of labor, it reinforced and re-created the racialized and gendered hierarchy of the labor market.[6] Those outside the labor market in need of economic assistance were either dependents on full-time wage earners or were relegated to second-tier, less generous, and more stigmatized public assistance, such as Aid to Families with Dependent Children or Old Age Assistance, programs generally falling into the category of "welfare." Women performing unpaid household labor were denied the benefits of economic citizenship, as were part-time and intermittent workers, who tended to be people of color.

But even among those who worked full-time, not all contributions to the labor market were equally valued.[7] Southern congressmen, insisting on control over the African American labor force, policymakers, and labor leaders, who prioritized the needs of the white male industrial worker, advocated circumscribed coverage of work-related benefits.[8] The factory worker became the prototype that informed assumptions about what constituted legitimate work and who qualified as a worker. Much of the paid work performed by women and African Americans, including domestic work, did not receive the benefits of social citizenship, establishing what historian Eileen Boris calls the "racialized gendered state."[9] Thus, New Deal labor policy further degraded domestic work through legal statutes.[10] The contradictory legacy of the New Deal makes clear that in the twentieth century, even as the United States seemed to embrace a more robust citizenship through the expansion of social welfare policy, legislators embedded stratification in the category of "social citizenship" by connecting it to race, gender, and one's position within the labor market. So social status and work, or more specifically, legal recognition of work, became the barometer for social citizenship. Those outside the labor market or in those occupations not included in New Deal social policy were more marginalized.

The Fair Labor Standards Act (FLSA) was a cornerstone of New Deal labor policy. Passed in 1938, it established the first federal minimum wage law, mandated overtime pay, and abolished child labor. The FLSA extended the power of the federal government, which was justified in terms of the government's right to regulate interstate commerce. Like other labor legislation, it excluded several categories of workers, such as those in retail, service, nonprofit, government, agricultural, and domestic work, jobs performed disproportionately by women and people of color. At the moment of passage, the FLSA covered only 20 percent of the American workforce and had the effect of privileging some forms of labor over others. Although the constitutional justification for the federal government's regulation of the workplace was rooted in the commerce clause, the definition of interstate commerce was malleable, and expanded over the course of the next forty years.[11]

Since the late 1930s, white labor feminists, including Esther Peterson, Frieda Miller, and members of the Women's Trade Union League, and black feminists such as Claudia Jones, Marvel Cooke, and Dorothy Height, had lobbied for extension of the federal minimum wage law and labor protections to domestic workers. In 1996 a political climate committed to alleviating poverty and inequality contributed to expansion of the law to cover farmworkers, nursing home employees, and school and hospital workers. By the early 1970s, domestic workers were the only significant category of workers excluded from minimum wage laws, and only three states—Wisconsin, Massachusetts, and New York—provided minimum wage for household workers.[12] So, even before the emergence of the HTA, labor activists and reformers had pushed to make the FLSA more inclusive.

The emergence of a domestic workers' rights movement added urgency and political pressure to this trend. The HTA, along with the NCHE and a coalition of civil rights, labor, and women's organizations, lobbied hard for passage of a congressional bill that would increase the minimum wage and expand minimum wage coverage to domestic workers. Domestic-worker representation and testimony proved to be an important component in the legislative debates. Congressional hearings and efforts to mobilize support for the bill provided a platform for domestic workers and their allies to publicly share their stories.

Shirley Chisholm, the first African American congresswoman, led the fight for the passage of a minimum wage bill. Chisholm's family was originally from Barbados, but Chisholm was born in Brooklyn. Her mother was a seamstress, although, like many other women of African descent, during the Great Depression she took on domestic work to help support her family. Chisholm tied her support for minimum wage for domestic work to her own family's history. In a speech before the House of Representatives in 1973, to enhance the power of her comments, she drew on that history: "My own mother was a domestic, so I speak from personal experience."[13] Chisholm's reference to her family history was another indication of the way in which personal stories of household labor became part of the discussion around the FLSA. Chisholm allied herself with the household technicians movement and attended the HTA founding convention as well as subsequent national gatherings. According to Geraldine Miller, "She was an outspoken advocate for the disadvantaged and the underdog. She was not big. She wasn't tall, but she was dynamite."[14] In 1972 Chisholm spoke before the national convention of domestic workers: "Organize and work together with the women's groups and labor and civil rights groups in your community," she urged them. "Hold meetings and rallies. Talk to the local press. Let everyone know that you are first-class citizens and that you will not settle for anything less than a fair and equal chance to share in the fruits of this country."[15] For Chisholm, labor protections were the most important indicator of equal citizenship, and she made passage of minimum wage for domestic workers one of her primary goals in Congress.[16]

The passage of amendments to the FLSA was a protracted process that took close to three years. It began in the summer of 1971, when the US House of Representatives Committee on Education and Labor held hearings to consider amendments to increase the minimum wage and expand coverage to government employees and domestic workers. The AFL-CIO and civil rights and women's organizations supported the bill, while the US Chamber of Commerce as well as some Republicans opposed it.[17] Both the House and the Senate passed a version of this legislation in 1972, but a conservative coalition in the House, fearful that the final bill would be more liberal, never sent it to a conference committee to iron out differences with the Senate. In 1973 Congress passed another minimum wage bill, but President Nixon, citing concerns about inflation and job loss, vetoed it. In March 1974 Congress passed a nearly identical minimum wage bill. This time, Nixon, feeling politically vulnerable in the midst of the Watergate scandal but also aware that Congress had the votes to override a veto, signed the bill. The 1974 law raised the minimum wage and extended it to domestic workers, as well as state and local employees. From the initial committee hearings until the bill became a law, household workers played a role in the legislative debates and the public dialogue about domestic workers' labor rights and mobilized support for the legislation.[18]

As Congress debated the bill to extend FLSA coverage in 1971, domestic workers gathered just a few miles away at the Marriot Motor Hotel for their first national convention in Washington, DC. Convention participants took advantage of their geographical proximity to Capitol Hill to lobby Congress. Over the course of the weekend, delegations of household workers visited congressional officials to make a case for passage of the legislation. Mary McClendon, for example, went with a delegation of thirty-six household workers to Representative John Conyers's office to rally support for the bill. In addition, Edith Sloan and Josephine Hulett testified in support of the legislation before a congressional committee. During the two-year period when the bills were debated, members of the HTA and the NCHE made powerful arguments about the value of their labor. Testifying before the House Subcommittee on Labor in 1973, Sloan framed domestic work as one of a number of options available for those entering the labor market. She argued that were it not for low wages, domestic work would be a better occupational choice than factory work: "We are convinced that one of the major reasons why many men and women choose monotonous assembly line positions in factories is that they have little choice. A more rewarding, interesting job caring for an infant or toddler or elderly person simply does not command a decent, living wage."[19] It is unclear whether or not higher wages alone would have attracted new recruits to the field of domestic service, given the low status, servile character, and demanding time commitments of the job.[20] Nevertheless, Sloan's comment is important because of her characterization of household labor as inherently superior to "monotonous assembly line positions." It reflected a widespread belief among domestic-worker activists that the work they performed was important and gratifying. Carolyn Reed explained: "I feel very strongly that I contribute just as much as my doctor contributes, you know. And that because he is a doctor does not make him better than me, as a household technician."[21] In this way, the campaign for minimum wage was connected to the struggle for dignity, recognition, and professionalization, as well as the goal of social citizenship, which assured household workers a level of economic security.

Sloan insisted that domestic work be afforded the same rights of social citizenship and New Deal benefits as other occupations: "Pay must be increased to provide a livable wage. Second, workers must receive the so-called 'fringe benefits,' which long ago stopped being 'fringes' in every other major American industry. At this time, household workers usually do not receive paid sick leave, vacations, or holidays. Coverage under unemployment and workmen's compensation is extremely limited and varies widely from state to state."[22] Mary McClendon similarly spoke of the disconnect in citizenship rights and civic responsibilities when she outlined the denial of basic benefits to household workers and concluded, "It is crystal clear that these workers have no constitutional protection of the law, yet their sons and relatives march off to Vietnam to die."[23] For McClendon and Sloan, the rights of social citizenship were precisely that—rights—rather than privileges or benefits. And domestic workers were entitled to the same economic rights as other American workers.

RACE, GENDER, AND WORK

The male-dominated congressional debate surrounding the minimum wage bill exposed the racial and gender assumptions about women, housework, race, and class embedded in social policy. Politicians and policymakers framed housework and domestic work as primarily women's work and cast minimum wage for domestic workers in terms of the rights of domestic workers versus the rights of housewives.[24] Legislators opposed the minimum wage bill because they claimed it would bring "the federal bureaucracy into the kitchen of the American housewife,"[25] and they wanted to protect the domain of white middle-class women.[26] Robert Thompson of the US Chamber of Commerce predicted a flood of "irate housewives," because the law would increase costs and prohibit some women from hiring domestic workers.[27]

By relegating the question of minimum wage for domestic workers to the "women's sphere," male politicians employed a rhetorical strategy that absolved them of any responsibility for the legal rights of domestic workers. They used the cloak of gender to dismiss the class and race politics that were central to the exclusion of domestic workers from labor legislation. They placed responsibility for low wages and poor treatment squarely on the shoulders of middle-class female employers—their "wives"—and framed domestic work as an occupation that took place in the privacy of the home, which legislators presumably could not regulate. This argument about the sanctity of the private sphere reinforced the artificial construction of the home as a personal space of refuge devoid of politics. Compounding the home/business distinction, policymakers also claimed that housewife-employers were incapable of complying with the law and keeping records, thus making the legislation impractical because housewives had minimal business knowledge. Secretary of Labor Peter Brennan explained: "Homemakers are not engaged in business in the traditional sense with experience in maintaining business records."[28] Brennan supported the minimum wage increase but opposed extending coverage to household workers, a position that reflected his class politics. Born and raised in New York City, Brennan was of working-class origin and a certified union man. He started off as a housepainter during the Depression—working, ironically, like household employees and housewives, in the domestic sphere. He rose up the ranks of the Painters Union and eventually became president of the Building and Construction Trades Council of

Greater New York. He served as secretary of labor under Presidents Nixon and Ford from 1973 to 1975. Although Brennan was an unwavering advocate for the rights of working people, his opposition to the minimum wage for domestic workers illustrates his somewhat narrow gender- and race-based view of labor.

Although Brennan seemed to discount the importance of household labor, a closer reading of the FLSA legislative debate underscores a deeper concern of congressmen and administration officials. They were fearful not only of "irate" housewives and their supposedly inadequate accounting practices but also of a potential disruption of the gender division of labor and its consequences. Clearly defining and recognizing domestic work posed a particular problem for male politicians, who quickly realized that raising the status of domestic workers meant raising the status of unpaid household work performed by many women. Senator Pete Dominick, an opponent of the bill, in his exchange with Secretary of Labor Brennan, expressed concern about the difficulty of defining domestic work and the impracticality of including domestic workers in the legislation. He argued that "the services provided by the householder ought to be included in the definition of what is or is not a minimum wage." Brennan elaborated on the problem this recognition posed: "Yes . . . you open the door to a lot of trouble. Your wife will want to get paid. I think we are going to be in trouble here because, as we say in here, there are many cases the wife cannot afford it; she will have to do it herself or someone in the family will have to. That means that you or I or we have to pay her. So we have to be very careful unless we are ready to do dishes."[29]

The legislative debates are striking because, although congressmen and administration officials rhetorically framed domestic work as an abstract and distant issue outside their domain, the question of domestic labor and FLSA coverage for household employees was deeply personal for some of them. Rather than arguing that domestic work was not really work, this discussion reveals how they were quite clear that the home was a site of work and the labor of household workers *was* work—work that they, as congressmen, did not want to perform. Their narrative exposed their understanding of the links between paid and unpaid household labor and the belief that the gender division of labor was a foundation for the social order.

Revaluing Household Labor

Domestic-worker organizers similarly made connections between paid and unpaid labor in the home, which enabled them to build a cross-class, cross-race gender alliance. In making their claim for minimum wage, domestic workers drew attention to the work that took place in the ostensibly private space of the home—both the work of social reproduction that was associated with women's unpaid household labor and work that was performed for pay primarily by women of color. By making this link, they shifted the conversation away from the responsibilities and shortcomings of white female employers toward the way that men characterized housework as women's work and left female employers and employees to deal with it. Household workers' understanding of the gendered nature of their employment and the common experiences of employer and employee prompted them to seek allies among middle-class women in the campaign for regulation of domestic work.

Domestic-worker advocates were acutely aware of the gendered middle-class conflict around household labor. They observed interactions within the homes of the more affluent and understood the implications of male politicians relegating housework to women's domain, especially in the context of a burgeoning women's movement. They used this to their advantage by driving a wedge between middle-class men and women and exploiting tensions about who needed to take responsibility for household labor. They claimed that failure to pass the amendments—rather than their passage—would result in a shortage of domestic workers because women would leave the occupation, suggesting that upgrading the occupation was necessary to retain domestic workers. But the loss of paid household labor, they argued, would not lead to double duty for housewives in the home, particularly in light of the women's movement's demands to be unshackled from household work and for greater employment opportunities outside the home.

Instead, they predicted the burden would fall on congressmen. Geneva Reid, a leader in the HTA, explained to a House committee in 1973 that if the shortage of domestic workers continued apace, "it may come to this, the affluent and Congressmen cleaning up after themselves because the women of the household have become liberated and have joined the work force and will not have time to cook, clean, wash, iron, and take care of the children."[30]

The domestic workers' rights movement saw itself as part of this burgeoning women's rights movement. Both Carolyn Reed and Geraldine Miller helped build a coalition of domestic workers and middle-class women's organizations in support of minimum wage legislation for domestic workers. Both had solid connections to a number of women's groups. Miller was president of the Bronx chapter of the National Organization for Women and the first president of the NOW Women of Color Task Force. She served at different points as president, co-president, and vice president in the National Congress of Neighborhood Women and rubbed elbows with prominent leaders such as Florence Kennedy and Bella Abzug. She saw her labor activism as feminist and her feminism as underpinning her labor activism. Miller reflected on the need for feminist alliances in the campaign for minimum wage legislation: "We really and truly needed the help of the other women who were of different nationalities to help us push for that, and that's the reason why we got under the Federal Minimum Wage."[31]

Carolyn Reed similarly found her first political allies among feminists. She was on the executive committee of the Women's Action Alliance, the steering committee of the National Women's Political Caucus, and a cofounder of the National Black Feminist Organization. She brought to her labor organizing a feminist sensibility rooted in her fierce independence and the aspirations of her childhood. As she explained, "I was happy to be involved with feminist groups. Before even knowing the word, I had always, in a sense been a feminist."[32]

Although both Miller and Reed, like other household technicians, claimed an identity as feminists, their relationship with the women's movement was somewhat tenuous. Paid household labor was largely an occupation of women employing women. As Mary McClendon explained in 1975: "Over work and under payment has been inflicted upon Household Technicians by white and black female employers, as well as white and black male employers. So many females have been slave masters of other females for over two hundred years."[33] Historically, domestic workers had strained relationships with their employers. The mistress of the household was often the source of domestic workers' most trying work experiences. Female employers were responsible for the day-to-day supervision of "their help," including establishing working hours and wages.[34] The occupation divided women by race and class by defining women who engaged in domestic work as "dirty" and the women who benefited from their labor as "clean."[35] The status, opportunities, and identity of middle-class women were inextricably linked to their access to domestic workers, who could attend to the time-consuming and unpleasant tasks that made for a well-run home.[36]

The women's movement of the 1960s complicated the potential alliance between domestic workers and middle-class women. The mainstream women's movement, which most often defined liberation in terms of paid employment outside the home, expressed disdain for domestic work. Betty Friedan, author of the seminal book *The Feminine Mystique*, described housework as boring and repetitious. As she explained: "Vacuuming the living room floor—with or without makeup—is not work that takes enough thought or energy to challenge any woman's full capacity."[37] The pitting of household labor against work opportunities outside the home contributed to negative perceptions about the value of this work. Middle-class women's claims that they needed jobs outside the home because housework lacked meaning inadvertently undermined the arguments of sectors of the women's movement that sought to revalue household labor and support the domestic workers' rights movement.

Carolyn Reed, on the other hand, saw a dirty house as an opportunity. "[Feminists'] theory was that housework is dirty work. I happen not to consider it dirty work and I had to get it across to them that the dirtier their places are, the more job security we have."[38] Household workers believed that middle-class women's low opinion of household labor contributed to the marginalized status of domestic workers.

The NCHE drew links between the degradation of domestic work and middle-class women's entry into the labor force.

"Underlying many difficulties that household workers face in trying to improve pay and working conditions," the organization stated in a document in 1976, "is a more subtle and pervasive problem of the household worker's image in our own eyes and the eyes of our employers. This image is deeply rooted in Americans' attitudes toward women and their traditional functions and toward the service professions generally. . . . Ironically, the changing attitudes that are giving many American women a new sense of their own worth and dignity, is working against the professional dignity of household workers. As women enter the work-force finding careers outside the home, they look on housework as demeaning drudgery."[39]

But the idea that housework was not meaningful and that women needed other sources of fulfillment represented only one component of the women's movement. There were multiple strands and competing perspectives among women's activists.[40]

Some socialist feminists had a different perspective from the mainstream women's movement. New York Radical Feminists was a staunch supporter of domestic workers. In October 1973, it cosponsored with the Professional Household Workers Union a speak-out on working-class women that was attended by seventy-five people. Invitees were encouraged to "hear what it's like to be a household worker," illustrating the importance of storytelling and testimony to convey ideas about the occupation. NYRF argued that working-class and middle-class women had closely aligned interests. Pointing to the economic vulnerability of middle-class women who were not financially independent, they suggested: "Most women . . . are only a step (or a man) away from a working-class job—if they are not already employed in one."[41]

Socialist feminists, like domestic workers, rethought the meaning and value of household labor. They offered a broad critique of American capitalism and its relationship to patriarchy. They argued that the devaluation of housework was a product of economic development—in particular the emergence of wage labor—and the consequent separation of public and private spheres. Women's reproductive labor, they believed, was absolutely essential to the functioning of the economy. Without it, American capitalism would not have a next generation of workers. Rather than viewing domestic labor as nonproductive labor, they suggested that it was productive and benefited capitalists because the costs of sustaining workers was borne by the unpaid labor of women.[42]

One offshoot of socialist feminism was the "wages for housework" movement. Spearheaded by Selma James and Maria Dalla Costa, the wages for housework movement, rather than seeing women's employment outside the home as the only path to liberation, attempted to reclaim housework as legitimate labor.[43] Much like welfare rights activists who made a claim for government assistance to support them in their work as mothers, members of the wages for housework movement advocated the commodification of household labor—attaching a wage to it as a way to revalue the work and compensate women. This argument for commodification was rooted in an understanding that wages were a measure of labor's worth in a capitalist economy. Moving domestic labor from the unpaid to the paid category, they believed, would upgrade the work. In a similar vein, Reed supported Social Security for housewives as a way to recognize that work, claiming, "they can all become household technicians."[44] Although this was a legitimate argument, the experiences of paid domestic workers offer a different perspective. Some domestic labor had been commodified since the emergence of capitalism. But as domestic workers repeatedly attested, a wage, in and of itself, did not raise the status of the work.[45] Socialist feminists offered promise for collaboration across feminist lines, but were, however, only a minority of women's activists.

As middle-class women won access to previously closed occupations and entered the workforce at a faster rate, the question of who would do the household labor became more pressing. As journalist Gail Sheehy wrote in the Boston Globe in 1980, "Behind just about every successful woman I know with a public as well as private life, there is another woman."[46] One employer who nominated her domestic worker for Atlanta's Maid of the Year testified about the need for household assistance to further her own goals: "Having Lula with the family made it possible for me to continue my education, and to do my research and teaching which I enjoy very much. If it had not been for Lula, I could not have worked toward and earned my PhD. . . . I never worried about [my children] coming home from school without me there because they came home to Lula's welcoming love. . . . Best of all, because she kept my house for me, I could spend all my time at home with my husband and daughters, because the chores were done."[47] Increasingly, middle-class women who saw personal empowerment bound up with employment outside the home wanted to free themselves from household labor. The goal for many in the women's movement became, as Angela Davis put it, "the abolition of housework as the private responsibility of individual women."[48]

Domestic work cut at the heart of the feminist dilemma of a desire for employment while still attempting to fulfill the responsibilities of mothering and housework. Feminist demands for greater contributions from male partners and government-funded child care to resolve this dilemma were less successful. The privatized solution of hiring someone else—preferably someone compliant and inexpensive—to do the work became the most viable one.[49] As *Essence* magazine explained in 1974: "It is the women who have fought sex discrimination in employment who are now discriminating against the Black women hired to work in their homes."[50] The goals of the mainstream women's movement increasingly narrowed to focus on the employment prospects of middle-class women and their individual achievements. Mary McClendon summarized the problem this way: "Nice ladies who have bought their freedom from household work at the expense of those who have no choice and must work for insulting and inadequate wages."[51] The most visible feminist heroes became those who broke through the glass ceiling rather than those who still labored downstairs but made possible the success of those at the top. The hiring of domestic workers as middle-class women went to work enabled feminist liberation for some without disrupting the gendered social order in middle-class homes.

Despite the fragility of the feminist coalition, household technicians forged ahead in developing a strategic alliance to pass the FLSA amendments. Domestic workers' stories mobilized the support of groups such as the National Organization for Women and the Business and

Professional Women's Club, as well as some socialist feminists.[52] The congressional debates provided a platform for domestic workers to speak out publicly, reach out to other women, and share their narratives of domestic labor. Their gendered analysis suggested that household labor, whether paid or unpaid, united women of different backgrounds.

HTA activists drew parallels between the plight of domestic workers and the dilemmas of the middle-class women who hired them. Both were responsible for housework. Both understood what maintaining a home entailed. Both experienced the devaluation of housework in the larger society. Josephine Hulett succinctly explained this in an interview: "After all, there's a sense in which *all* women are household workers. And unless we stop being turned against each other, unless we organize together, we're never going to make this country see household work for what it really is—human work, not just 'woman's work': a job that deserves dignity, fair pay, and respect."[53] Similarly, Geraldine Miller argued that "as we upgrade the household worker, we will upgrade the woman in the home."[54]

Many feminists, like those at Gloria Steinem's fund-raiser, grappled with the ethical issues of paid household help, and for political and personal reasons did not want to replicate hierarchical or exploitative relationships. Domestic workers acknowledged feminist unease and assured them that there was nothing wrong with hiring household help as long as workers were well paid and treated as professionals. Josephine Hulett recalled her interactions with middle-class women who were hesitant about hiring domestic help. "I've also met women involved in the Women's Movement who feel guilty about employing another woman, and who even fire their household worker and try to do without. I explain to them that we need the job; it's a *good* job. We just want to be respected—and to be decently paid."[55]

Domestic workers argued that even if employers experienced financial constraints, the demand for decent pay was nonnegotiable and family budgets shouldn't be balanced on the backs of household workers. Hulett believed female employers should demand more money from their bosses or their husbands to make ends meet. "I've run into employers who say, 'But how can I pay that? I don't have any money myself.' I sympathize with those women. I know we're all pretty badly off. . . . But if you didn't have the price of a car, you couldn't talk the dealer down—you'd just have to get along without it. And that's the way it should be with household help too. Maybe if women employers see it that way, they'll make more trouble with their husbands or their own employers, and get proper pay for themselves and their sisters."[56] Domestic workers framed gender solidarity in terms of privileged women's support for poor women's work and suggested that middle-class women's advocacy of domestic worker rights would benefit all women.

Domestic workers forged a diverse coalition with a small group of feminists. Their ability to ally with feminists of very different political orientations is a testament to the significance of this issue and the ways in which different categories of women were connected to it. Household workers didn't gloss over the vast differences between poor and middle-class women. But they did find a common thread that linked them. Through their testimony and storytelling, domestic workers articulated an alternative vision that claimed housework as real work and tied the degradation of the occupation to both women's unpaid household labor as well as the history of racism. Domestic workers' claims of household work as labor powerfully resonated with middle-class women who felt burdened by their domestic responsibilities.

The underlying tension between middle-class women and household workers became more clear when attempts were made to enforce the new minimum wage legislation. After passage of the amendments in 1974, HTA and NCHE made a commitment "to increase knowledge of and compliance with fair labor standards among household employers and the general public."[57] Gloria Steinem was asked to head the program and mobilize local women's organizations to ensure compliance with the FLSA.[58] Steinem pledged the active support of the women's movement. Carolyn Reed had a great deal of respect for Steinem. "When I think of people who've supported us, the first name that comes up is Gloria Steinem . . . she is accessible without the whole fanfare. She was the person who has been most consistent—really putting her money and her actions where her mouth is, just constantly doing it and not really seeking publicity for it. . . . You can call on her and get action."[59] Steinem also appreciated her alliance with the Household Technicians, especially because it projected a different image of the women's movement. She said about Reed in 1993: she was "exactly the kind of person who should get recognized and doesn't and then people think only three of us are feminists and we all wear suits."[60] Carolyn Reed did not wear a suit, but for her a maid's uniform could be as fiercely feminist as the attire of those climbing the corporate ladder.

The goal of the NCHE minimum wage–enforcement campaign was to get ten thousand employers to place a sticker in the window of their homes that read "This is a Fair Labor Standards Household." This harkened back to a New Deal strategy to encourage businesses that complied with federal regulations to display a blue eagle. Despite the support of individuals like Steinem and their laudable efforts, enforcement remained an insurmountable problem, even among feminists. Educating millions of employers was a massive undertaking and many employers were simply unable or unwilling to comply on their own. As middle-class and working-class women of different racial backgrounds joined the workforce, they relied more on paid household workers. The situation was especially difficult for working-class women for whom a generous wage for a child-care worker or housekeeper would have likely stretched them beyond their limits. Did they have alternatives? It seems not, given the competing demands of working and having children at home to care for. Yet, poor women, such as household workers, struggled with this same conundrum and rarely had the option of hiring someone to do this work for them. And because cutbacks and political attacks on welfare increasingly required welfare recipients to take paid employment outside the home, staying home to take care of their own children was less of an option. Day care was one solution. In 1968, Dorothy Bolden and the NDWUA in Atlanta hoped to start a worker-run day-care program because "far too many of the women have no child care so their children are left alone during the day."[61] In 1976, the NCHE's "Program Priorities" called for government-funded affordable day-care programs to meet the child-care needs of household workers and other poor women.[62] Government-funded day care, also advocated by some feminist groups, never gained traction, however. Household workers who were mothers patched together unreliable caretaking options—they turned to friends, family, and unregulated day care, or left children home alone. And they rarely had the luxury of returning to a clean house after a long day at work. As Bolden explained: A typical day for her was to "get up at 4 a.m. to leave home by 6 a.m., and be on the job by 8 a.m., perform all those duties necessary to the proper management of a household for eight hours, leave there by 4 p.m. to be home by 6 p.m. where I would do the same things I've done all over again for my own family."[63] Working-class women's hardship is not something all women should suffer. But recognizing those hardships could and should prompt us to consider solutions to meet the needs of all families, regardless of their economic status.

THE MEANING OF RIGHTS

The passage of the FLSA amendments in 1974 was an important milestone in African American history and the history of social rights. It won labor rights for this excluded sector of workers and brought them into the fold of legally recognized labor. An NCHE press release claimed: "Minimum wage coverage for household workers gives to these one and a half million employees a legal mandate, a recognition of the value of their services and basic equality with other workers. . . . For the domestic worker, whether she is Black, White, Red or Brown, or lives in the North, East, South or West, it means a new respect—for her service and her person—and the ability to support herself and family."[64] The passage of minimum wage legislation was one of several victories for household workers in the postwar period. In 1950 they won the right to Social Security assistance. In 1974, they came under minimum wage laws. And in 1976, they obtained access to unemployment insurance. This body of legislation addressed a fundamental inequality that had structured social rights since the 1930s and marked the postwar period as one of racial progress. Although they never achieved full equality—domestic workers are still excluded from the National Labor Relations Act, the Occupational Safety and Health Act, and civil rights laws—these advances were important and represented the movement's effort to upgrade household labor.

Household workers' struggles were part of a broader campaign for economic rights among social justice advocates. Activists in the 1960s and 1970s utilized divergent strategies, including demanding reparations for slavery and a guaranteed annual income to bring all Americans to a minimum standard of living, but the most common approach was seeking legislative equity in the workplace. Mainstream feminist and civil rights activists lobbied for the Equal Pay Act and the Civil Rights Act, both of which attempted to ameliorate racial and gender discrimination in employment. Passed in 1963, the Equal Pay Act, spearheaded by the Women's Bureau, amended the FLSA and prohibited unequal wages between men and women for the same work. Women in occupations already covered by the FLSA would be assured equality with their male counterparts. Title VII of the Civil Rights Act of 1964 prohibited discriminatory practices in the workplace and gave employees a means to file claims with the Equal Employment Opportunity Commission to challenge race and sex discrimination. These acts helped end widespread practices of discrimination in the labor force, opened up previously closed occupations, and made hiring and evaluation processes more transparent.[65]

But there was a tension between the antidiscrimination approaches of the Equal Pay Act and the Civil Rights Act—which focused on the rights of individual workers' equal access to previously closed occupations or equal pay for men and women in certain occupations—and broader campaigns to expand the social safety net, include unprotected workers in labor law, and upgrade occupations. The individual rights approach, according to historian Alice Kessler-Harris, benefited middle-class women most and left poor women vulnerable. Scholar Venus Green, for example, argues that NOW's adoption of a narrow, gender-based concept of inequality in its battles with Sears and AT&T failed to adequately address the needs of black women. Similarly, the campaign for comparable worth, which sought equal pay between women and men for jobs of similar skill level, didn't address the growing divide among women in occupations of different skill level. Most working-class women were not competing with men for jobs, but were in gender-segregated occupations. Consequently, white women benefited much more from these decisions than did African American women.[66] Antidiscrimination laws enabled middle-class and professional women opportunities in previously male-dominated occupations while the continued devaluation of care work assured them access to an underpaid labor force of domestic workers, home care attendants, and nursing home workers, to whom they could outsource household responsibilities. Individual women and people of color benefited from the equal-rights approach, but the vast majority were stuck in occupations that continued to devalue their labor and underpay them. So, Title VII and the Equal Pay Act may actually have exacerbated the divide among women.[67] Antidiscrimination law did not restructure the workplace and did not revalue occupations such as care work.

Domestic workers' campaign for social citizenship rights was part of this larger struggle for justice in the workplace. They were more closely aligned with union campaigns to upgrade certain occupations and the goals of social movements, such as the welfare rights and wages for housework movements, to revalue household labor.[68] Many African American women leaving domestic service undoubtedly fought for equal access to other kinds of employment and an end to discrimination within those workplaces. But the thrust of this movement was to upgrade their jobs and change the terms of social citizenship by extending labor rights to their current occupation. Annie Love, a mother of four, household worker and organizer in Miami, expressed her view: "A lot of people talk about training household workers to be something else. It isn't that I haven't been interested in another kind of job, it's just that this is what I really want to do."[69] Less concerned about individual access to new jobs, and perhaps aware of the obstacles that poor black women faced in escaping low-wage jobs, they aimed to transform the political and economic status of an entire occupation and gain federal recognition of their work.[70] Even training and education were less about obtaining new jobs than improving old ones. Geraldine Roberts attended a community college, but wanted to "still continue as a domestic worker."[71] Household workers' claims for rights and recognition of their work of social reproduction disrupted long-standing notions of both labor and citizenship and expanded the definition of "worker" that had been circumscribed in the 1930s. They intended to raise the status of the work of social reproduction and reverse the marginalization of African American women domestic workers in labor law.

Minimum wage legislation for domestic workers didn't fully achieve the expected results and had a mixed legacy. The granting of formal rights to domestic workers absolved the state of its most blatant exclusions, reinforcing and strengthening the abstract construct of universal equality without creating a mechanism for enforcement. The end result was a turn away from state responsibility toward individual employer responsibility. Once domestic workers were legally protected, it was assumed that the real obstacles were employers who refused to comply. The decentralized nature of the work and its location in the home— issues that historically made regulation difficult—still impeded enforcement. The Department of Labor had little power and few tools to ensure compliance. Moreover, the ideology of the home as a private sphere continued to hold sway over the public imagination in a way that inhibited people from acknowledging the home as a workplace.[72]

The FLSA legislation also excluded important categories of domestics, including live-in workers and home-health-care aides, who, along with babysitters, were defined as providing "companionship" services.[73] Home care was distinct from private household labor because it was funded by state agencies and often had a third-party employer. These new exclusions became even more important as the occupation shifted. At the turn of the twenty-first century, home-care assistance was one of the fastest-growing industries because of changes in health-care administration, state funding patterns, and greater stratification in health-care delivery. Domestic workers, especially African American women, increasingly left private household labor for home-care work as well as institutional employment as nurses, cleaners, and cafeteria workers. Thus, those who became home-health-care aides left one unprotected occupation only to find themselves in another unprotected occupation. The other exclusion of live-in workers also became important with the influx of immigrant workers. As live-ins, these new workers were not entitled to minimum wage protection. So the legal recognition of the category of domestic work also narrowed that definition and removed protections for some. The reforms of the 1970s attempted to mitigate stratification within labor law but created new forms of stratification at the same time.[74]

THE STRUGGLE FOR EQUALITY

In the 1970s, domestic workers forged an alliance with middle-class women and waged a campaign for full citizenship rights by insisting that domestic work was legitimate work deserving of the same labor protections as other occupations. Since the 1930s, they had been excluded from labor legislation and were marginalized in both their work and their legal status. Domestic workers claimed their labor as legitimate work and built a broad-based alliance to suport the passage of minimum-wage legislation.

In their campaigns, domestic workers' voices and experiences and their participation in the policymaking process were critical elements of the legislative debate. Their analysis of the gendered nature of domestic labor told through stories of racial exclusion, hardship, and unmet expectations, as well as their hope to revalue household labor served as a basis for a feminist alliance. Although passage of minimum wage legislation was an important victory for domestic workers, it was also limited, offering domestic workers legal status but little political leverage.

Domestic workers' campaigns for equality in the 1960s and 1970s were never solely about labor legislation and citizenship rights. Although the question of social and economic rights was critical for domestic workers, most did not see these rights as the ultimate goal but rather as one part of a broader agenda. Concerns about dignity and respect were also crucial. As Josephine Hulett explained: "Raising pay by inclusion under FLSA is not an end in itself. But coverage under FLSA is a vital prerequisite—a vital *means* of achieving a larger aim—which, from the employee's view is to provide her with a profession that is respected and pays adequately."[75] Domestic workers viewed the degradation of their work as deeply rooted and informed by the racialization of the occupation as well as the lack of value placed on household labor.

The struggle for social citizenship was a step toward achieving rights and respect for this sector of the African American community and aimed to remedy the marginalization that resulted from decades-long inequality in social citizenship. Edith Barksdale Sloan wrote in the NCHE newsletter, "Many employers are slowly beginning to realize that there has been a revolution in the kitchen, and like it or not, there is a new force and a determined new worker who will no longer work unreasonable hours under unreasonable conditions for unjust wages, some leftover food and a worn-out garment."[76] Domestic workers' victorious passage of the FLSA amendments pushed the boundaries of American citizenship and managed to redefine the very meaning of work that had been so circumscribed by New Deal labor legislation. The shifting, contingent, and contested notions of work and citizenship suggest that this has been an important arena of political struggle for marginalized groups—a struggle that is still unfinished.

CHAPTER 7

WOMEN, WORK, AND IMMIGRATION

*It is important to realize that, in the past, our sisters left us
a legacy of organizing that we can follow today.*

—BONITA JOHNSON

WOMEN, WORK, AND THE END OF HOUSEHOLD LABOR

In 1973 the renowned sociologist Lewis Coser published an article in a prominent academic journal declaring the obsolescence of domestic servants. Paid household labor, he argued, was an antiquated occupation that had no place in industrialized society.[1] Coser and other social commentators in the 1970s had come to believe that hired domestic labor was out of step with the democratic ideals of a modern society. Moreover, they argued that technological advances, new consumer products, and shifting cultural patterns made the need for in-home household employees a thing of the past. Such assertions were not entirely new. In 1953 *House and Garden* magazine promised that electrical appliances would be the "servant that never takes a day off" and that convenience foods were the equivalent of "1001 servants in your kitchen."

In the mid- to late 1970s, labor economists, feminists, and countless journalists once again lauded a turn toward capitalist innovation as a solution to the problem of household labor. Working mothers no longer had to spend hours in front of the stove when they could easily pick up fast food or prepared supermarket items, such as frozen TV dinners and instant soup. Dishwashers, self-cleaning ovens, washing machines, vacuum cleaners, and wrinkle-free fabrics eased the burdens of cleaning. And institutional child care would make nannies unnecessary. The free market, it seemed, would relieve middle-class women of the crushing burden of household labor.

In addition to market solutions, changing expectations of how to keep house—or more accurately, declining standards—reduced the time spent on housework. Many middle-class women had come to believe that a clean house was only marginally important, and may have been a sign of misplaced priorities. Beginning in the mid-1960s, women did less household labor, even when no one else picked up the slack.[2] As Geraldine Roberts observed in 1977, "So many employers have seemed to adopt the style that it is not that important anymore about how well the house is kept clean."[3]

Despite declining standards and the proliferation of household appliances and prepared foods, the problem of household labor persisted as the number of women in the workforce continued to grow. By 1980 the labor force participation rate of married women was 49 percent.[4] Some women joined the labor force because of second-wave feminist ideas that employment and an independent income led to personal liberation. Other women were less moved by ideology and went to work out of sheer necessity as a shrinking manufacturing sector, rising inflation, and high unemployment generated an economic crisis. Single mothers often relied on paid employment to support themselves and their children, especially as welfare increasingly came under attack. And as middle-class and lower-middle-class families found it hard to maintain their standard of living on a single income, women's employment became the salve for an aching economy. Many families now depended upon two incomes.[5]

While the drudgery and time devoted to household labor seemed to have lessened given technological advances and changing expectations, the promises that paid domestic labor would soon be a thing of the past were overly optimistic. Market innovations were limited. Ready-made foods were not considered nutritious enough. Institutional day care was perceived to be inadequate by many middle-class families that were bombarded with messages about the importance of one-on-one attention for healthy growth and development of their children. And hopes and expectations that modern-day men would shoulder more of the household chores never materialized. In effect, the overall workload for newly employed women increased because of their double day. Both the "care gap" and the cleaning gap needed to be filled. As in earlier periods, low-paid household workers seemed to be the most feasible solution.[6]

A new employer-employee relationship emerged in the 1970s because of growing unease with the master-servant model. A *New York Times* author described it this way: "Relations between the two groups are fraught with feelings of anxiety, guilt and helplessness, all on the part of the employers, none on the part of the employees."[7] Female employers sought greater distance from their employees and were increasingly uncomfortable with their role as employers, perhaps because of the way in which the relationship had come to symbolize racial hierarchy among women. A divorced mother employed in the public relations department of a large food company and interviewed by *Westchester Illustrated* magazine explained that she hired a white housekeeper because "I didn't want to present the stereotype of the black maid doing a white woman's work to my kids." Another employer despised feeling responsible for all her employee's problems: "I hate having inherited another person's life in return for having my tub scrubbed and my floor waxed." Most employers guarded their privacy and were not interested in the personal relationship that characterized the occupation a generation earlier. A speech pathologist explained: "When my kids were small, I had intimate relationships with the people who cared for them. I knew about their dates and their agonies. Now, I simply don't want to be bothered. . . . I don't want an intimate observer at dinner time serving my family. . . . I don't even like to be at home when my housekeeper's there. . . . Someone who cleans for you doesn't have to be patronized as a child or treated as a member of the family if she's not."[8]

Their detached approach sometimes led to a lack of clear instructions. Although employers didn't want to micromanage or dictate to their workers, they also had high expectations for how care should be provided and tasks completed. One employer explained: "I want a competent person to come into my house, look around, know what's to be done and do it. I want a housekeeper who's as expert in her job as I am in mine."[9] The hope was that employees would be independent and take initiative, and, at the same time, conform to their bosses' often unspoken standards. Household work was shifting because of workers' initiatives as well. As scholar Mary Romero has argued, Chicano workers transformed household labor into a business relationship wherein they worked for multiple employers and established set wage rates. This gave workers greater control over the work process and better suited employers' hands-off approach. The emphasis on day work, however, did not eliminate the ongoing need for care workers, which tended to be full-time employment and, in many cases, live-in. Nevertheless, by the 1980s, there was a distinct change in the occupation. Household worker agitation and a new crop of employers combined to dismantle the paternalism and patterns of servitude that characterized the mid-twentieth century.[10]

Black Women in a New Era

In the mid-1970s, African American women, who had been the primary domestic-labor force since the early twentieth century, were a shrinking percentage of domestic workers. They had been steadily leaving household labor since World War II and choosing, when given the opportunity, to take formal-sector jobs.[11] This trend accelerated with the victories of the black freedom movement, which removed barriers to employment discrimination and increased educational opportunities for African Americans.

Some African American women moved out of domestic service into clerical, sales, and professional jobs such as teaching, nursing, and social work that were previously closed to them.[12] Geraldine Roberts observed: "I think, more than ever now, domestics at this time, at this period, 1977, are beginning to go to school and seek out higher education for themselves . . . women all began to help themselves as individuals saying I'm going to go back to school, try to improve myself because I'm tired of being worked as a slave in this country without a decent wage, tired of being ignored."[13] Other African American women, with less education and fewer employment prospects, ended up on welfare and were relegated to "second tier" public assistance benefits. The bifurcation between the more privileged and the less privileged characterized the shifting employment prospects of African American women, where some moved up and others simply moved out of employment and were further marginalized.[14] The net effect was a decline in the number of African American household workers. So, while 42 percent of employed black women were domestics in 1950, by 1970 only 19.5 percent of employed black women worked as domestics. This proportion had dropped to 6 percent by 1980.

Ironically, working-class black women who left private household labor often ended up in occupations that resembled the social reproductive labor they had previously engaged in, albeit in different settings. They shifted "over" rather than "out," thus re-creating the racial and gender inequality in the workforce. The proliferation of hospitals, schools, nursing homes, and restaurants changed the nature of social reproductive care and relocated some of the work that had previously taken place in the home into institutional settings. Dorothy Bolden was aware of growing opportunities for black women in these employment areas. NDWUA's training proposal prepared participants for one of two career tracks: private household work or "service delivery and management for institutions" such as for-profit businesses and nonprofit organizations.[15] Institutions offered women, and many men, formal-sector jobs that included nurturant care, as well as other kinds of social reproductive work like cleaning, laundry, and food preparation. Women working in institutions were still often relegated to largely female service occupations. But even within this predominantly female workforce, inequalities persisted, with women of color performing the lowest-paid menial work—the "back-room jobs" such as changing bedpans and serving in cafeterias—and white women engaging in nurturant work such as registered nursing and teaching.[16]

One instance of this widening racial gap in institutional care is evidenced in the home-health-care industry. Over the course of the twentieth century, the health-care industry underwent enormous changes with the creation of occupational hierarchies, including professionalization of certain jobs and the implementation of cost-cutting measures. Government policy encouraged the expansion of home health care—where individuals paid by private or government agencies provided services to the sick or disabled in their homes. Home health care enabled hospitals to outsource patient care to low-wage workers, many of whom were former welfare recipients, domestic workers, or family members of those needing care. This burgeoning field was made up largely of women of color, who worked long hours performing multiple tasks that included nursing and patient hygiene and bodily care, as well as household chores such as cooking and cleaning. These jobs were not vastly different from the labor provided by private household employees for generations. But because home-health-care aides were legally categorized as casual babysitters with the passage of the 1974 amendments, they were excluded from the provisions of the FLSA. Occupations such as home health care proved to be an important outlet for poor black women, and many immigrant women, fleeing private household work.[17] So black women, although less important in private household service, continued doing low-paid reproductive care in institutional settings.

Mary McClendon's life illustrates these trends. After almost fifty years as a private household worker, McClendon enrolled in a community college to become certified as a home-care aide. In some ways, this transition was a logical extension of her efforts to upgrade household labor through professionalization and training. In 1977 McClendon took a job with the city of Detroit as a home-care attendant. She signed a one-year contract with the city's Neighborhood Services Department to work as a homemaker aide and described her job, which involved cleaning, cooking, and caring for the elderly or disabled, as "household technician work." But the autonomy she might have hoped for with "professional" status didn't materialize. Her supervisors called to check in every day, monitored her closely, and required her to inform them if she left her place of employment for any reason. They even instructed her how to dress for Friday meetings and what to say to the seniors she cared for.[18]

The work was physically demanding and McClendon suffered from long-term ailments that she attributed to lifting clients as a home-care attendant. In 1980 she sued the city of Detroit for workers' compensation because of chronic back pain. By that time, she was unemployed, received general assistance—a welfare program for the poor without young children—and lived in Highland Park, an impoverished black city within the municipal boundaries of Detroit. At issue in the lawsuit was whether McClendon was an independent contractor or directly employed by the city. This distinction, while seemingly a technicality, was enormously important in shaping the status, rights, and political leverage of home-care attendants. The city claimed she was a contractor and therefore couldn't make any claims as an employee. McClendon offered examples of how frequently supervisors checked up on her as evidence of her status as an employee of the city's agency. McClendon lost her legal case, an indication of how home-health-care workers found it more difficult to challenge working conditions, bargain collectively, or bring lawsuits against their employers for unfair labor practices. Her situation exemplifies the continuities in African American women's low-wage labor both inside and outside domestic service—and, in particular, how labor rights were curtailed.

Migrant Domestic Workers

The exodus of African American women from private household work led to shifting demographics in the occupation. Changes in immigration law in the 1960s created a much larger pool of low-wage immigrant workers, many of whom ended up as household laborers. The Hart-Celler Immigration Act of 1965 abolished the discriminatory national-origins immigration formula established in the 1920s that gave preference to northern and western Europeans and completely excluded Asians and Africans. The new law established a per-country quota, which prioritized immigrants' skills and family unification, and placed new restrictions on the number of legal immigrants from the western hemisphere. These restrictions regulated a border that was previously unregulated and heightened the number of undocumented immigrants coming to the United States. The loosening of certain restrictions enabled greater numbers of immigrants from other parts of the world to come to the US and expanded the pool of vulnerable immigrants without legal papers. These new immigrants, many of whom were in search of employment, became available for those seeking household workers.[19]

The turn to immigrant labor as a source of household workers was not unprecedented. Immigrant women were the primary domestic-service labor force in the nineteenth and early twentieth centuries. In the post–World War II period, women were recruited from the southern United States, Puerto Rico, the Caribbean, Mexico, and Europe. For example, Domestic Service, Inc., a Manhattan employment agency started in 1950 by Lee Ahneman, specialized in connecting European household workers with employers in the United States. Usually paid between $100 and $150 a month, workers signed one-year contracts. In its first five years, the company placed about six thousand domestics; by 1961, ten thousand were entering the country every year. They came from all over Europe, but especially Britain and Ireland, because of fluency in English and high immigration quotas. A reporter identified another reason why some nationalities were less represented: "No Scandinavians are brought in by the firm, for an interesting reason. They don't want to come. Domestics in these countries have recently organized and work only an eight-hour day. If longer, they get time-and-a-half." So, the workers ending up in the United States were very likely less demanding of their rights. Despite the best efforts of companies like Domestic Service however, recruitment agencies could not meet the demand for European workers.[20]

Another possible source for domestic workers was Puerto Rico. The long-standing colonial relationship made travel back and forth fairly easy and Puerto Ricans' status as American citizens enabled an unlimited number of people to go to the continental US. Since the early twentieth century, a steady stream of Puerto Ricans, middle-class and working-class voluntary migrants and contract laborers, had arrived in the mainland US, especially New York and Chicago, and some ended up in or were shuttled into domestic work. Puerto Ricans quickly became the second-largest Spanish-speaking community next to Mexicans.[21]

Private companies recruited contract workers from Puerto Rico. One of the most well-publicized cases was in Chicago. In September 1946, after signing an agreement with the Puerto Rican Department of Labor, a Chicago employment agency, Castle, Barton and Associates, recruited men to work in foundries and women and some men to work in private households with one-year labor contracts. Although the contracts were not legally binding, the agency used them as a form of coercion. The agency head told one employer that if a worker broke a contract, "we could blackball them successfully from any other job."[22] Close to four hundred women, most who had never before worked as maids, served as live-in domestics. To combat workers' isolation, the Chicago YWCA organized Thursday-afternoon teas for the migrants. Although they were not tea drinkers, the domestic workers seized the opportunity to establish solidarity and share information about their jobs.[23] They expressed dissatisfaction with both working and living conditions.

A group of University of Chicago students learned of the plight of the workers and began to document complaints of underage labor, fifteen-hour workdays, mistreatment, and underpayment. They found that employers had deducted money for transportation to and from Puerto Rico from workers' monthly wages, leaving them with far less than they expected. Carmen Isales, a Puerto Rican social worker who happened to be vacationing in Chicago at the time, confirmed the students' findings and also discovered that Puerto Rican women earned far less than their African American and white counterparts.[24] Low wages seemed to be another form of labor control. One employer testified that the agency told him that if they paid more "it might make [the workers] 'flighty.'"[25] The program was hardly a success. Half the household workers left before their contract was up. Alarming press reports suggested that the "girls" had turned to prostitution and that there was now a "displaced-persons" problem.[26] Because of the growing publicity, the Puerto Rican Senate launched an investigation and halted the Castle, Barton and Associates contract-labor program.[27]

In addition to private initiatives, there were government-sponsored programs. In 1947 the Puerto Rican Department of Labor launched the development project known as Operación Manos a La Obra, or Operation Bootstrap, designed to transform Puerto Rico from an agricultural economy to an industrial economy.[28] Operation Bootstrap encouraged migration of working-class, unskilled, and rural Puerto Ricans to the mainland United States as a way to alleviate poverty and unemployment. The Migration Division trained workers, offered information about employment opportunities, organized contract-labor programs with assistance from the US Federal Division of Territories and Island Possessions, and launched a public relations campaign that touted the benefits of hiring Puerto Rican workers. They hoped, in part, to avoid the scandal associated with the recent recruitment efforts in Chicago. In 1948 the Puerto Rican government hired L. Frances Phillips, an African American woman, as assistant to the Puerto Rican commissioner of labor in New York and employment manager of the Metropolitan Household Offices of the New York State Department of Labor. She trained and placed Puerto Ricans in household jobs. Phillips had worked for the New York State Department of Labor since 1935 and was instrumental in trying to eliminate the "slave markets" of the Depression era by creating a registration and placement program for household workers. In 1948, the first twenty-one Puerto Rican workers were placed in homes in Scarsdale, an affluent community just north of New York City. Although the program was hailed as a solution to the shortage of domestic labor, the workers encountered numerous problems, much like the domestics in Chicago, including isolation, overwork, and a language barrier.[29]

Despite the difficulties, hiring foreign domestic workers still appealed to employers. The benefits were evident in the documents of one employment agency. In 1967, the Frances Green Employment Agency, with offices in Maryland, New York, and Pennsylvania, promised "the services of an English-speaking South American or West Indian domestic." The owners assured potential clients that they "go to South America and Jamaica every month to personally interview, select and approve all applicants" and offered to take care of all paperwork, such as obtaining a permanent work visa for the domestic. The three-page contract specified workers' rights and responsibilities. They were expected to clean, do laundry, care for children, and cook, but not wash windows outside, shovel snow, wash cars, or garden. Workers were advised by the company: "In some homes you may be required to scrub a kitchen and/or bathroom the good old fashioned way on your hands and knees. Some employers feel that this is the only way to get all the corners, baseboard and floors clean. Since it is your employer's home and she is paying you a good salary you are obligated to comply."[30] The agency suggested that on their days off, maids "go to church" and urged them to "choose your friends wisely." They compiled a dossier for each worker with a photo, references, and "a questionnaire reflecting the applicant's personality, attitude, intelligence and personal habits." The agency promised clients a "one-year unconditional replacement guarantee."[31] The detailed contract of the Frances Green Employment Agency is revealing both for what it promised employers—hardworking, morally upstanding, and reliable employees—and its obvious attempt to discipline workers in both their social habits and work expectations.

The Frances Green Agency's target of "South American" and "West Indian" domestics reflected the growing interest in hiring women from the Caribbean. Caribbean women had a long history of immigration to the United States, but the number increased in the 1970s and 1980s. Mary McClendon experienced this firsthand. In 1970, the HWO in Detroit explained in its newsletter, *Household Workers Employment News*, the way Jamaican workers were exploited: "Some employers of household workers are hiring foreigners, such as Jamaicans. . . . The only real compensation that they receive is that they are allowed to stay in America. . . . The wages of the Jamaican ladies are so small it's like robbing the helpless, and the contracts that they are expected to keep along with keeping their living quarters and duties again is slavery."[32] Many Caribbean women were employed in their countries of origin, although not necessarily as domestic workers, and migrated in search of economic opportunity as Caribbean nations experienced shrinking job opportunities, growing debt, and greater vulnerability to austerity policies imposed by agencies such as the International Monetary Fund. Some Caribbean women migrants who were mothers left their children in the care of friends or relatives and sent remittances back home. Those who brought children with them had to juggle their own child-care responsibilities while serving as a nanny for someone else. Although hired as "nannies," Caribbean domestic workers were expected to do a great deal of housework as well. Immigrant Caribbean women may have been middle-class prior to their relocation and were shocked at their poor treatment, which was exacerbated in situations where employees were sponsored by or dependent upon employers for their green card or permanent residency status. According to scholar Shellee Colen, "The central issue discussed by all the women is the lack of respect shown to them by their employers."[33]

The other growing group of domestic workers was Chicanas and Mexican immigrants, who had been an important low-wage workforce since the expansion of the US empire in the nineteenth century, especially in the Southwest. But new legal limits on Mexican migrants in 1965 fueled undocumented immigration because of the way in which migrants were increasingly criminalized for crossing the border without papers. Both Mexican Americans and Mexican immigrants, especially those labeled "illegal," were vulnerable to abuse and exploitation.[34] An employer's guide, titled *Your Maid from Mexico: A Home Training Course for Maids*, published in 1959, indicated how Mexicans were viewed as desirable domestics. Several nonprofits operated to mitigate the negative impact. The International Institute of Los Angeles found that Mexican domestic workers were paid as little as thirty cents an hour. The director, Robert Armendariz, described the employment of Mexican immigrants as "coerced labor." Bert Corona of the Autonomous Center for Social Action (CASA), a Los Angeles advocacy group that organized Mexican immigrants, explained: "These dowager ladies in society circles hire them to take care of their babies" so they can do charity and benefit work. "They want to help the poor but they are exploiting the poor at home."[35]

Immigrants, even undocumented immigrants, in this period were protected by US labor law. Only much later, in 1986, did it become illegal to hire undocumented workers, and almost twenty years after that, claims of unfair labor practices by undocumented workers began to be curtailed by the Supreme Court. But even in the period when they were entitled to make legal claims, undocumented workers were often unable to assert their rights because of their vulnerability. Employers had the power to report, or threaten to report, employees who lacked proper papers. Immigrants were sometimes unaware of US labor law, may not have been fluent in English, and had few support networks in their communities. Grace Gil Olivarez, Chicana activist and chairman of the National Committee on Household Employment, explains: "If you're very low on the economic ladder, if you have only one skill, you don't protest. You have no options in the event the protest backfires."[36]

The periodic turn to immigrant domestic workers is one iteration in a long history of racialized labor practices that sought to address the shortage of cheap domestic workers and problem of labor control. In the late nineteenth and early twentieth centuries, the mammy stereo-type cast African American women as ideal domestic servants. Isabel Eaton, who wrote a report on domestic work as part of W. E. B. Du Bois's classic 1899 study, *The Philadelphia Negro*, found that employers in the city believed that African Americans were "industrious" and "a great deal better workers and decidedly better cooks than the whites."[37] Other groups in this period also experienced racialization through paid domestic labor. Chinese men were constructed as servile and emas-culated and therefore good workers, and Irish Catholic women were deemed unrefined, rebellious, and in need of training in household labor.[38] While the particular situation of black domestic workers was distinctive—most obviously because African Americans were not vol-untary migrants—employers constructed both African American and immigrant domestic workers as racially different, rendering them invis-ible and justifying low pay and poor working conditions.

As the demographics changed, so too did ideas about race and do-mestic labor. In part because of civil rights and domestic-worker-rights activism, by the 1970s African Americans were increasingly viewed as "uppity," difficult to control, demanding, and lazy. *Essence* reported in 1974: "Black household workers are banding together to demand improvements. They are becoming more militant and less inclined to settle for crumbs." NCHE recognized the shift, stating in one report: "Many employers would rather hire a white or oriental alien—legal or illegal—than a black U.S. citizen."[39] African American women, no lon-ger the ideal mammy, were now reconstructed in popular discourse as the lazy welfare recipient. In contrast, immigrants, it was believed, were malleable, controllable, and exploitable. Native-born whites and Eu-ropeans—who were always highly sought after—and new immigrants became the preferred household workers, imbued with their own racialized stereotypes about what made them good workers. Want ads for household workers frequently specified "European preferred" or "Oriental preferred."[40]

Reliance on immigrant workers and the ways in which certain groups of women were characterized as ideal domestic workers illustrates how the politics of race informed the occupation. Domestic work produced ideas about race as much as it reflected them.[41] In the 1940s, for example, Puerto Rican women were perceived as having qualities that made them inherently suited for domestic work. Stories of Puerto Rican women as good maids appeared in the popular press. A 1949 *New York Times* article suggested that despite poverty and overcrowded conditions, Puerto Rican women were "instinctively tidy."[42] Caribbean women in the 1980s were characterized as being clean, well-educated, and having a good work ethic. By the early part of the twenty-first century, however, as other groups of immigrant women became available, there was growing concern that Jamaican women were "too aggressive."[43] Latina women were especially valued for their ability to speak Spanish and believed to be more nurturing nannies. Filipino women were seen as hardworking, respectful, and compliant. These racial ideas didn't describe innate traits, or even cultural patterns. Rather they justified, in the employer's mind, why particular groups of women at particular moments in time might serve as good household workers. And, as was the case for African American women, they could be easily redefined. The ways in which different groups of people enter and exit household labor illuminate the centrality of race relations in shaping and transforming domestic work and the malleability of worker stereotypes.

"THE SAME VICIOUS CYCLE OVER AND OVER"

Domestic-worker organizers like Josephine Hulett and Geraldine Miller saw their core constituency as African American women. But from the outset, they grappled with the question of immigrant domestic workers and were committed to creating a racially inclusive organization. Things did not always go smoothly, as was clear in 1970, as NCHE, which at that time was led by middle-class reformers, was about to launch the Household Technicians of America. Elva Ruiz, a Mexican American staff member of NCHE, issued a press release, signed by several Mexican American organizations, criticizing the organization for its inattention to the needs of the Mexican American community. The NCHE called the release "inaccurate" and "slanderous" and fired Ruiz shortly after that.[44] This difficult beginning, however, may have prompted the organization to think more about issues of racial diversity. The next year, the HTA board of directors, at one of its first meetings, discussed how to contact white, Chicana, and Native American household workers, proposed to write a pamphlet in Spanish, and decided to invite underrepresented constituencies to join the board.[45] In 1971, Edith Sloan reached out to Francisca Flores, a Chicana activist in Los Angeles and editor of the magazine *Carta Editorial.* Flores prioritized issues of low-income Mexican American women and, in 1972, formed the Chicana Service Action Center. In her letter, Sloan explained the HTA's desire to work with Chicanas: "We are very much interested in increasing the participation of Chicanos in all facets of NCHE's operations." The formation of the HTA, she suggested, "makes the immediate identification and inclusion of workers from the Mexican American community of the utmost concern to us." The NCHE, she explained, was considering sponsoring an Autumn Southwest Regional Conference on Household Employment, "the bulk of whose participants will be either American Indians or Mexican Americans."[46] In 1973, the NCHE translated the Code of Standards, Model Contract, and pamphlet on "How to Organize Household Workers" into Spanish.[47] In addition, the NCHE Western Regional field officer, Curt Moody, in 1973 developed an ongoing relationship with Ding Ho, a household training program for Chinese-speaking women in San Francisco. Ding Ho never became an NCHE affiliate, but did collaborate with the organization, and its members attended some national conferences.[48]

It is not clear that anything tangible resulted from these efforts. The sentiment was significant nonetheless. Organizers in the NCHE and HTA understood immigration issues and racial division as complicating their effort to better the status of domestic workers. Curt Moody wrote to Edith Sloan about the situation in southern California: "Families seeking slave labor are importing and hiring Mexican Nationals at the rate of $25.00 per week with no benefits."[49] Geraldine Miller also explained employer preference for an immigrant workforce: "Immigrants were coming in and [employers] were hiring them instead of the African American because they were cheap labor and they could get by with it. You know, they could threaten the woman with deportation and they can't threaten us, we'd a been threatened already, and we're still here."[50] In outlining its priorities in 1976, the NCHE reflected on the complicated problem of immigration, including the perceived reluctance of immigrants to defend their rights: "When household workers are trying to improve their working conditions and pay, unfair competition from illegal aliens is a serious problem . . . immigrants working illegally undermine our efforts to improve pay and working conditions because their illegal status makes them afraid to complain to their employers or to seek help from any government agency."[51]

The NCHE saw the influx of immigrant domestic workers as altering the balance of supply and demand and giving greater leverage to employers. The availability of immigrant workers and the reluctance of those workers to claim their rights, in many ways, undermined the substance of the FLSA. A 1975 NCHE study concluded that "employers in many areas offered wages well below the legally established minimum wage, and . . . these employers could easily obtain persons willing to work for less than the law demands."[52] Anita Shelton, executive director of the NCHE, explained in March 1976 before the annual convention, "Thus it becomes an employer's market and a worker's nightmare."[53] "The rule of supply and demand, which governs the production and sale of apples and oranges, automobiles and motorboats, or stocks and bonds," she argued, "cannot be allowed to apply to human beings and their labor." And she promised that the NCHE would "see that household workers take their rightful place in the economy and society."[54]

Despite the way that immigration empowered employers and weakened the bargaining position of domestic workers, the leaders of the NCHE refused to buy into the larger discourse circulating about deportation. Domestic workers' advocates could have taken a xenophobic

position. They did not. NCHE's "Program Priorities," adopted and ratified in 1976, declared: "Humanly, it is hard to say that illegal aliens in
great numbers should be deported so that US citizens can have their
jobs."[55] It also committed the organization to bringing into the fold the
new immigrants: "We will make special efforts to expand the Committee
to include the national groups most affected by household employment
issues, e.g., Spanish-speaking, Caribbean and Vietnamese groups."[56]
Carolyn Reed was also a stalwart supporter of cross-race cooperation
and considered ways to bring nonblack women into the organization:
"In household work, it is not just Black women that are being exploited,
and how do I set up an atmosphere so that white women will feel comfortable about coming into the organization. The only way that I can
do that is by example of what we do, as an organization, and how we
set it up. How do we get more Hispanic women who are doing it to feel
comfortable within the organization. The only way that I can do that is
by example—and saying, 'Okay. Why don't I take the effort to do this
newsletter in English and in Spanish?'"[57]

By the late 1970s, the HTA had established a few more immigrant
affiliates. In Washington, DC, the Asociación Internacional de Tecni-
cas del Hogar (International Association of Household Technicians)
emerged out of the Spanish Catholic Center in 1977. Sister Manuela, the
nun who ran the center, spoke highly of Carolyn Reed, but also believed
"our problem is more complicated" because many of the two hundred
members worked for diplomats and were live-ins.[58] These employers
had diplomatic immunity, which made protecting workers against labor law violations very difficult. As the Sister explained, workers in her
organization struggled for "the right to not be a prisoner in the employer's home."[59] In another case, Carolyn Reed trained Haitian refugee
women as household technicians and taught them their rights "as a way
of helping Haitian women in New York City get jobs to help them become self-sufficient and financially independent—making the way for
a better life." She wanted to ensure their "ability to function properly
in their new home by knowing their rights and getting paid for what
they are worth."[60] The HTA's and NCHE's concerted effort to reach
out to immigrant workers reflected an awareness that the constraints of

the occupation were similar regardless of ethnic and racial background or citizenship status. And this extended beyond national borders. The HTA had an ongoing relationship with organized domestic workers in South Africa. After a visit with Madame Leila Tutu of the Domestic Workers Project of South Africa in 1982, the organization wrote in the newsletter, "We found that household workers in their country had much in common with workers here in the United States."[61] So even though household-worker organizers rooted their analyses in the particular racial history of African Americans, they were able to transcend the particularity of their experiences and make, or attempt to make, connections with other workers.

In a draft article for *Ms.* magazine in 1972 that was later revised and published, Josephine Hulett wrote about the cross-racial experience of household work: "The problems are similar for the 1.5 million people engaged in this field, the Blacks, the Chicanas, the white ethnics."[62] She recounted going to a meeting where a Chicana worker explained that every Monday morning she was given for lunch the "doggy" bag from the employer's Saturday night out. She told of an Italian American household worker who had never received a paid vacation. Geraldine Miller similarly drew parallels between African American migrants from the South and immigrant workers from abroad. "I feel as though these people are being brought in as a workforce to be exploited, as we were to begin with. It's the same vicious cycle over and over again regardless of where the person is coming from whether it's out of the country or from the South and if they don't know their rights then they're going to be exploited."[63] By embracing undocumented immigrant workers, household-worker activists expressed an understanding that labor rights were not confined to those with formal citizenship. Their vision was one in which all domestic workers, regardless of legal status, would be equally rewarded for their labor.

Bringing together household workers of different racial backgrounds proved to be a tough task. In early 1974, Washington, DC, Household Technicians reported a "certain degree of latent animosity" between the immigrant household workers and the native-born household workers. Despite hopes that the two groups would "work harmoniously together," the Jamaican leadership of the group concluded that "maintaining a truly bi-cultural organization may be unrealistic and impossible."[64] Geraldine Miller acknowledged the lack of real integration in the movement: "If we had more groups of various nationalities fighting for the same thing, I think that we'd be much further along, but as it is, it's been the black woman fighting for the rights of household workers when there are many Irish women, many Polish women . . ."[65] Despite the difficulty of bringing African American and immigrant workers together as household technicians, the HTA's strategy was politically important because it illustrates the commitment to interracial organizing on the part of African American domestic workers. As the organization outlined in a press release in 1978: "It is in low-paying jobs that brown and black women are pitted against each other by unscrupulous employers thereby creating an employer's market because the workers have no means of uniting for mutual benefit."[66] They believed there was potential for domestic workers of whatever racial, cultural, or linguistic background to find common cause as workers. Similarly, Geraldine Roberts was committed to supporting and working with women of all backgrounds: "We have attorneys standing by that we can contact at any time if we discover any domestic employees whether she's a member here or not that's been abused. Whether she's from an island or from Europe. It doesn't make any difference. If she's been abused we immediately become concerned, and begin to do something and take actions immediately on this."[67]

BUILDING BRIDGES AMONG "PRACTICAL WORKERS"

In addition to reaching out to domestic workers of all racial, ethnic, and national backgrounds, the NCHE launched campaigns that more broadly addressed low-wage women's work. In 1975 the organization planned a testimonial, "'Speak-Out for Economic Justice': Poor Women in the Economy," before a congressional panel that included, among others, Representative Shirley Chisholm of New York, Senator Alan Cranston of California, and Representative Yvonne Brathwaite Burke of Los Angeles. As NCHE explained: "The purpose of the

Speak-Out is to focus public attention on the deplorable situation of women who are left out of the mainstream of the nation's economic concerns and are confined to the backwaters of the country's economic and social life." The event brought together "women workers who have been particularly hard hit by the economic recession coupled with inflation."[68] Domestic workers, sugarcane cutters, farm workers, hotel workers, office workers, cafeteria workers, and hospital workers testified. Phoenix resident Antonia Diaz, for example, spoke of waitresses earning only a dollar an hour, and female farm workers who "during the rainy season . . . cannot work and have no compensation at all." Gil Foon Hong, a fifty-seven-year-old San Francisco household worker and widowed mother of six from Hong Kong, spoke about her low pay and lack of benefits. In 1974, she joined the Ding Ho Housekeeping Training program. Speaking through a translator, she stated, "If my employer decides to take three months in the summer for a vacation, I don't get paid. I'm out of a job for three months. . . . I am a woman. . . . I don't know English, I'm too old to learn a new skill."[69] Edith Sloan, in her keynote address, lamented the declining status of these workers in a tight labor market and the ways in which their concerns were neglected: "Those in the heady world of economics tell us that it's what's on the bottom line that counts. They are wrong, we are the bottom line and, clearly we don't count."[70] Two years later, in 1977, NCHE made the theme of its fifth national conference in Charlotte, North Carolina, a "Practical Workers' Congress," which included household technicians, hotel and restaurant employees, porters, school aides, health aides, migrant workers, and janitors. The conference was deemed a "national salute to the practical workers of America, who are the backbone of the American economy."[71]

Household workers' embrace of other low-wage women workers was a strategic move that enabled domestic workers to build coalitions, but it also represented a critical perspective about "women's issues" at a moment when feminism was gaining worldwide currency. In 1975 the United Nations declared the first International Women's Year and dubbed 1976–85 the United Nations Decade for Women. Edith Barksdale Sloan and Josephine Hulett attended, and Sloan presented on a plenary on Women and Trade Unions at the 1975 international gathering in Mexico City. Two years later twenty thousand women gathered in Houston to develop a US National Plan of Action around the UN Declarations. NCHE participated in that convening and endorsed the plan, but had some criticisms. "NCHE firmly supports the 26 planks of the National Plan of Action for the International Decade for Women . . . but also believes the National Plan does not effectively represent the interests of the nation's low income women." In 1978 the organization issued its own "Low Income Woman's International Woman's Year Action Plan" endorsed by the NCHE national membership. It agreed on the need "to end discrimination based on sex" but also wanted to "restate, expand upon, and supplement the recommendations" and consider the "special impact upon low income women . . . [who] bear the triple jeopardies of sex, poverty, and ethnicity." NCHE suggested that including the problems of disability, rural residence, age, child care, and health would deepen the analysis of "women's issues."[72]

Domestic workers' alliance with other low-wage workers opened up a dialogue between domestic workers and other workers who were also outside the mainstream of labor organizing and had been denied basic labor protections. By building an alliance among marginalized workers, the NCHE highlighted the bigger gulf between less privileged and more privileged workers, between those who were unionized and those who were not. It also spoke to the growing importance of low-wage women service workers in a deindustrializing economy. The DC Household Technicians changed its name to the DC Professional Service Workers Association, with the motto: "Working to better the lives of all unorganized workers in service occupations."[73] Drawing attention to the way in which low-wage women workers had difficulty making ends meet for themselves and their families, it overturned assumptions that women workers were "secondary earners" who didn't play a substantial role in supporting the family. This alliance of low-wage workers foreshadowed efforts in the first part of the twenty-first century to form a national coalition, an "Excluded Workers Congress" (later renamed the United Workers Congress)—taxi drivers, domestic workers, restaurant workers, guest workers, farm workers, and formerly incarcerated workers—that built bridges among workers in different occupations outside the formal labor movement.

"New World Domestic Order"

The institutional legacy of the NCHE and the HTA was relatively short lived. The HTA never achieved the independence it hoped for, and over time its goals and leadership merged with the NCHE. In 1975 the NCHE became a membership organization for household workers and constituted a new board made up of household workers. This change was an acknowledgment of the ineffectiveness of HTA to operate independently but also reflected the new orientation of the NCHE as an organization run and represented by workers.[74] But even the NCHE was unable to sustain itself, encountering difficulties with fund-raising and administration. In 1976, Edith Sloan left the organization and Josephine Hulett was let go as field officer because of financial constraints. That year, the Ford Foundation, the primary financial backer of the NCHE, insisted that its grant be handled through a third party because of the organization's inability to raise funds from other sources. The NCHE board voted to affiliate with the National Urban League, a move of desperation considered "the only way to save the organization."[75] The membership of NCHE stood at ten thousand in 1980—still substantial, but well below its peak a few years earlier.

By the time the formal movement of household workers began to wane, the occupation had shifted dramatically since the early twentieth century, when "Mammy" reigned as the most recognizable domestic worker. Annie Love, household worker and head of the Miami Household Technicians, testified about this change: "Back not so long ago we worked just like slaves. They always made us use a separate plate and fork to eat from and a separate glass to drink out of. It was degrading. Now I tell our women they have a profession to be proud of. We provide an important, necessary service—no different from a secretary. We expect to be treated no different than any employer would treat any employee."[76] It is hard to quantify exactly how much domestic-worker organizing can be credited for this transformation. Undoubtedly, broader economic and political trends, from consumer innovations to changing household structure, account for some of the changes in the status of household workers. Nevertheless, by the end of the 1970s a very different sensibility about African American household workers had entered the public consciousness.

Perhaps this was most evident with the hugely popular television sitcom *The Jeffersons*, which originally aired in 1975. The show centered on an affluent African American couple and their outspoken and wisecracking African American household worker, Florence. In one episode Florence decides to form a union, "The United Sisterhood of Household Technicians," advocating for health insurance, higher wages, paid sick days, and pension plans for the racially diverse group of women working in the building. The Jeffersons are good employers, and when Florence seeks to have a meeting at their apartment, Louise Jefferson, a former maid herself, is fully supportive. Her husband, George, initially reluctant, is won over when a white employer insults Louise as she explains the importance of the union. So, both the racial politics of domestic work and household workers' need for labor protection and rights take center stage in this episode, in many ways reflecting the orientation of the HTA. Marla Gibbs, the actress who played Florence on *The Jeffersons*, was an ally of household workers. She attended the 1978 NCHE annual conference in Washington, DC, and was honored at a special Saturday-evening banquet.[77] And whereas Alice Childress was a member of the black left writing for a largely black audience in the 1950s, *The Jeffersons* was a mainstream show on network television, enjoyed by people of all racial backgrounds. Perhaps, more than anything else, the episode about household workers forming a union illustrates how popular perceptions of black household workers had shifted so dramatically in a period when race relations were being redefined.

In addition to contributing to new attitudes about household workers, the significance of the movement in the 1970s was its distinctive model of organizing. Poor African American women who overcame obstacles of inadequate education and limited opportunity were committed to organizing poor women of all racial backgrounds for dignity and justice. Moreover, they had a sense that their struggle was not about them as individuals, but about a larger movement for change. Geraldine Roberts explained years later her views of leadership: "An individual should not be the life of an organization or be the life of the people . . . if it was just Geraldine Roberts then the cease of my activities would mean the organization would be over."[78] Similarly, Carolyn Reed discussed stepping back from her role as leader in the movement in order to give someone else a chance: "I never want things to be centered around an individual, but I see some people who won't let go—the Roy Wilkins complex."[79]

The domestic-worker-rights movement holds other lessons for labor organizers. Mainstream approaches to union organizing established in the early twentieth century were premised on a worker's long-term association with a single employer, often in the manufacturing sector. The decline in manufacturing—a process that began in the 1950s but accelerated in the 1970s—the rise of the service sector, increasing women's employment, and a greater reliance on immigrant labor transformed employment. And the mainstream labor movement was not well equipped to address the needs of this new workforce. As powerful as the mid-twentieth-century labor-organizing models were, they were less effective at mobilizing a workforce of women service workers in nontraditional settings.

The domestic workers' rights movement of the 1960s and 1970s prefigured a model of labor organizing that would go on to become one of the most promising strategies of the labor movement. African American domestic workers' approach to organizing—their use of public spaces as recruiting venues, one-on-one negotiation, legislation that would protect all workers, not only those who were organized, a focus on women of color, the inclusion of workers of diverse nationalities and legal statuses, and push for professionalization—spoke to the specific realities of their occupation. Household labor, where work was always uncertain and labor protections minimal, foretold the shifting realities of a new economy that was not yet full blown. As other forms of employment emulated the character of domestic work—with its lack of security, uneven benefits, and largely women-of-color workforce— the models of organizing pioneered by African American women in the 1960s and 1970s became increasingly important. HTA's victories and the changing political landscape put the domestic workers' rights movement on the cusp of a new era, one in which they were unable to flourish. But their closing epilogue would become the prologue for a new generation of activists.

Contrary to public declarations about the inevitable demise of domestic work in the 1970s, the occupation began to expand in the 1990s. The new norm of the dual-earner household in conjunction with neoliberal economic restructuring created a "crisis of social reproduction" that resulted in fewer institutional supports for care work and household responsibilities. Declining public support for single mothers, fewer preschool and after-school programs, cuts in health programs, and limited elder-care programs, made day-to-day living more taxing. And many families relied on hiring someone to assist with household chores and caring for those needing assistance. These broad economic trends—women's employment outside the home, declining state support for families, and lower wages—which hit most Americans hard, were mitigated by the employment of low-wage workers who could help maintain a semblance of domestic social order. With their help, the basic tenets of the nuclear family could remain intact.

Neoliberal restructuring also led to economic impoverishment in Third World countries. Markets were flooded with cheap foreign products, which undermined local industry. International Monetary Fund (IMF) policies demanded cutbacks in state services. And large-scale World Bank development projects resulted in massive displacement of poor and rural populations. Immigrants came to the US from a wide range of places including the Philippines, the Indian subcontinent, Mexico, Indonesia, Brazil, and Central America. The abundance of low-wage immigrant labor inhibited state-based or even market-based solutions to the problems of who would clean the house and take care of the kids, resulting in what Pierrette Hondagneu-Sotelo has called the "new world domestic order."[80]

These new immigrant domestic workers, like the earlier generation of workers, didn't remain silent. They came together outside the formal labor movement, often in community- or neighborhood-based associations or workers centers to challenge the conditions under which they labored.[81] Barbara Young is one of these women. Born Barbara Cumberbatch in Barbados in 1947, she, her parents, brother, and two sisters were tenants on a plantation. Upon finishing high school, she took a hotel training course and worked as a hotel maid and in a knitting factory. Then she landed a well-paid position with the state-run Barbados Transport Board as a bus conductor, collecting money from passengers and totaling receipts at the end of the day. She worked for the board for twenty years, but was laid off in 1992 after the IMF mandated, through its structural adjustment policies, that government services be cut back and conductors replaced by fare boxes. Young received unemployment for a while, but found it hard to pay for her house and support her three children.[82]

The following year, in 1993, Young went to New York hoping to find a job. In her Queens neighborhood, she met a Jamaican woman employed in a hospital who told her about a patient being discharged and needing a caretaker. Young worked forty-five to fifty hours a week for $250 a week. She received no benefits and no paid overtime. Her second job, which she got through an agency, was a live-in nanny position on Long Island for $225. For seven years, she cleaned, cared for two children, did laundry, and cooked. Young was on duty in the evenings when the couple went out, and thus had no guaranteed time to herself. Her salary eventually increased to $370. Her next job, which she started in 2001, was in Tribeca. Young slept in the same room with the baby and got up at night when the child needed soothing, essentially working twenty-four hours a day. She also cleaned and did the child's laundry. Her pay: $500 a week. Young worked for the family for only ten months before they moved. But it was at this job that she first learned of Domestic Workers United (DWU), a newly formed New York City–based rights group for household workers.

Young was in a park with the child she cared for when another household worker, Erline Brown, approached her. Erline had a stack of newsletters from DWU and told her about a training session being offered at Hunter College. Barbara politely declined, saying that she didn't need training. Erline persisted, explaining that through the session

Barbara could earn a CPR certificate. Barbara was convinced. When she attended her first DWU meeting in Brooklyn, made up largely of women from the Caribbean, she explained: "People were telling the stories about the work that they were doing, not getting vacation, not getting paid for holidays. It was the first time I was hearing stories from workers coming together." One woman, for example, explained that she didn't get holidays on Labor Day, the Fourth of July, or Thanksgiving. Her employer told her that these were "American" holidays, and since she is not "American," she was expected to work. "It was heartbreaking to hear. All of those stories . . . was very, very painful to listen to and to hear people one after the other." DWU mobilized women of different racial, ethnic, linguistic, and national backgrounds, women from Central America, the Philippines, and South Asia, as well as women from Africa. Despite the diverse origins, all the stories seemed to resonate with one another. As Barbara Young put it: "Some people had different stories but similar stories."

Although this was Young's first foray into household-worker organizing, she had a history of labor organizing. Almost all her jobs in Barbados were unionized and she served as a grievance officer in the Barbados Workers Union. In addition, while employed for the bus company, she attended a three-week residential college course on labor history and organizing, which provided her with an intellectual background that would serve her well as she became involved in DWU.

In those early DWU meetings, Young learned about the history of the occupation and made a link between the history of slavery and the exclusions of household workers from labor protections: "The work that domestic workers were doing in the home . . . working for the slave masters and farm laborers were working in the fields. And these were the two categories of workers that were excluded from labor protections in this country." All leaders of DWU were required to take a leadership course, which covered the history of African Americans, Irish immigrants, and Mexican Americans as household workers.[83] The history enabled Young to place her struggle in a broader historical context, understand how different women experienced the occupation, but also recognize the continuities. "This is a different era . . . but people . . . are still working in slave-like conditions."

Young and other DWU organizers also took note of and were inspired by the history of organizing. The contemporary struggle for domestic-worker rights draws on historical examples to build a movement of household workers. As Young explained: "We looked back on the history of domestic worker organizing. . . . We learned of the success of Dorothy Bolden in Atlanta." Those earlier instances of organizing "gave me hope that we would eventually succeed. We even look back as far as Rosa Parks. . . . The resistance of Rosa Parks gives us strength. . . . It was a movement behind her that caused her to say, well, this is enough."[84]

Young was hired by the National Domestic Workers Alliance (NDWA) in March 2011 as a full-time organizer. NDWA formed in 2007 when thirteen local domestic-workers' rights groups—including DWU—came together to establish a national organization. Young provides support for local chapters and serves as a liaison with the national organization. Today she is one of the leaders, traveling around the world to share the work of the National Domestic Workers Alliance. She went to Amsterdam for an international gathering of domestic workers rights groups and to Geneva, Switzerland, to advocate for the 2011 International Labor Organization's Convention on Domestic Work. The convention established global standards for household labor, such as a written agreement of terms of employment, freedom from discrimination, violence, and harassment, collective bargaining rights, abolition of child labor, and decent working and living conditions. Countries that ratify the convention are obligated to enforce it, although only a handful of countries have thus far ratified.

Like their predecessors, household workers in the twenty-first century adopted distinctive organizing strategies rooted in their particular social location. Local groups very often emerged out of ethnic and community-based organizations. They reached out to other workers in public spaces and advocated legislative protections or "bills of rights" for household workers. They drew public attention to egregious violations

of the rights of workers to shame employers and insisted on model contracts and detailed agreements about rights and responsibilities. And
they organized employers as well as employees. Storytelling was an important component of their strategies: As Ai-Jen Poo, the executive director of the National Domestic Workers Alliance, explained in 2010:
Organizing "taught us the ways in which workers' stories can play a crucial role in drawing people into a struggle."[85] Because domestic workers
still lack the right to organize and bargain collectively, are often not paid
minimum wage, have few benefits, work in precarious occupations with
little job security, and in many cases have multiple employers, they have
come to signify the prototype of the modern-day worker. Their employment conditions and circumstances resemble what an increasing number of working people—both men and women—are experiencing. And
to the extent that that is true, both their example and that of the earlier
generation of organizers offer instruction on how workers can begin to
tackle and transform this new political climate.[86]

History and Organizing

History has always been important in the struggle for domestic workers' rights. As the struggle of the 1970s illustrates, the family lore passed
down in household workers' families, the collective memory crafted
from African American women's history, and workers' shared personal
histories facilitated the development of a mass movement. If their personal experiences were the building blocks of the movement, the process of sharing, of storytelling, was the cement that fused those blocks
into a larger whole. Stories of the "slave markets," stories of Rosa Parks,
and stories of struggle and empowerment circulated among household
workers in the 1970s. By 1980, the NCHE began to more consciously
acknowledge the importance of the history of organizing among household workers and embrace the example of working-class black wom-
en's resistance. These household workers seemed acutely aware of the
historical significance of their organizing and how it fit into a broader
trajectory of activism among domestic workers. In addition, as the academic field of black women's history emerged, they attempted to shape

the larger narrative and carve out a space for a distinctive working-class perspective on African American women. Although not scholars, they claimed and had an investment in scholarly interventions.

The powerful example of Rosa Parks that inspired Georgia Gilmore and Dorothy Bolden continued to resonate with household workers. Anita Shelton, in her executive director's report in 1976, invoked the model of Rosa Parks: "May I recall for you the name of a pioneer in the movement, Rosa Parks, who one day . . . decided she just was not going to move to the back of the bus anymore. On that day, that one woman by a single act breathed a new life into the civil rights movement. And beyond that, she gave women of whatever color everywhere, a new dimension. Had it not been for Rosa Parks, some of us may still be satisfied being one husband away from poverty." Shelton analyzed Parks's struggle through a feminist lens and went on to draw a parallel between Parks's bravery and a contemporary household worker, who in her mind exhibited similar courage: "Jesse Mae Wooten is a household worker in Raleigh, N.C., who stood up for her rights to a minimum wage when her employer failed to pay her the rate she is entitled to by law. This past summer her *employer* was *found guilty* of *violation* of the Fair Labor Standards Act."[87] (Italics in the original.)

In 1979 the NCHE appointed Carolyn Reed as its new executive director—the first time a domestic worker had ever held this position. One of Reed's first projects in this role was to present a formal history of African American women and household labor. Reed was well positioned to do so, as her organizational work increasingly intersected with the emerging field of women's history. In November 1979 the National Council of Negro Women (NCNW) organized a conference, directed by Bettye Collier-Thomas, entitled "Black Women: An Historical Perspective, The First National Scholarly Research Conference on Black Women." During her presentation at the conference, Reed made a claim for inclusion of the voices of black working-class women and insisted that documentation needed to include "all women and all of the truth." In 1979 a reporter observed of Reed: "Her reading about labor and social history combined with her background and experience . . . form [her] into a socialist of the oldest and most utopian of schools."[88] Coinciding with the conference was the opening of the Mary McLeod Bethune Memorial Museum, which housed the newly established National Archives for Black Women's History in Washington, DC. It was around this time that Reed donated the papers of the NCHE to the National Archives for Black Women's History.[89]

The NCNW conference was part of a growing attention to women's history and black women's history specifically as an area of scholarly study. Rosalyn Terborg-Penn, Angela Davis, Darlene Clark Hine, Sharon Harley, Paula Giddings, Evelyn Brooks Higginbotham, among others, were writing about black women's history and shaping it as a discipline. Just one month before the NCNW conference, the Association of Black Women Historians (ABWH) was formed, and Rosalyn Terborg-Penn served as the first national director for the first four years. The ABWH would become the most important institutional voice for black women's history.

In 1977 Reed and other household workers participated in a Sarah Lawrence College conference, "The Future of Housework." Two years later Reed attended a two-week Institute on Women's History at Sarah Lawrence College. The Sarah Lawrence Institute was an intensive learning experience—a crash course that included lectures, seminars, workshops, and independent study—designed to provide leaders of women's organizations with a deeper understanding of women's history. The goal was "to bridge the gap between the theory and practice of feminism." Household workers were deeply interested in both the theory and practice of feminism. As Geraldine Miller explained: "Having a theory and doing something with it are two different things. . . . It's the thinking about it, the theory, putting it down on paper, and doing nothing about it means nothing. But having a theory and then trying to see how it will work is different."[90] The forty-five attendees of the institute examined the history of families, sexuality, the domestic sphere, and collective action. At the conference, Reed met Bettye Collier-Thomas, Gerda Lerner, Barbara Omolade, Alice Kessler-Harris, and Amy Swerdlow, all of whom were considered pioneers in the field of women's history. Participants of this conference, including Carolyn Reed, resolved to launch a National Women's History Week to be celebrated in March. And after much persistence, the group succeeded when President Jimmy Carter signed a proclamation in 1980 declaring a National Women's History Week.[91]

While she was at Sarah Lawrence, Carolyn Reed also met Bonita Johnson, a history graduate student. Johnson was deeply influenced by Gerda Lerner's pathbreaking 1972 collection of primary source documents about African American women, *Black Women in White America*, which included an interview with Dorothy Bolden. Lerner had founded and was directing the master's program in women's history at Sarah Lawrence, the first of its kind. Lerner's influence convinced Johnson that the history of household workers was central to the academic study of black women, and she subsequently enrolled in the Sarah Lawrence master's program in women's history. Reed and Johnson developed a collaborative relationship, with Reed helping her with her thesis on the history of household workers, but also suggesting ways for Johnson to contribute to the movement.[92] Reed was thrilled about "meeting a person like Bonnie Johnson, who's really into history, and saying to her, 'Gee, I really want you to do a history project for us, because I feel it's most important.' And really having that sistership with her that has developed with working with her, so that I take her to conferences with me and let people hear her ideas about household work."[93] Reed eventually recruited Johnson to launch an NCHE history project called "Our Right to Know."

"Our Right to Know" consciously integrated black women's history of labor and resistance into current organizing efforts by both assuring the presence of household workers in black women's history and thinking of history as a component of organizing. The project was designed in part to address the paucity of historical studies about household labor. As Johnson explained: "Until very recently, historians have ignored household employment as a topic of research. For the most part, women have been left out of history and women working in traditionally female occupations have been totally bypassed." Examining that history brought value and respect to their work and also exposed the ways in which black working-class women had wielded power and agency as workers. Speaking before an NCHE advisory board meeting, Johnson stated, "I believe that every household worker has a right to know the part she has played in the history of the United States. House-hold workers have helped to build this nation."

Johnson opened the October 1980 NCHE national conference at Memphis State University with a lesson about African American wom-en's history and domestic labor. She encouraged the 125 attendees to share the stories of their mothers and grandmothers and advised them that "history can be used as an organizing tool."[94] Carolyn Reed un-derscored this point about family and community when she closed the conference. They were meeting, she noted, "not in some fancy Hyatt-Regency but where your roots are—in a church in the heart of Mem-phis' black community."[95] The "Our Right to Know" project centered the experiences of African American household workers and hoped to "gather and record their own history," including documents and photo-graphs and "family stories passed down from generation to generation." As Johnson had written in the organization's newsletter just a couple of months earlier about the history project: "The most important part of the project are household workers themselves. Each and every techni-cian has a lifetime of experiences that individually and collectively make up a rich history that deserves documentation. These life histories will draw a picture of household employment today. They will also connect us with our past and guide us in the future!"[96]

Epilogue

I have often been asked why I chose to write about domestic workers. Certainly, part of the reason can be traced to my own family history. My great-grandmother worked as a domestic in South Africa for most of her life. My mother and grandmother both worked briefly as household laborers when they were young. My great-great-grandparents traveled as indentured servants from India to South Africa around the end of the nineteenth century. There was no written family history—not one of my grandparents was literate. So much of what I know about my history was passed down orally.

It never occurred to me to ask my grandmother about her early work experience when she was alive. My father told me how, on her way to work in the home of a white South African family, she regularly passed by the home of the man who would become my grandfather. That commute was how they first met, leading to their eventual marriage. My mother told me stories about her own experience of growing up in apartheid South Africa. She attended school only through the eighth grade and then, as the oldest daughter, dropped out to care for her siblings and supplement the family income. Because her father's wages from a job at a rubber factory were not enough to sustain the family, she washed clothes for a white family to help pay the school fees of her brothers. The patriarchal politics that privileged boys' over girls' education, as well as the racialized and gendered politics of apartheid that created this work opportunity, had long-term consequences for my mother. Not completing school was one of her biggest regrets. After coming to the United States and working in a factory for ten years to put my father through school, she finally upgraded to a part-time secretarial job, which enabled her to take classes at the local high school.

Equally illuminating for me was the gendered division of labor that persisted throughout my childhood, which allocated the bulk of household chores to my mother, my sister, and me (a cycle I have broken in my own family, as my children and husband will attest). But perhaps more important was seeing how my mother came to value and respect all forms of labor through the various working-class jobs she held. Similarly, my aunt, who immigrated to the United States in the 1980s and has since worked as a "housecleaner," as she calls herself, has always spoken positively of her work. So the dignity, the humanity, and the intelligence of the women I researched resonated with me because it mirrored the women in my family who labored in similar ways.

In addition to my personal connections, I have intellectual reasons for writing about household labor. This book offers an incredibly powerful, little-known story about working-class African American women told through their own words. The history of household laborers is usually told from the perspective of employers or middle-class reformers. A key point in this book is self-representation, and the domestic-worker activists profiled here offer a trove of information, through firsthand accounts of their perceptions of domestic work and their aspirations for rights. But these stories are not unmediated. The archival material consists of oral histories, interviews, newspaper clippings, public appearances, organizational papers, and legislative documents. Domestic workers didn't write extensively or collect an abundance of material that historians might consider important. But the stories that the movement generated offer us a rare window into the lives and sentiments of these workers.

In writing about domestic-worker organizing, I have limited my focus to African American women because it was African American women who were at the forefront of these campaigns. In addition, the stories of black domestic workers gained currency in the early 1970s in part because the struggle for black freedom dominated the political landscape. But my emphasis on African American women is also a reflection of the sources that have been preserved in the public domain, the stories that were retold by journalists, and the ones that resonated in popular culture. The overwhelming quantity of material on African

American women may stem from the fact that, given the historical moment, the occupation was closely associated with the struggle for racial equality and presented one path to achieving racial justice.

Although rich sources are available, there are also gaps and unanswered questions. Because of the nature of historical documentation, our knowledge of these women's lives remains incomplete. There is a profound silence around the issue of sexual harassment, abuse, and rape, for example. We know from other research that sexual abuse was a widespread problem in the occupation of domestic service, where employees confined to their employers' domestic spaces were often vulnerable. Yet I have found little evidence of workers who advocated reform of the occupation raising the issue of sexual violence. Perhaps that's because in telling their stories, they refused to be seen or represent themselves as victims. The discussions of victimhood as it related to domestic work often lay, for them, in the past—in the lives of their mothers and grandmothers, on the street corners of New York in the 1930s. They were not victims seeking compensation. They were a new generation of workers deserving of and demanding their rights.

A major theme of this book is storytelling as a political strategy and form of activism. I focus on the stories that domestic workers told about their own history or their remembered history to help construct and make sense of their present. Storytelling became a means of building community, motivating participation, and shaping political perspectives; and storytelling is, of course, intimately tied to history, since it is those stories we remember or choose to remember that we tell. Storytelling became a way to construct the past and convey ideas. I found activists' use of storytelling to be strategic. The significance of these narratives has less to do with objectivity and truth than with their explanatory power—their ability to express women's sense of themselves and their current predicaments. So their stories are not simply interesting to read, but reflective of a particular moment. For the women I write about, what they remembered became a form of action and a way to disrupt conventional wisdom and construct new identities.

My academic training has forced me to think critically about history and the way history is told. All historians are storytellers. We decide to tell some stories and not others—albeit according to a set of criteria different from that of political actors. The stories I tell as a historian are influenced in part by gaps in the literature—narratives that marginalize and mute the voices of working-class women, archival material that has been accessed by only a handful of scholars, and circumscribed ideological categories that shape how we understand historical periods.

Since entering the academy, I have been drawn to a social justice approach to writing and teaching, meaning that I gravitate to topics that have relevance to ordinary people. I try to offer perspectives that are less likely to be a part of the academic or popular discourse—perspectives that I believe will enrich, rather than supplant, how issues are discussed. This also means that I stay connected to contemporary activists, both because I'm committed to social transformation and because I learn from their advocacy and hope to offer my skills and my support in return. Social justice education, I believe, needs a permanent space in the academy. It offers one avenue for how those inside the academy can speak to those outside the academy. At the same time, it creates an opportunity for broader engagement with ideas emerging from scholarly research. Academic ideas are not isolated from the outside world, and the academic sphere does not have a monopoly on intellectualism. My participation in grassroots organizing has also convinced me that academic scholarship matters.

I have been an ally of the contemporary struggle for domestic workers' rights since I first learned about the vibrant movement of household workers and their frequent demonstrations on the streets of New York about ten years ago. As a scholar-activist, I simultaneously buried myself in archival material and made an effort to attend domestic-worker meetings, and was struck by the use of storytelling in both venues. Contemporary participants reminded me very much of the women who populate this book—mature women with life experience and a sharp political analysis. I aided the organizations in whatever way I could, and however I was asked.

Women like Erline Brown, Narbada Chhetri, Joyce Gil-Campbell, Allison Julien, Christine Lewis, Linda Oalican, Barbara Young, and many others helped me realize that what we were told about the decline of the labor movement was simply wrong, and that images of immigrant workers conveyed by the popular press were based on a partial truth. These women were deeply committed to an expansive vision of justice, had a clear sense of how to organize, and were critical of neoliberal economic transformations. I was, and continue to be, inspired. I watched as Domestic Workers United grew from a small, struggling organization to one that was hundreds strong and lobbied successfully for both a New York City law governing employment agencies and a state bill of rights. It is now part of both a national and an international federation of domestic workers' rights groups.

The world, at times, seems full of despair. Yet in my reading of history and through the resurrection of voices rarely heard I don't find despair but rather enormous hope, even when people face seemingly insurmountable obstacles.

My family history, study of history, and commitment to social change have fostered a belief that ordinary people can and must speak out and that in order to develop a vision about how to frame justice and how to engage in social change, we can and must listen.

Acknowledgments

Books are rarely written in isolation. They are woven into and emerge from the fabric of everyday life. The intellectual work for this book was shaped in the archives, as well as in daily conversations and seemingly unrelated experiences. The many household workers I have known over the course of my life are reflected in these pages. I owe my first thanks to them for enabling me to understand this occupation in a way I otherwise would not have. They include the members of Domestic Workers United, Adhikaar, Mujeres Unidas Y Activas, Damayan, and the National Domestic Workers Alliance.

Numerous archivists and librarians facilitated access to material and assisted in the research process: Kenneth Chandler of the National Archives for Black Women's History at the Mary McLeod Bethune Council House, Abby Lester at Sarah Lawrence College, archivists at the Southern Labor Archives at Georgia State University, Margaret Jessup at Smith College, Joellen El Bashir at the Moorland-Spingarn Research Center at Howard University, Andrew Salinas at the Amistad Research Center at Tulane University, Tom Hodgdon at the Louis Round Wilson Special Collections Library at the University of North Carolina, Sarah Moazeni at the Tamiment Library and Robert F. Wagner Labor Archives at New York University, Shannon O'Neill at the Barnard College Library, Walter LeFeber and Kristen Lynn Chinery at the Walter Reuther Library at Wayne State University, and Sarah Hutcheon at the Schlesinger Library. I was lucky to have access to interviews of domestic worker activists conducted by other researchers. They include Gerda Lerner, Robert Hamburger, Tamar Carroll, Loretta Ross, Martha Sandlin, Donna Van Raaphorst, Chris Lutz, Malaika Lumumba, and Debra Bernhardt. Their foresight to document the lives of household worker activists provided a foundation for this book, as did the work of numerous black feminist scholars and women's historians who began to write about black working-class women's history many decades ago. Unfortunately, I did not have the opportunity to meet any of the household workers from the 1970s featured in this book. I did have a chance to speak to Mary McClendon a few times on the telephone, although she felt unable to have a face-to-face interview. Sadly, as I was completing the final round of edits, I learned from her granddaughter that she had passed away.

Funding from the PSC-CUNY Research Foundation, Barnard College; the Center for the Humanities at the CUNY Graduate Center; and the Center for Place, Culture, and Politics at the CUNY Graduate Center enabled me to conduct research and complete the writing. I had the opportunity to share portions of the manuscript at a number of seminars: the Center for the Humanities; the Center for Place, Culture, and Politics; the Columbia University Social Rights and Democracy Workshop; Sister Scholars; the Boston Seminar on the History of Women and Gender; the Penn Program on Democracy, Citizenship, and Constitutionalism; the Barnard Center for Research on Women's Gender, Justice, and Neoliberal Transformations Workshop; and the Intimate Labors Conference at the University of California–Santa Barbara.

I have the good fortune of being a part of enriching academic and nonacademic communities that helped make this book what it is. Individuals who influenced me in one way or another include Mimi Abramovitz, Patricia Antoniello, Bill Ayers, Rosalyn Baxandall, Asha Best, Martha Biondi, Grace Chang, Amy Chazkel, Yvette Christianse, Cathy Cohen, Kathy Coll, Sarah Covington, Aimee Cox, Grace Davie, Angela Davis, Dana-Ain Davis, Gina Dent, Lindsey Dayton, Bonnie Thornton Dill, Bernardine Dohrn, Sujatha Fernandes, Leon Fink, Jennifer Fish, Bill Fletcher, Eric Foner, Pablo Foster, Pablo Foster Jr., Valerie Francisco, Zinga Fraser, Josh Freeman, Pam Galpern, Ruth Gilmore, Stephanie Gilmore, Harmony Goldberg, Linda Gordon, Dayo Gore, Anna Gueverra, Beverly Guy-Sheftall, Victoria Haskins, Nancy Hewitt, Cheryl Hicks, Elizabeth Kai Hinton, Tarry Hum, Tera Hunter, Lynette Jackson, Janet Jakobsen, Anne Jonas, Amy Jordan, Temma Kaplan, Robin Kelley, Alice Kessler-Harris, Madhulika Khandelwal, Alice Kim, Lisa Lee, David Levine, Manning Marable, Vanessa May, Sonya Michel,

Keesha Middlemass, Nara Milanich, Nancy Mirabal, Michele Mitchell, Chandra Mohanty, Leith Mullings, Lisa Murray, Cheryl Mwaria, Celia Naylor, Alondra Nelson, Immanuel Ness, Mae Ngai, Mojubaolu O. Okome, Francois Pierre-Louis, Michael Ralph, Sheri Randolph, Beth Ritchie, Sam Roberts, Gunja Sengupta, Carla Shedd, Irene Sosa, Marie Cruz Soto, Pam Sporn, Rosalyn Terborg-Penn, Jeanne Theoharis, James Thindwa, Ethel Tungahon, Peter Vellon, KC Wagner, Rhonda Williams, Barbara Winslow, and Komozi Woodard. Barbara Ransby, Peter Sporn, Jason Ransby-Sporn, and Asha Rosa Ransby-Sporn are like family. Barbara has for decades been an important source of support and love. I have been especially impressed by Asha's growing commitment to activism and her demonstrated leadership on and off Columbia's campus. I appreciate Lelanie Foster-Sporn finding the time to take an author photograph for me. Special thanks to Linda Burnham, research director of the National Domestic Workers Alliance, whose sharp insight and decades-long commitment to organizing has taught me a great deal, and to Ai-Jen Poo, whose unwavering dedication was so important to building the local and national movement of household workers. Eileen Boris has been a friend and collaborator on research and writing related to domestic worker organizing for many years.

Several people read portions of the manuscript and provided feedback: George Aumoithe, Eileen Boris, Dorothy Sue Cobble, Nancy Cott, Lisa Levenstein, Erik McDuffie, Ruth Milkman, Celia Naylor, Annelise Orleck, Barbara Ransby, Mary Romero, Robyn Spencer, Lisa Tiersten, and Lara Vapnek. Their brilliance and insight made this a better book. Two research assistants, Jessica Mendez and Tess Domb Sadof, helped me at critical moments in the completion of the book.

When I started this project, I was teaching at Queens College, an institution with dedicated faculty and students with unmatched maturity and life experience. Although I am no longer at Queens, I still deeply value its mission of public education. I also had the privilege of serving as visiting Endowed Chair in Women's Studies at Brooklyn College, where I developed lasting friendships. My move to Barnard has exceeded my expectations. I have a fabulous set of colleagues, both in my department and across the college and the university, and an outstanding chair, Lisa Tiersten, who made my transition into Barnard a smooth one. The Barnard Center for Research on Women has been a particularly supportive space to think and talk about household worker activism. I am impressed by the sense of community, as well as the intellectually stimulating environment, at Barnard.

Gayatri Patnaik, Rachael Marks, Susan Lumenello, Marcy Barnes, Melissa Dobson, and the entire staff at Beacon have been a real pleasure to work with. Even in those moments when I was in my writing doldrums, Gayatri and Rachael always knew exactly what to say to guide me through to the other side. They cheered me when I needed cheering and pushed me when they thought it would be productive. I thank them for their faith in the project and their insightful feedback as the book underwent many rounds of revisions.

Friends and family members helped out in big and small ways. John Johnson, Luciano Dos Santos, David Fletcher, Jeffrey Palichuck, Nicole Martin, Dave Martin, Amina Khalil, Jaycinth Hyman, and Robyn Spencer and her daughter Sira all serve as surrogate family. My extended family in South Africa, especially my aunt Saroj and cousins Anthony, Rajes, Deysie, Leo, Tracy, and Marshall and their children, are dear to my heart. Kasie and Sheila Padayachee hosted me in Michigan while I visited the Reuther Library, and Nicole Nadasen took care of my daughter. Sally Gladstone, Allan Hruska, Peggy Calkins, Andy Calkins, Emily Coombs, Kitty Gladstone, and all my nieces and nephews—Charlie, Caroline, Jack, Bonnie, Liza, Grace, and David—always have an abundance of love to share. I am grateful for the love and support of Denise Nadasen, Tom Reynolds, Jeff Nadasen, Carol Nadasen, Timothy, Clay, Jeremy, Jackie, Zoe, Mitchell, and Sophia. Denise read drafts of chapters and encouraged me to carry on. Clay Nadasen-Reynolds made a trek to the library for me, for which I am grateful.

This book prompted me to think more about my own family history. Although my mother passed away as I embarked on this project, I spoke to a number of family members about her early life. I have also begun interviewing my father and have come to appreciate his own hardships and struggles—from dirt poor to tenured professor late in life. Despite his rise in status, he has always carried himself with humility. Bill

Gladstone, Tyler Nadasen-Gladstone, and Indira Nadasen-Gladstone were all enormously patient and supportive through the process of writing this book. I know it took its toll on them, as I was often holed away during family vacations, and, ironically, as I was intellectualizing about the value of household labor, they ensured that not only their but my chores were completed. Both Tyler and Indira have turned out to be magnificent human beings—filled with compassion, intelligence, self-confidence, and a clear sense of justice. Bill has gone above and beyond the call of duty, not only reading drafts and running the household while holding down his own job but doing so with humor and grace. He is a model partner, whose love sustains me.

NOTES

INTRODUCTION

1. Patrice O'Shaughnessy, "Long Island Case Turns Spotlight on Hundreds Trapped as Slaves," *New York Daily News*, June 28, 2008; Corey Kilgannon, "Long Island Couple Convicted of Enslaving Two Domestic Workers for Years," *New York Times*, December 18, 2007; Paul Vitello, "From Stand In Long Island Slavery Case, A Snapshot of a Hidden US Problem," *New York Times*, December 3, 2007.

2. For more on contemporary domestic workers, see, for example, Grace Chang, *Disposable Domestics: Immigrant Women Workers in the Global Economy* (Cambridge, MA: South End Press, 2000); Pierrette Hondagneu-Sotelo, *Doméstica: Immigrant Workers Cleaning and Caring in the Shadows of Affluence* (Berkeley: University of California Press, 2001); Rhacel Salazar Parreñas, *Servants of Globalization: Women, Migration, and Domestic Work* (Stanford, CA: Stanford University Press, 2001); Tamara Mose Brown, *Raising Brooklyn: Nannies, Childcare, and Caribbeans Creating Community* (New York: New York University Press, 2011); Monisha Das Gupta, *Unruly Immigrants: Rights, Activism, and Transnational South Asian Politics in the United States* (Durham, NC: Duke University Press, 2006).

CHAPTER 1
"Conversations" About Domestic Labor

1. Alice Childress, *Like One of the Family: Conversations from a Domestic's Life* (Boston: Beacon Press, 1986), 2.

2. Mary Helen Washington, "Alice Childress, Lorraine Hansberry, and Claudia Jones: Black Women Write the Popular Front," in *Left of the Color Line: Race, Radicalism, and Twentieth-Century Literature*, ed. Bill V. Mullen and James Edward Smethurst (Chapel Hill: University of North Carolina Press, 2003).

3. For more on Childress, see Trudier Harris, *From Mammies to Militants: Domestics in Black American Literature* (Philadelphia: Temple University Press, 1982), 111–33; Kathlene McDonald, *Feminism, the Left, and Postwar Literary Culture* (Jackson: University Press of Mississippi, 2012), chapter 3; Cheryl Higadisha, *Black Internationalist Feminism: Women Writers of the Black Left, 1945–1995* (Urbana: University of Illinois Press, 2011).

4. Letter to Trudier Harris, January 7, 1980, cited in Mary Condé, "Some African American Fictional Responses to *Gone with the Wind*," *Yearbook of English Studies* 26 (1996): 212.

5. See, for example, Bonnie Thornton Dill et al., "For the Good of Family and Race: Gender, Work, and Domestic Roles in the Black Community, 1880–1930," *Signs* 15, no. 2 (Winter 1990): 336–49.

6. Faye Duddan, *Serving Women: Household Service in Nineteenth-Century America* (Middletown, CT: Wesleyan University Press, 1983); David Katzman, *Seven Days a Week: Women and Domestic Service in Industrializing America* (New York: Oxford University Press, 1978); Andrew Urban, "Irish Domestic Servants, 'Biddy,' and Rebellion in the American Home, 1850–1890," *Gender and History* 21, no. 2 (August 2009): 263–86.

7. Mary Romero, *Maid in the USA* (New York: Routledge, 1992), 27.

8. Duddan, *Serving Women*; Katzman, *Seven Days a Week*. According to Vicki Ruiz, domestic labor was the most common form of employment for Mexican and Mexican American women in the first half of the twentieth century, especially during the open-border period prior to the 1930s. See Vicki L. Ruiz, "By the Day or Week: Mexicana Domestic Workers in El Paso," in *To Toil the Livelong Day: America's Women at Work, 1780–1980*, ed. Carol Groneman and Mary Beth Norton (Ithaca, NY: Cornell University Press, 1987), 269–83, and *Women on the US-Mexico Border: A Response to Change*, ed. Vicki Ruiz and Susan Tiana (Boston: Allen & Unwin, 1987). See also Evelyn Nakano Glenn, *Issei, Nisei, War Bride: Three Generations of Japanese American Women in Domestic Service* (Philadelphia: Temple University Press, 1986); Romero, *Maid in the USA*; Kyle E. Ciani, "Hidden Laborers: Female Day Workers in Detroit, 1870–1920," *Journal of the Gilded Age and the Progressive Era* 4, no. 1 (2005): 23–51; Daniel T. Hobby, "We Have Got Results: A Document in the Organization of Domestics in the Progressive Era," *Labor History* 17, no. 1 (1976): 103–8.

9. Lucy Maynard Salmon, *Domestic Service* (orig., c. 1897; New York: Arno Press, 1972); Lara Vapnek, *Breadwinners: Working Women and Economic Independence, 1865–1920* (Urbana: University of Illinois Press, 2009); Linda Martin and Kerry Segrave, *The Servant Problem: Domestic Workers in North America* (Jefferson, NC: McFarland & Co., 1985).

10. Susan B. Carter et al., *Historical Statistics of the United States: Earliest Times to the Present* (New York: Cambridge University Press, 2006), table Ba1061–74, "Major Occupational Groups—Females: 1860–1990," table Ba1103–16, "Major Occupational Groups—White Females: 1860-1990," and table Ba1117–30, "Major Occupational Groups—Nonwhite Females: 1860–1990."

11. Vanessa May, *Unprotected Labor: Household Workers, Politics, and Middle-Class Reform in New York, 1870-1940* (Chapel Hill: University of North Carolina Press, 2011).

12. Carter et al., *Historical Statistics of the United States*, tables Ba1061–74, Ba1103–16, and Ba1117–30. For more on demographics of the occupation, see Mignon Duffy, *Making Care Count: A Century of Gender, Race, and Paid Care Work* (Piscataway, NJ: Rutgers University Press, 2011), chapter 2.

13. Danielle Phillips argues that "constructions of blackness also played a critical role in demarcating the domestic workplace as a site where the boundaries of race and citizenship were imagined and contested daily." See Danielle Taylor Phillips, "Moving with the Women: Tracing Racialization, Migration and Domestic Workers in the Archive," *Signs* 38, no. 2 (Winter 2013): 379–404. See also Rebecca

Sharpless, *Cooking in Other Women's Kitchens: Domestic Workers in the South, 1865–1960* (Chapel Hill: University of North Carolina Press, 2013); Mahnaz Kousha, "African American Private Household Workers, White Employers and Their Children," *International Journal of Sociology and Family* 25, no. 2 (1995): 67–89.

14. K. Sue Jewell, *From Mammy to Miss America and Beyond: Cultural Images and the Shaping of US Social Policy* (New York: Routledge, 1993).

15. Cheryl Thurber, "The Development of the Mammy Image and Mythology," in *Southern Women: Histories and Identities*, ed. Virginia Bernard (Columbia: University of Missouri Press, 1992), 87–108; Grace Elizabeth Hale, *Making Whiteness: The Culture of Segregation in the South, 1890–1940* (New York: Vintage, 1999); Micki McElya, *Clinging to Mammy: The Faithful Slave in 20th Century America* (Cambridge, MA: Harvard University Press, 2007). See also Elizabeth Ross Haynes, "Negroes in Domestic Service in the United States: Introduction," *Journal of Negro History* 8, no. 4 (1923): 384–442.

16. Kimberly Wallace-Sanders, *Mammy: A Century of Race, Gender, and Southern Memory* (Ann Arbor: University of Michigan Press, 2008), 106. Wallace-Sanders uses the phrase "mammy prism" to illustrate how the mammy figure reflected the broader politics of race.

17. Joan Marie Johnson, "'Ye Gave Them a Stone': African American Women's Clubs, Frederick Douglass, and the Black Mammy Monument," *Journal of Women's History* 17, no. 1 (2005): 62–86.

18. Mary Church Terrell, *Washington (DC) Evening Star*, February 10, 1923. Quoted in Johnson, "'Ye Gave Them a Stone,'" 62.

19. Ella Baker and Marvel Cooke, "The Slave Market," *Crisis* 42 (November 1935): 330–31.

20. Alana Erickson Coble, *Cleaning Up: The Transformation of Domestic Service in Twentieth-Century New York City* (New York: Routledge, 2006).

21. See Dayo F. Gore, *Radicalism at the Crossroads: African American Women Activists in the Cold War* (New York: New York University Press, 2011); Carole Boyce Davies, *Left of Karl Marx: The Political Life of Black Communist Claudia Jones* (Durham, NC: Duke University Press, 2008); Erik McDuffie, *Sojourning for Freedom: Black Women, American Communism, and the Making of Black Left Feminism* (Durham, NC: Duke University Press, 2011).

22. Louise Thompson Patterson, "Toward a Brighter Dawn," *Woman Today*, April 1936.

23. Claudia Jones, "An End to the Neglect of the Problems of the Negro Woman!," *Political Affairs*, June 1949, reprint, National Women's Commission, CPUSA.

24. Washington, "Alice Childress, Lorraine Hansberry, and Claudia Jones," 195.

25. Other domestic-worker unions emerged during the 1930s as well. In 1942, United Domestic Workers formed in Baltimore as CIO Local 1283 and managed to increase the wages and reduce working hours for its members. The union also attempted to include sick leave and vacation pay as part of its member benefits. By the end of the war, however, it had stopped functioning. Domestics in El Paso, Texas, like black women in New York City, formed a domestic workers association to demand higher wages. See Rosalyn Terborg-Penn, "Survival Strategies Among African-American Women Workers: A Continuing Process," in *Women, Work, and Protest: A Century of US Women's Labor History*, ed. Ruth

Milkman (London: Routledge, 2013), 139–55; Vicki Ruiz, "By the Day or By the Week: Mexican Domestic Workers in El Paso," in *Women on the US-Mexico Border: A Response to Change*, ed. Vicki Ruiz and Susan Tiana (Boston: Allen & Unwin, 1987).

26. May, *Unprotected Labor*, 158.

27. Esther Victoria Cooper, "The Negro Woman Domestic Worker in Relation to Trade Unionism" (MA thesis, Fisk University, 1940), 54.

28. May, *Unprotected Labor*. See also Stephen H. Norwood, "Organizing the Neglected Worker: The Women's Trade Union League in New York and Boston, 1930–1950," *Labor History* 50, no. 2 (2009): 163–85.

29. Mary Helen Washington coined the term "black left feminism."

30. Mary L. Dudziak, *Cold War Civil Rights: Race and the Image of American Democracy* (Princeton, NJ: Princeton University Press, 2011); McDuffie, *Sojourning for Freedom*, 192.

31. Of the 10,005 black women workers in Montgomery in 1955, 5,087 worked as domestics in the homes of white families. All but 47 were live-out workers. Robert Heinrich, "Montgomery: The Civil Rights Movement and Its Legacies" (PhD diss., Brandeis University, 2008), 28. See also Susan Tucker, *Telling Memories Among Southern Women: Domestic Workers and Their Employers in the Segregated South* (Baton Rouge: Louisiana State University Press, 2002).

32. Mary Fair Burks, "Trailblazers: Women in the Montgomery Bus Boycott," in *Women in the Civil Rights Movement: Trailblazers and Torchbearers, 1941–1965*, ed. Vicki L. Crawford, Jacqueline Anne Rouse, and Barbara Woods (Bloomington: Indiana University Press, 1993), 71–83; David Garrow, ed., *The Montgomery Bus Boycott and the Women Who Started It: The Memoir of Jo Ann Gibson Robinson* (Knoxville: University of Tennessee Press, 1987). Belinda Robnett, *How Long? How Long? African American Women in the Struggle for Civil Rights* (New York: Oxford University Press, 1997), discusses women's role as bridge leaders, linking the formal leaders and the community. On women's leadership in the civil rights movement, including the participation of working-class women, see Bernice McNair Barnett, "Invisible Southern Black Women Leaders in the Civil Rights Movement: The Triple Constraints of Gender, Race, and Class," *Gender and Society* 7, no. 2 (June 1993): 162–82.

33. Mrs. Allean Wright, age forty-five to fifty, cook, interview by Willie M. Lee, January 24, 1956, box 4, folder 3, Preston and Bonita Valien Papers, Amistad Research Center, Tulane University (hereafter ARC).

34. Mrs. Beatrice Charles, maid, age forty-five, interview by Willie M. Lee, January 20, 1956, box 4, folder 3, ARC.

35. "Statement in Response to Question As to Why the People in Montgomery, Alabama Walk?," March 15, 1956, interview by J. Harold Jones, box 4, folder 2, ARC.

36. Henry Hampton, Steve Fayer, and Sarah Flynn, *Voices of Freedom: An Oral History of the Civil Rights Movement from the 1950s through the 1980s* (New York: Bantam, 1991), 25–26.

37. Irene Stovall, cook and maid, age thirty-five to forty, interview by Willie M. Lee, February 1, 1956, box 4, folder 3, ARC.

38. A domestic of about forty years old working in a white retail area, interview by Willie M. Lee, January 1, 1956, box 4, folder 3, ARC.

39. Beatrice Charles interview.

40. Dealy Cooksey, domestic, about age forty, interview by Willie M. Lee, January 24, 1956, box 4, folder 3, ARC. For the sake of clarity, I have corrected misspellings in the transcription that reflect bias or seem to emphasize pronunciation unnecessarily.

41. See Jeanne Theoharis, *The Rebellious Mrs. Rosa Parks* (Boston: Beacon Press, 2013), and Danielle McGuire, *At the Dark End of the Street: Black Women, Rape, and Resistance—A New History of the Civil Rights Movement from Rosa Parks to the Rise of Black Power* (New York: Vintage, 2011).

42. McGuire, *At the Dark End of the Street*, 75.

43. McGuire referred to the boycott as a "women's movement for dignity" (ibid., 108).

44. Marisa Chappell, Jenny Hutchinson, and Brian Ward, "'Dress modestly, neatly . . . as if you were going to church': Respectability, Class and Gender in the Montgomery Bus Boycott and the Early Civil Rights Movement," in *Gender in the Civil Rights Movement*, ed. Peter J. Ling and Sharon Monteith (New York: Garland, 1999), 69–100.

45. Robin D. G. Kelley makes an argument about the militancy of black working-class bus riders. See Robin D. G. Kelley, "'We Are Not What We Seem': Rethinking Black Working-Class Opposition in the Jim Crow South," *Journal of American History* (June 1993): 75–112.

46. Willie Mae Wallace, store maid, age thirty to thirty-five, interview by Willie M. Lee, January 27, 1956, box 4, folder 3, ARC. Again for the sake of clarity, I have corrected misspellings in the transcription that reflect bias or seem to emphasize pronunciation unnecessarily.

47. Mrs. H. N. Blackwell, interview by Anna Holden, February 2, 1956, box 3, folder 13, ARC.

48. Mrs. Lydia S. Prim, interview by Anna Holden, January 27, 1956, box 3, folder 13, ARC.

49. Taylor Branch, *Parting the Waters: America in the King Years, 1954–63* (New York: Simon & Schuster, 1988), 136.

50. Willie Mae Wallace interview.

51. Irene Stovall interview.

52. Virginia Foster Durr, *Outside the Magic Circle: The Autobiography of Virginia Foster Durr* (Tuscaloosa: University of Alabama Press, 1985). For more on the relationship between white employers and black domestics in the South, see Katherine Von Wormer, David W. Jackson III, and Charletta Sudduth, *The Maid Narratives: Black Domestics and White Families in the Jim Crow South* (Baton Rouge: Louisiana State University Press, 2012); and Tucker, *Telling Memories*.

53. Gilmore also worked as a tie changer for the railroad.

54. Interview with Georgia Gilmore, Blackside Films and Media, February 17, 1986, for *Eyes on the Prize: America's Civil Rights Years (1954–1965)*, Washington University Libraries, Film and Media Archive, Henry Hampton Collection.

55. Georgia Gilmore, Montgomery bus boycott trial transcript, March 19, 1956, Alabama Department of Archives and History, Montgomery, 351–52.

56. Ibid., 353.

57. Ibid., 350–51.

58. Nikki Silva and Davia Lee Nelson, *Hidden Kitchens: Stories, Recipes, and More From NPR's The Kitchen Sisters* (Emmaus, PA: Rodale, 2005), 199. Georgia Gilmore was thirty-five at the time.

59. Hampton, Fayer, and Flynn, *Voices of Freedom.*

60. Johnnie Carr, quoted in *Hidden Kitchens*, 205.

61. Vernon Jarrett, "Raised Funds for Blacks: 'Club From Nowhere' Paid Way of Boycott," *Chicago Tribune*, December 4, 1975.

62. Ibid.

63. Gilmore interview, Blackside Films.

64. Ibid.

65. Jarrett, "Raised Funds for Blacks."

66. Silva and Nelson, *Hidden Kitchens*, 199.

67. "The Club from Nowhere: Cooking for Civil Rights," National Public Radio Special Series, *Hidden Kitchens: The Kitchen Sisters*, March 4, 2005, http://www .npr.org/templates/story/story.php?storyId=4509998.

68. When her son Mark was beaten up by police for walking through a whites-only park on his way to the hospital where he worked, Gilmore, aided by movement leaders, sued the city (*Gilmore v. City of Montgomery*) and won.

69. *Hidden Kitchens*, 202.

70. Robert Heinrich, "Montgomery: The Civil Rights Movement and Its Legacies" (PhD diss., Brandeis University, 2008), 77.

71. Thomas Jordan, quoted in *Hidden Kitchens*, 206.

72. Jarrett, "Raised Funds for Blacks."

73. See Patricia Hill Collins, "Learning from the Outsider Within: The Sociological Significance of Black Feminist Thought," *Social Problems* 33, no. 6 (October–December 1986): S14–S32.

74. Barnett, "Invisible Southern Black Women Leaders," 212. See also Vernon Jarrett, "'Club from Nowhere' Paid Way of Boycott," *Chicago Tribune*, December 4, 1975.

75. Hazel Carby, "White Women Listen! Black Feminism and the Boundaries of Sisterhood," in *The Empire Strikes Back: Race and Racism in 70s Britain*, ed. Centre for Contemporary Cultural Studies (New York: Routledge, 1982).

76. Childress, *Like One of the Family*, 140–41.

CHAPTER 2

Women, Civil Rights, and Grassroots Mobilization

1. Dorothy Bolden, interview by Chris Lutz, August 31, 1995, Transcript L1995–12, p. 22, Southern Labor Archives, Special Collections and Archives, Georgia State University Library, Atlanta.

2. Ibid.

3. Ibid.

4. The historical literature on domestic service work is extensive. See, for example, Eileen Boris and Premilla Nadasen, "Domestic Workers Organize!," *Working USA: The Journal of Labor and Society* (December 2008): 413–37; David Katzman, *Seven Days a Week: Women and Domestic Service in Industrializing America* (New York: Oxford University Press, 1978); Phyllis Palmer, *Domesticity and Dirt:*

Housewives and Domestic Servants in the United States, 1920–1945 (Philadelphia: Temple University Press, 1991); Evelyn Nakano Glenn, *Issei, Nisei, War Bride: Three Generations of Japanese American Women in Domestic Service* (Philadelphia: Temple University Press, 1986); Mary Romero, *Maid in the USA* (New York: Routledge, 1992); Donna Van Raaphorst, *Union Maids Not Wanted: Organizing Domestic Workers, 1870–1940* (Santa Barbara, CA: Praeger, 1988); Judith Rollins, *Between Women: Domestics and Their Employers* (Philadelphia: Temple University Press, 1987); Dorothy Sue Cobble, *The Other Women's Movement: Workplace Justice and Social Rights in Modern America* (Princeton, NJ: Princeton University Press, 2004); Tera Hunter, *To 'Joy My Freedom: Southern Black Women's Lives and Labors After the Civil War* (Cambridge, MA: Harvard University Press, 1997); Cecilia Rio, "'On the Move': African American Women's Paid Domestic Labor and the Class Transition to Independent Commodity Production," *Rethinking Marxism* 17, no. 4 (October 2005): 489–510; Bonnie Thornton Dill, *Across the Boundaries of Race and Class: An Exploration of Work and Family Among Black Female Domestic Servants* (New York: Garland, 1993); Peggie R. Smith, "Regulating Paid Household Work: Class, Gender, Race, and Agendas of Reform," *American University Law Review* (1999): 851–918; Soraya Moore Coley, "And Still I Rise: An Exploratory Study of Contemporary Black Private Household Workers" (PhD diss., Bryn Mawr College, 1981). For sources on the National Domestic Workers Union of America (NDWUA), see Premilla Nadasen, "Power, Intimacy, and Contestation: Dorothy Bolden and Domestic Worker Organizing in Atlanta in the 1960s," in *Intimate Labors: Cultures, Technologies, and the Politics of Care*, ed. Eileen Boris and Rhacel Parreñas (Stanford, CA: Stanford University Press, 2010); Cobble, *The Other Women's Movement*; Elizabeth Beck, "The National Domestic Workers Union and the War on Poverty," *Journal of Sociology and Social Welfare* 28, no. 4 (December 2001): 195–211; Lars Christiansen, "The Making of a Civil Rights Union: The National Domestic Workers Union of America" (PhD diss., College of Social Sciences, Florida State University, 1999).

5. The domestic workers' rights movement fits into the scholarly trajectory of black working-class activism. Recent scholarship on the black freedom movement has examined how campaigns for economic justice were part and parcel of the civil rights movement. Civil rights campaigns, such as Operation Breadbasket in Chicago and the 1963 March on Washington for Jobs and Freedom, included an economic component. In addition, black workers participated in a number of unionization efforts in the public sector and in the tobacco and textile industries, where they fought for inclusion and equal treatment.

6. Dorothy Bolden resumé, box 1624, folder 31, National Domestic Workers Union Records (hereafter NDWU Records), Southern Labor Archives, Special Collections and Archives, Georgia State University, Atlanta.

7. In 1930, 90 percent of employed black women in Atlanta were domestic workers. Julia Kirk Blackwelder, "Quiet Suffering: Atlanta Women in the 1930s," *Georgia Historical Quarterly* 61, no. 2 (Summer 1977): 116.

8. Bolden, interview by Lutz, 4.

9. Bolden attended David T. Howard Junior High School. Dorothy Cowser Yancy, "Dorothy Bolden, Organizer of Domestic Workers: She Was Born Poor but She Would Not Bow Down," *Sage* 3, no. 1 (Spring 1986): 53–55; Dorothy Bolden,

interview by Gerda Lerner, September 1978, Transcript, box 6, folder 218, Papers of Gerda Lerner, 1924–2006, Schlesinger Library, Radcliffe Institute, Harvard University, Cambridge, MA.

10. Carole C. Marks, "The Bone and Sinew of the Race: Black Women, Domestic Service and Labor Migration," in *Families on the Move: Immigration, Migration, and Mobility*, ed. Barbara H. Settles, Daniel E. Hanks, and Marvin B. Sussman (New York: Haworth Press, 1993).

11. Isabel Wilkerson, *The Warmth of Other Suns: The Epic Story of America's Great Migration* (New York: Vintage, 2010); Gretchen Lemke-Santangelo, *Abiding Courage: African American Migrant Women and the East Bay Community* (Chapel Hill: University of North Carolina Press, 1996); James R. Grossman, *Land of Hope: Chicago, Black Southerners, and the Great Migration* (Chicago: University of Chicago Press, 1991); Joe Trotter, ed., *The Great Migration in Historical Perspective: New Dimensions of Race, Class, and Gender* (Bloomington: Indiana University Press, 1991); Nicholas Lemann, *The Promised Land: The Great Black Migration and How It Changed America* (New York: Vintage, 1992). For a discussion of African American domestics and migration, see Elizabeth Clark-Lewis, *Living In, Living Out: African American Domestics and the Great Migration* (New York: Kodansha, 1996).

12. Bolden, interview by Lutz, 11.

13. Ibid., 13.

14. Bolden resumé, NDWU Records.

15. Dorothy Bolden, "Organizing Domestic Workers in Atlanta, Georgia," in *Black Women in White America: A Documentary History*, ed. Gerda Lerner (New York: Vintage, 1972), 234.

16. Bolden, interview by Lerner.

17. Barbara Ransby, *Ella Baker and the Black Freedom Movement: A Radical Democratic Vision* (Chapel Hill: University of North Carolina, 2003).

18. Tomika Brown-Nagin, *Courage to Dissent: Atlanta and the Long History of the Civil Rights Movement* (New York: Oxford University Press, 2011).

19. Winston A. Grady-Willis, *Challenging US Apartheid: Atlanta and Black Struggles for Human Rights, 1960–1977* (Durham, NC: Duke University Press, 2006); Clayborne Carson, *In Struggle: SNCC and the Black Awakening of the 1960s* (Cambridge, MA: Harvard University Press, 1995).

20. Hunter, *To 'Joy My Freedom*.

21. Kathryn L. Nasstrom, "Down to Now: Memory, Narrative, and Women's Leadership in the Civil Rights Movement in Atlanta, Georgia," *Gender and History* 11, no. 1 (April 1999): 124; Julia Kirk Blackwelder, "Quiet Suffering: Atlanta Women in the 1930s," *Georgia Historical Quarterly* 61, no. 2 (1977); Karen Jane Ferguson, *Black Politics in New Deal Atlanta* (Chapel Hill: University of North Carolina Press, 2001).

22. Bolden, quoted in Christiansen, "The Making of a Civil Rights Union," 159.

23. Louise Bradley, quoted in Christiansen, "The Making of a Civil Rights Union," 149.

24. Bolden, interview by Lutz, 28.

25. NDWUA Minutes, November 7, 1968, box 1633, folder 173, NDWU Records; Christiansen, "The Making of a Civil Rights Union," 165.

26. Ransby, *Ella Baker*; Charles Payne, *I've Got the Light of Freedom: The Organizing Tradition and the Mississippi Freedom Struggle* (Berkeley: University of California Press, 2007); Wesley Hogan, *Many Minds, One Heart: SNCC's Dream for a New America* (Chapel Hill: University of North Carolina Press, 2009); Carson, *In Struggle.*

27. For more on SNCC's Atlanta Project, see Grady-Willis, *Challenging US Apartheid*, chapter 4.

28. Bolden, interview by Lutz, 28.

29. Christiansen, "The Making of a Civil Rights Union," 160–61.

30. Dorothy Bolden, "National Domestic Workers, Inc.," in *Nobody Speaks for Me: Self Portraits of American Working-Class Women*, ed. Nancy Seifer (New York: Simon & Schuster, 1977), 156–57.

31. Bolden, interview by Lutz, 28.

32. "Board Considers New Site for Vine City High School," *Atlanta Daily World*, June 11, 1964; Dorothy Bolden biography, box 1624, folder 31, NDWU Records.

33. George M. Coleman, "Domestic Work Now a Virtue Because of Dorothy Bolden," *Atlanta Daily World*, March 23, 1975.

34. Bolden resumé, box 1624, folder 31, NDWU Records.

35. Bolden, "National Domestic Workers, Inc.," 146.

36. Gerda Lerner, ed., *Black Women in White America: A Documentary History* (New York: Vintage, 1972), 235.

37. Bolden, interview by Lutz, 17.

38. Ibid., 31.

39. Yancy, "Dorothy Bolden."

40. Julian Bond, quoted in Christiansen, "The Making of a Civil Rights Union," 163–64.

41. "In Town Extra," *Atlanta Journal-Constitution*, January 6, 1983.

42. Bolden, interview by Lerner, 2.

43. NDWUA Minutes, September 19, 1968, box 1633, folder 173, NDWU Records.

44. NDWUA Minutes, September 26, 1968, and October 3, 1968, box 1633, folder 173, NDWU Records.

45. NDWUA brochure, box 1, Dorothy Lee Bolden Thompson Collection, Atlanta-Fulton Public Library System, Auburn Avenue Research Library on African American Culture and History, Atlanta, GA.

46. NDWUA Minutes, October 3, 1968, box 1633, folder 173, NDWU Records.

47. Bolden, interview by Lutz, 30.

48. Ibid., 15.

49. Ibid., 12.

50. Ibid., 14.

51. Ibid., 29.

52. Geraldine Roberts, interview by Donna Van Raaphorst, March 30–June 29, 1977, Cleveland, Program on Women and Work, Institute of Labor and Industrial Relations, University of Michigan, Walter P. Reuther Library, Wayne State University, 37.

53. Ibid., 37.

54. Ibid., 41–42.

55. Ibid., 42.

56. US Commission on Civil Rights, *A Time to Listen, A Time to Act: Voices from the Ghettos of the Nation's Cities* (Washington, DC: US Commission on Civil Rights, November 1967).

57. Roberts, interview by Van Raaphorst, 77.

58. Ibid., 42–43.

59. Ibid., 56.

60. Ibid., 46.

61. Ibid., 45–46.

62. Geraldine Roberts, interview with Malaika Lumumba, August 1, 1970, Ralph J. Bunche Oral History Collection, Moorland-Spingarn Research Collection (MSRC), Howard University accession no. 593, p. 10.

63. For more on bridge leaders such as Turner, see Belinda Robnett, *How Long? How Long? African American Women in the Struggle for Civil Rights* (New York: Oxford University Press, 2000).

64. Rhonda Williams, *The Politics of Public Housing: Black Women's Struggles Against Urban Inequality* (New York: Oxford University Press, 2005); Matthew Countryman, *Up South: Civil Rights and Black Power in Philadelphia* (Philadelphia: University of Pennsylvania Press, 2007); Thomas Sugrue, *Sweet Land of Liberty: The Forgotten Struggle for Civil Rights in the North* (New York: Random House, 2008); Jeanne F. Theoharis and Komozi Woodard, ed., *Freedom North: Black Freedom Struggles Outside the South, 1940–1980* (New York: Palgrave Macmillan, 2003); Lisa Levenstein, *A Movement Without Marches: African American Women and the Politics of Poverty in Postwar Philadelphia* (Chapel Hill: University of North Carolina Press, 2010); Donna Murch, *Living for the City: Migration, Education, and the Rise of the Black Panther Party in Oakland, California* (Chapel Hill: University of North Carolina, 2010).

65. Harry Margulis and Todd Michney, "Constrained Communities: Black Cleveland's Experience with World War II Public Housing," in *Places of Their Own: African American Suburbanization in the Twentieth Century*, ed. Andrew Wiese (Chicago: University of Chicago Press, 2004); Todd M. Michney, "Race, Violence, and Urban Territoriality: Cleveland's Little Italy and the 1966 Hough Uprising," *Journal of Urban History* 32, no. 3 (March 2006): 404–28.

66. Lewis Robinson, *The Making of a Man: An Autobiography* (Cleveland: Green and Sons, 1970).

67. Ruth Turner, interview by Robert Penn Warren, May 7, 1964, Transcript and Digital Audio File, Louie B. Nunn Center for Oral History, University of Kentucky Libraries, http://nyx.uky.edu/oh/render.php?cachefile=03OH32RPWCR21_Turner.xml; Leonard Nathaniel Moore, "The School Desegregation Crisis in Cleveland, Ohio, 1963–1964: The Catalyst for Black Political Power in a Northern City," *Journal of Urban History* 28, no. 2 (January 2002): 135–57.

68. "The Scars of Hough," *Cleveland Plain Dealer*, July 20, 1966.

69. Turner, interview by Warren; Moore, "The School Desegregation Crisis in Cleveland, Ohio."

70. Cleveland was also the city where, in 1961, the Revolutionary Action Movement was founded by Herman Ferguson, Max Stanford, and others. Stanford attended Cleveland CORE meetings. Robert Williams's *Negroes with Guns* was published in 1962 and may also have helped the shift to self-defense. There were also rent strikes in Cleveland in January–February 1964.

71. Roberts, interview by Van Raaphorst, 44. Henry Hampton, Steve Fayer, and Sarah Flynn, *Voices of Freedom: An Oral History of the Civil Rights Movement from the 1950s through the 1980s* (New York: Bantam, 1991), chapter 22.
72. Roberts, interview by Van Raaphorst, 60.
73. Ibid., 82.
74. Ibid., 50.
75. Ibid., 94.
76. Ibid., 44–45.
77. Ibid., 50.
78. Ibid., 46.
79. Faith Corrigan, "Domestic Workers Organize Group to Help Themselves," *Cleveland Plain Dealer*, September 16, 1965.
80. Roberts, interview by Lumumba, 11.
81. Roberts, interview by Van Raaphorst, 98.
82. Corrigan, "Domestic Workers Organize Group."
83. "Maids Ask Clean Sweep of Job Benefits," *Cleveland Plain Dealer*, October 22, 1967.
84. "Clothing Drive Is Under Way," *Cleveland Plain Dealer*, September 4, 1966. CORE and the NAACP offices were drop-off points.
85. Roberts, interview by Van Raaphorst, 99.
86. Roberts, interview by Lumumba, 7.
87. Roberts, interview by Van Raaphorst, 49.
88. Ibid., 52.
89. Ibid., 51.
90. Ibid., 71.
91. Ibid., 52.
92. Ibid., 47.
93. Ibid., 62–63. See also "10 NAACP Members Return Happy from Mississippi March," *Cleveland Plain Dealer*, June 28, 1966.
94. Roberts, interview by Lumumba, 8.
95. Corrigan, "Domestic Workers Organize Group."
96. Roberts, interview by Van Raaphorst, 94.
97. James C. Scott, *Weapons of the Weak: Everyday Forms of Peasant Resistance* (New Haven: Yale University Press, 1985). Robin Kelley has applied this concept to African American struggle: Robin D. G. Kelley, *Race Rebels: Culture, Politics, and the Black Working Class* (New York: Free Press, 1994). See also Mahnaz Kousha, "African American Private Household Workers and 'Control' of the Labor Process in Domestic Service," *Sociological Focus* 27, no. 3 (August 1994): 211–28.
98. For more on connections between the civil rights movement and the domestic-worker rights movement, see Premilla Nadasen, "Power, Intimacy, and Contestation: Dorothy Bolden and Domestic Worker Organizing in Atlanta in the 1960s," in *Intimate Labors: Cultures, Technologies, and the Politics of Care*, ed. Eileen Boris and Rhacel Parreñas (Stanford, CA: Stanford University Press, 2010); Lars Christiansen, "The Making of a Civil Rights Union: The National Domestic Workers Union of America" (PhD diss., Florida State University, 1999); Elizabeth Beck, "The National Domestic Workers Union and the War on Poverty," *Journal of Sociology and Social Welfare* 28, no. 4 (December 2001): 195–211.

99. Cobble, *The Other Women's Movement*, and Dorothy Sue Cobble, "'A Sponta-neous Loss of Enthusiasm': Workplace Feminism and the Transformation of Women's Service Jobs in the 1970s," *International Labor and Working-Class History* 56 (Fall 1999): 23–44.

CHAPTER 3
A New Day for Domestic Workers

1. Edith Barksdale Sloan, "NCHE: Gaining Respect for Household Workers," *Essence*, July 1974, 67.
2. Ibid.
3. Edith Barksdale Sloan, "Statement for the First Black Woman's Institute," 1972 Hunger Convocation, April 21, 1972, National Archives for Black Women's History, Mary McLeod Bethune Council House National Historic Site, Landover, MD, DcWaMMB; National Committee on Household Employment Records, series 003, subseries 01, box 11, folder 31 (hereafter NCHE Records).
4. "Edith Barksdale Sloan," *Washington Post*, February 27, 1977.
5. Sloan, "NCHE," 67, 69.
6. Jolie A. Jackson-Willett, "Edith Barksdale Sloan," in *The African American National Biography*, ed. Henry Louis Gates Jr. and Evelyn Brooks Higginbotham (New York: Oxford University Press, 2008).
7. See Peggie R. Smith, "Regulating Paid Household Work: Class, Gender, Race, and Agendas of Reform," *American University Law Review* (1999): 851–918.
8. US Department of Labor, *American Women: Report of the President's Commission on the Status of Women* (Washington, DC: GPO, 1963), 34–35.
9. For more on labor feminists, see Annelise Orleck, *Common Sense and a Little Fire: Women and Working-Class Politics in the United States, 1900–1965* (Chapel Hill: University of North Carolina Press, 1995); Dorothy Sue Cobble, *The Other Women's Movement: Workplace Justice and Social Rights in Modern America* (Princeton, NJ: Princeton University Press, 2004); Stephen H. Norwood, "Organizing the Neglected Worker: The Women's Trade Union League in New York and Boston, 1930–1950," *Labor History* 50, no. 2 (2009): 163–85; Ruth Milkman, *Gender at Work: The Dynamics of Job Segregation by Sex During World War II* (Urbana: University of Illinois Press, 1987); Nancy Felice Gabin, *Feminism in the Labor Movement: Women and the United Auto Workers, 1935–1975* (Ithaca, NY: Cornell University Press, 1990); Dennis Deslippe, *Rights, Not Roses: Unions and the Rise of Working-Class Feminism, 1945–1980* (Urbana: University of Illinois Press, 2000).
10. Orleck, *Common Sense*; Norwood, "Organizing the Neglected Worker."
11. Frieda Miller, "Household Employees in the United States," *International Labour Review* (1951): 319–20.
12. Frieda Miller, "Can We Lure Martha Back to the Kitchen?" *New York Times*, August 11, 1946.
13. Cobble, *The Other Women's Movement*, chapter 7; Dorothy Sue Cobble, "Friendship Beyond the Atlantic: Labor Feminist International Contacts After the Second World War," *Worlds of Women, International Material in ARAB's Collections* (2012), http://www.arbark.se/publikationer/worlds-of-women/.

14. Dorothy Height, *Open Wide the Freedom Gates: A Memoir* (New York: Public Affairs, 2003), 8. Mary Romero also discusses the consequences of being a maid's daughter. See Mary Romero, *The Maid's Daughter: Living Inside and Outside the American Dream* (New York: New York University Press, 2011).

15. NCHE, "Second Annual Meeting," October 4, 1967, p. 7, box 12, folder 253, Frieda S. Miller Papers, Schlesinger Library, Radcliffe Institute, Harvard University, Cambridge, MA (hereafter Miller Papers); Frieda Miller, "Women in the Labor Force," *Annals of the American Academy* 251 (May 1947): 35–43.

16. Bureau of Labor Statistics, US Department of Labor, "Changes in Men's and Women's Labor Force Participation Rates," *TED: The Economics Daily*, January 10, 2007, http://www.bls.gov/opub/ted/2007/jan/wk2/art03.htm.

17. Elizabeth Waldman, "Labor Force Statistics from a Family Perspective," *Monthly Labor Review* (December 1983): 16–20.

18. Mignon Duffy, *Making Care Count: A Century of Gender, Race, and Paid Care Work* (New Brunswick, NJ: Rutgers University Press, 2011).

19. See Anne McLeer, "Practical Perfection? The Nanny Negotiates Gender, Class, and Family Contradictions in 1960s Popular Culture," *NWSA Journal* 14, no. 2 (Summer 2002).

20. Mary Romero, *Maid in the USA* (New York: Routledge, 1992); Elizabeth Clark-Lewis, *Living In, Living Out: African American Domestics and the Great Migration* (New York: Kodansha, 1996).

21. C. Arnold Anderson and Mary Jean Bowman, "The Vanishing Servant and the Contemporary Status System of the American South," *American Journal of Sociology* 59, no. 3 (November 1953): 215–30.

22. "The Servant Problem: Trials, Triumphs on the Servant Trail of a Working Mother with Her Maids," *Life*, April 7, 1961, p. 109. See also *Ebony* editorial, "Goodbye Mammy, Hello Mom," *Ebony*, March 1947, 36–37.

23. "Help Wanted!" *Woman's Day*, July 1967.

24. Beatrice Vincent, "One Party After Another," *Cleveland Press*, December 20, 1966, NCHE Records, series 003, subseries 01, box 17, folder 04.

25. Mary D. Schlick, "Taking the Dust off Household Jobs," *Manpower Magazine*, July 1969, 25, box 58, folder 1118, Esther Peterson Papers, Schlesinger Library, Radcliffe Institute, Harvard University, Cambridge, MA (hereafter, Peterson Papers). For more on the history of welfare, see Lisa Levenstein, *A Movement Without Marches: African American Women and the Politics of Poverty in Postwar Philadelphia* (Chapel Hill: University of North Carolina Press, 2010); Marisa Chappell, *The War on Welfare: Family, Poverty, and Politics in Modern America* (Philadelphia: University of Pennsylvania Press, 2010); Premilla Nadasen, *Welfare Warriors: The Welfare Rights Movement in the United States* (New York: Routledge 2005); Felicia Kornbluh, *The Battle for Welfare Rights: Politics and Poverty in Modern America* (Philadelphia: University of Pennsylvania Press, 2007); Annelise Orleck, *Storming Caesar's Palace: How Black Mothers Fought Their Own War on Poverty* (Boston: Beacon Press, 2005); Jennifer Mittelstadt, *From Welfare to Workfare: The Unintended Consequences of Liberal Reform, 1945–1965* (Chapel Hill: University of North Carolina Press, 2005); Rhonda Williams, *The Politics of Public Housing: Black Women's Struggles Against Urban Inequality* (New York: Oxford University Press, 2004).

26. In May 1967, on the Chicago campus of the University of Illinois, the NCHE cosponsored a conference on the status of household employment with the Women's Bureau and the Chicago YWCA. Mary Dublin Keyserling, "Summary—Our Task Ahead," Consultation on the Status of Household Employment, Conference Proceedings, May 20, 1967, p. 1.

27. Women's Bureau and NCHE, "If ONLY I Could Get Some Household Help!," pamphlet, 1969 (reprint), box 58, folder 1118, Peterson Papers.

28. Keyserling, "Summary—Our Task Ahead," 3.

29. Carolyn Lewis, "Panel Told Skill Makes Housekeeping a Profession," *Washington Post*, February 25, 1966, box 57, folder 1111, Peterson Papers.

30. Esther Peterson, "Household Consultations," speech transcript, May 20, 1967, box 57, folder 1113, Peterson Papers.

31. Elizabeth Duncan Koontz, "Household Employment: The Quiet Revolution," speech transcript, Northern Virginia Conference on Household Employment, Alexandria, VA, April 14, 1969, p. 3, reprinted by US Department of Labor, NCHE Records, series 003, subseries 01, box 12, folder 15.

32. NCHE, *Improving the Status of Household Employment: A Handbook for Community Action*, revised October 1969, box 199, folder 12, Gloria Steinem Papers, Sophia Smith Collection, Smith College, Northampton, MA.

33. Carolyn Lewis, "Uncle Sam Dons Apron for Sweeping Study," *Washington Post*, February 24, 1966, box 57, folder 1111, Peterson Papers.

34. NCHE, *Improving the Status of Household Employment*.

35. "Homemaker Service Demonstration Project—Kansas State University," May 8, 1968, box 57, folder 1113, Peterson Papers.

36. Myra MacPherson, "Proper Diction Is Part of Program to Elevate Status of Domestics," *New York Times*, April 5, 1968, National Archives for Black Women's History, Series 003, Subseries 04, box 1, folder 8.

37. NCHE, "Second Annual Meeting," October 4, 1967, p. 6 F, box 12, folder 253, Miller Papers.

38. Edith Barksdale Sloan, "NCHE: Gaining Respect for Household Workers," *Essence*, July 1974, p. 66.

39. The NCHE also wanted fifteen "minority group members" to serve as board members. Edith B. Sloan, memorandum to Task Force on Committee Development, September 22, 1969, box 58, folder 1118, Peterson Papers.

40. Anna Halsted to Esther Peterson, May 8, 1970, box 58, folder 1119, Peterson Papers.

41. Frieda Miller, "Household Employees in the United States," *International Labour Review* (1951): 336–37.

42. For examples of other literature on identity formation in the African American community, see Michele Mitchell, *Righteous Propagation: African Americans and the Politics of Racial Destiny After Reconstruction* (Chapel Hill: University of North Carolina Press, 2004); Walter Rucker, *The River Flows On: Black Resistance, Culture, and Identity Formation in Early America* (Baton Rouge: Louisiana State University Press, 2006); Arlene Keizer, *Black Subjects: Identity Formation in the Contemporary Narrative of Slavery* (Ithaca, NY: Cornell University Press, 2004); Adam Green, *Selling the Race: Culture, Community, and Black Chicago, 1940–1955* (Chicago: University of Chicago Press, 2007).

43. Josephine Hulett, interview by Janet Dewart, "Household Help Wanted: Female," *Ms.*, February 1973, pp. 46–48, 105–7.
44. Ibid., 47.
45. Ibid., 105.
46. Ibid.
47. Josephine Hulett, "Profiles in Household Work," June 20, 1972, draft article for *Ms.* (published in revised form February 1973), Ms. Magazine Records, series 7, box 39, folder 12, Sophia Smith Collection, Smith College, Northampton, MA.
48. Hulett, *Ms. Magazine*, 48.
49. Ibid., 106.
50. Ellen Graham, "Home Work: To Household Help, Difficult Times Are a Normal Way of Life," *Wall Street Journal*, February 13, 1975.
51. Auburn Household Technicians, Progress Report, March 1971–October 1972, NCHE Records, series 003, subseries 01, box 02, folder 04.
52. Hulett, *Ms. Magazine*, 46.
53. Josephine Hulett to Anna R. Halsted, November 3, 1970, box 58, folder 1120, Peterson Papers.
54. Jessie Williams of Auburn, AL, was there. There is no indication that Geraldine Roberts and Dorothy Bolden attended.
55. Jeannette Smyth, "Union Maid: A Two Way Street," *Washington Post*, July 17, 1971.
56. Edith Barksdale Sloan, "Keynote Address," July 17, 1971, NCHE Records, series 003, subseries 03, box 02, folder 06.
57. "Farewell to Dinah," *Newsweek*, August 2, 1971.
58. Susan Fogg, "Domestics Meet for 'First Step,'" *Sunday Canton (OH) Repository*, August 1, 1971, box 2, folder 6, Mary Upshaw McClendon Papers (hereafter McClendon Papers), Wayne State Labor Archives, Wayne State University, Detroit.
59. Jacqueline Trescott, "600 Domestics Confer," *Washington (DC) Evening Star*, July 17, 1971, box 2, folder 6, McClendon Papers.
60. "Domestics Fight for a New Way of Life," *Chicago Defender*, August 21, 1971. Four days after the conference, Fauntroy introduced a minimum wage bill into Congress.
61. Ibid.
62. Trescott, "600 Domestics Confer."
63. Anne Valk and Leslie Brown, *Living with Jim Crow: African American Women and Memories of the Segregated South* (New York: Palgrave Macmillan, 2010), 154–56.
64. North Carolina Fund Records, 1962–1971, series 6, subseries 6.7, folder 7035, Southern Historical Collection, Wilson Library, University of North Carolina at Chapel Hill.
65. Fogg, "Domestics Meet for 'First Step.'"
66. "The Annual Meeting of the National Committee on Household Employment," Minutes, November 10, 1971, NCHE Records, series 003, subseries 03, box 01, folder 06.
67. Minutes, first meeting of committee on the formation of a national association of household workers, 1971, p. 2, box 8, folder 19, National Archives for Black Women's History, series 003, subseries 01.

68. NCHE, "Proposal to Sachem Fund," June 9, 1972, p. 1, NCHE Records, series 003, subseries 01, box 03, folder 02.
69. Cobble, *The Other Women's Movement*; and Phyllis Palmer, "Housework and Domestic Labor: Racial and Technological Change," in *My Troubles Are Going to Have Trouble with Me: Everyday Trials and Triumphs of Women Workers*, ed. Karen Brodkin Sacks and Dorothy Remy (New Brunswick, NJ: Rutgers University Press, 1984), 80–91.

CHAPTER 4
Intimacy, Labor, and Professionalization

1. NDWUA brochure, p. 18, NDWU Records.
2. Proclamation by Governor Gilligan, March 28, 1974, NCHE Records, series 003, subseries 01, box 12, folder 26.
3. "Maids' Honor Day Nomination," box 1627, folder 79, NDWU Records.
4. Feminist scholars have debated the impact of commodification of care work and have disagreed about the supposed tension between "love and money"—or the imperatives of the market versus the nurturing aspects of care work. Viviana Zelizar has argued against the assumption that love and money are incompatible or hostile worlds. Similarly, Nancy Folbre suggests that both love and money can be motivating factors. See Deborah Stone, "Caring by the Book," in *Care Work: Gender, Labor, and the Welfare State*, ed. Madonna Harrington Meyer (New York: Routledge, 2000); Nancy Folbre and Julie Nelson, "For Love or Money—or Both?," *Journal of Economic Perspectives* 14, no. 4 (2000): 123–40; Viviana Zelizar, *The Purchase of Intimacy* (Princeton, NJ: Princeton University Press, 2007); Arlie Russell Hochschild, *The Commercialization of Intimate Life* (Berkeley: University of California Press, 2003); Nancy Folbre, *For Love and Money: Care Provision in the United States* (New York: Russell Sage Foundation, 2012).
5. Josephine Hulett, "Profiles in Household Work," June 20, 1972, draft article for *Ms.*, Ms. Magazine Records, series 7, box 39, folder 12, Sophia Smith Collection, Smith College, Northampton, MA.
6. See for example, Rollins, *Between Women*, Palmer, *Domesticity and Dirt*, and Evelyn Nakano Glenn, *Forced to Care: Coercion and Caregiving in America* (Cambridge, MA: Harvard University Press, 2010).
7. Boris, *Home to Work: Motherhood and the Politics of Industrial Homework in the United States* (New York: Cambridge University Press, 1994).
8. Faye Duddan tracks the shift from task-based work to time-based work, which occurred with the emergence of employer women's efforts in the nineteenth century.
9. Mrs. E. T. Barwick, Maids' Honor Day Nomination for Leola King, April 1973, box 1627, folder 87, NDWU Records.
10. Mrs. Ralph Toon, Maids' Honor Day Nomination for Jeannette C. Everhart, May 1976, box 1628, folder 90, NDWU Records.
11. Mrs. E. T. Barwick, Maids' Honor Day Nomination for Mrs. Amanda Rebecca Jones, May 1973, box 1627, folder 87, NDWU Records.
12. Mrs. James W. Coody, Maids' Honor Day Nomination for Sophie Duncan, May 1973, box 1627, folder 87, NDWU Records.

13. Anne T. Winston, Maids' Honor Day Nomination for Rosie Lee Powell, May 1972, box 1627, folder 87, NDWU Records.

14. Betty Talmadge, Maids' Honor Day Nomination for Lucille Kelley, May 30, 1974, box 1628, folder 89, NDWU Records.

15. J. Wallace Rustin Family, Maids' Honor Day Nomination for Mary Williams, April 1971, box 1627, folder 80, NDWU Records.

16. "Maids' Honor Day Nomination," box 1627, folder 79, NDWU Records.

17. Elizabeth Runyan to National Domestic Workers of America, May 25, 1976, box 1628, folder 90, NDWU Records; Flo Anne Menzler to National Domestic Workers of America, May 24, 1976, box 1628, folder 90, NDWU Records; Evelyn and Alton Reeves to National Domestic Workers of America, May 24, 1976, box 1628, folder 90, NDWU Records.

18. Sue Sturges, Maids' Honor Day Nomination for Mrs. Jewel Adams, May 1971, box 1627, folder 81, NDWU Records.

19. Dorothy Bolden, "Message from the President," Maids' Honor Day, 1972, box 1628, folder 97, NDWU Records.

20. Frances X. Clines, "About New York: Cleaning Women: Why Sit and Cry?" *New York Times*, June 22, 1978. Soraya Moore Coley argues that members of domestic-worker-rights groups had a more positive view of the occupation than nonmembers. See Soraya Moore Coley "And Still I Rise: An Exploratory Study of Contemporary Black Private Household Workers" (PhD diss., Bryn Mawr College, 1981).

21. Vivian Castleberry, "Maids Organize for Better Image and Benefits," *Dallas Times Herald*, July 26, 1976, box 443, folder 13, National Urban League Records (hereafter NUL Records), Library of Congress.

22. Two-part interview of Geraldine Miller filmed at Saint Peter's College, Jersey City, NJ, April 18, 2000, available on the website of Neighborhood Women Williamsburg-Greenpoint, http://neighborhoodwomen.org/category/nwwg/nwwg-media/movies-nwwg/.

23. Hazel Garland, "Early Morning TV Can Be Very Informative," *Pittsburgh Courier*, February 9, 1980. Feminist scholars have debated the impact of commodification on care work. See, for example, Arlie Russell Hochschild, *The Commercialization of Intimate Life: Notes from Home and Work* (Berkeley: University of California Press, 2003); Deborah Stone, "Caring by the Book," in *Care Work: Gender, Labor, and the Welfare State*, ed. Madonna Harrington Meyer (New York: Routledge, 2003), 89–111; Mona Harrington, *Care and Inequality: Inventing a New Family Politics* (New York: Routledge, 2000); Nancy Folbre, ed., *For Love and Money: Care Provision in the United States* (New York: Russell Sage Foundation, 2012); Viviana Zelizar, *The Purchase of Intimacy* (Princeton, NJ: Princeton University Press, 2005).

24. Susan Strasser, *Never Done: A History of American Housework* (New York: Pantheon, 1982).

25. Charlotte Perkins Gilman, *Women and Economics: A Study of the Economic Relation Between Men and Women as a Factor in Social Evolution* (Small, Maynard & Co, 1898).

26. Geraldine Roberts, interview by Donna Van Raaphorst, March 30–June 29, 1977, Cleveland, Ohio, Program on Women and Work, Institute of Labor and

Industrial Relations, University of Michigan, Walter P. Reuther Library, Wayne State University, p. 46.

27. Pat Burstein, "A Convention on Domestic Policy," *Newsday*, March 20, 1973.

28. Vanessa May, *Unprotected Labor: Household Workers, Politics, and Middle-Class Reform in New York, 1870–1940* (Chapel Hill: University of North Carolina Press, 2011); Tera Hunter, *To 'Joy My Freedom: Southern Black Women's Lives and Labors After the Civil War* (Cambridge, MA: Harvard University Press, 1997).

29. Alice Childress, *Like One of the Family: Conversations from a Domestic's Life* (Boston: Beacon Press, 1986), 42–43.

30. Maids' Honor Day Nomination, box 1627, folder 79, NDWU Records.

31. Maids' Honor Day Nomination, box 1627, folder 79, NDWU Records.

32. Vivian Gornick, "There Once Was a Union Maid/Who Never Was Afraid," *Village Voice*, November 29, 1976, Ms. Magazine Records, series 7, box 39, folder 12, Sophia Smith Collection, Smith College.

33. Arlie Russell Hochschild, *The Managed Heart: The Commercialization of Human Feeling* (Berkeley: University of California Press, 1983).

34. Roberts, interview by Van Raaphorst, 71.

35. Darlene Clark Hine, "Rape and the Inner Lives of Black Women in the Middle West," *Signs* 14, no. 4 (1989): 912–20. Judith Rollins, *Between Women: Domestics and Their Employers* (Philadelphia: Temple University Press, 1985).

36. Josephine Hulett, interview by Janet Dewart, "Household Help Wanted: Female," *Ms.*, February 1973, p. 48, NCHE Records, series 003, subseries 01, box 11, folder 17.

37. Gornick, "There Once Was a Union Maid/Who Never Was Afraid."

38. Several scholars have discussed the issue of naming and deference. See Bonnie Thorton Dill, *Across the Boundaries of Race and Class: An Exploration of Work and Family Among Black Female Domestic Servants* (New York: Garland, 1994); Susan Tucker, *Telling Memories Among Southern Women: Domestic Workers and Their Employers in the Segregated South* (Baton Rouge: Louisiana State University Press, 1988); Phyllis Palmer, *Domesticity and Dirt: Housewives and Domestic Servants in the United States, 1920–1945* (Philadelphia: Temple University Press, 1991); Katherine Van Wormer, *The Maid Narratives: Black Domestic and White Families in the Jim Crow South* (Baton Rouge: Louisiana State University Press, 2012); Mary Romero, *Maid in the USA* (New York: Routledge, 1992); Rollins, *Between Women*.

39. Roberts, interview by Van Raaphorst, 53.

40. EBS, "Keynote Address," July 17, 1971, NCHE Records, series 003, subseries 03, box 02, folder 06.

41. Roberts, interview by Van Raaphorst, 70.

42. Leslie Maitland, "They Still Call Us Girl," *New York Times*, February 15, 1976.

43. Carolyn Reed, interview by Robert Hamburger, 286, Robert Hamburger Transcripts and Research Materials, Schomburg Center for Research in Black Culture, New York Public Library.

44. Geraldine Miller, interview by Loretta Ross, transcript of video recording, p. 30, October 14, 2004, Voices of Feminism Oral History Project, Sophia Smith Collection, Smith College, Northampton, MA.

45. NDWU, "Proposal to Implement a Training Program for Household Management Technicians in Metro-Atlanta," June 26, 1974, p. 4, box 1625, folder 52, NDWU Records.

46. Charlotte Robinson, "Organizing Household Workers," n.d. (c. 1975?), *Detroit Free Press*, box 2, folder 8, McClendon Papers.
47. Roberts, interview by Van Raaphorst, 53.
48. Judith Rollins et al., "African American Private Household Workers and 'Control' of the Labor Process in Domestic Service," *Sociological Focus* 27, no. 3 (August 1994): 211–28.
49. NDWU, *National Domestic Workers of America, Inc.*, booklet, n.d. (c. 1977?), NDWU Records.
50. The code was established before formation of the Household Technicians of America (HTA) under NCHE in 1967 and was patterned after the Minnesota Commission on the Status of Women. Mary Dublin Keyserling, "Summary— Our Task Ahead," Consultation on the Status of Household Employment, Conference Proceedings, May 20, 1967, p. 6.
51. "NCHE: Gaining Respect for Household Workers," *Essence*, July 1974, p. 35.
52. DC Household Technicians, "A Code of Standards," 1974, p. 2, NCHE Records, series 003, subseries 01, box 06, folder 12.
53. Dorothy Bolden, "Statement Before the Democratic Platform Committee," June 9, 1972, p. 4, box 1625, folder 44, NDWU Papers.
54. Roberts, interview by Van Raaphorst, 55.
55. Geraldine Roberts, interview with Malaika Lumumba, August 1, 1970, Ralph Bunche Oral History Collection, Moorland-Spingarn Research Collection, accession no. 593, p. 14.
56. Geraldine Miller, interview by Debra Bernhardt, June 18, 1981, audio recording, New Yorkers at Work Oral History Collection, Tamiment Library and Robert F. Wagner Labor Archive, New York University.
57. NDWU, "Proposal to Implement a Training Program for Household Management Technicians in Metro-Atlanta," June 26, 1974, box 1625, folder 52, NDWU Records.
58. NDWUA, "A Manpower Development, Training and Placement Program," 1975, box 1625, folder 53, NDWU Records.
59. NDWUA, "A Proposal: To Research Techniques of Assistance in Developing a Training Program for Household Employees," n.d. (probably late 1968), box 1625, folder 52, NDWU Records.
60. "Household Workers Organization," leaflet (minimum wage), n.d. (probably 1973), box 2, folder 4, McClendon Papers. The meeting took place at 8245 Linwood Ave.
61. Mary McClendon, autobiography, box 1, folder 1, McClendon Papers.
62. Cassandra Spratling and Patrice Williams, "Obama on the Ballot: They Never Thought They'd See the Day: Rise of Black Senator Symbolizes a Dream Realized," *Detroit Free Press*, October 31, 2008.
63. Mary McClendon (probably), speech, "Household Workers Organization," n.d. (probably late 1972 or early 1973), box 1, folder 3, McClendon Papers.
64. Cassandra Spratling, "Black Women Who Cleaned Whites' Houses Look Back," *Detroit Free Press*, August 14, 2011.
65. Author telephone interview with Mary McClendon, October 2013.
66. Jeannette Smyth, "Union Maid: A Two Way Street," *Washington Post*, July 17, 1971.

67. Ibid.

68. Household Workers Organization (HWO), proposal, "Household Workers, Inc., Job Descriptions for Household Technicians," June 18, 1970, box 2, folder 19, McClendon Papers.

69. "Appendix II," Training Proposal, n.d., box 2, folder 23, McClendon Papers.

70. HWO, "Household Workers, Inc., Job Descriptions for Household Technicians."

71. Helen May, "Household Workers Push Wage Battle," May 26, 1972, *Detroit Free Press*, box 2, folder 6, McClendon Papers.

72. *You and Your Household Help*, pamphlet, 1971, box 2, folder 28, McClendon Papers. The wage recommendations came from the Michigan Employment Securities Commission.

73. Unnamed author, "Letter to Mary McClendon," June 29, 1973, box 2, folder 17, McClendon Papers.

74. Charlotte Robinson, "Organizing Household Workers," n.d. (1975?), *Detroit Free Press*, box 2, folder 8, McClendon Papers.

75. HTA, minutes, board of directors meeting, April 12, 1972, p. 4, NCHE Records, series 003, subseries 01, box 8, folder 18.

76. Judith Rollins argued that the social and psychological components of domestic-service work perpetuated notions of inequality. Judith Rollins, *Between Women: Domestics and Their Employers* (Philadelphia: Temple University Press, 1987). Dorothy Sue Cobble explained: "Dismantling the 'mammy' stereotype with its expectations of self-sacrifice and deference required an assault against multiple ideologies of domination." Dorothy Sue Cobble, "'A Spontaneous Loss of Enthusiasm': Workplace Feminism and the Transformation of Women's Service Jobs in the 1970s," *International Labor and Working-Class History* 56 (Fall 1999): 23–44.

77. Dorothy Bolden, *Nobody Speaks for Me: Self Portraits of American Working-Class Women*, ed. Nancy Seifer (New York: Simon & Schuster, 1977), 167.

78. Philip Shabecoff, "To Domestics, a Minimum Wage Is a Raise," *New York Times*, June 6, 1973.

79. Alan Wolfe argues that boundaries and distinctions are not always bad and can function to enhance group solidarity. See Alan Wolfe, "Democracy Versus Sociology: Boundaries and Their Political Consequences," in *Cultivating Differences: Symbolic Boundaries and the Making of Inequality*, ed. Michele Lamont and Marcel Fournier (Chicago: University of Chicago Press, 1992).

80. Roberts, interview by Van Raaphorst, 71.

CHAPTER 5

Space, Place, and New Models of Labor Organizing

1. Geraldine Miller, interview by Debra Bernhardt, June 18, 1981, audio recording, New Yorkers at Work Oral History Collection, Tamiment Library and Robert F. Wagner Labor Archive, New York University.

2. Geraldine Miller, interview by Loretta Ross, transcript of video recording, p. 26, October 14, 2004, Voices of Feminism Oral History Project, Sophia Smith Collection, Smith College, Northampton, MA.

3. Two-part interview of Geraldine Miller filmed at Saint Peter's College, Jersey City, NJ, April 18, 2000, available on the website of Neighborhood Women Williamsburg-Greenpoint, http://neighborhoodwomen.org/category/nwwg /nwwg-media/movies-nwwg/.

4. Peggie Smith, "Organizing the Unorganizable: Private Paid Household Workers and Approaches to Employee Representation," 79 *North Carolina Law Review* 45 (2000).

5. Geraldine Miller, "Geraldine Miller: Household Technician and Social Activist," in *Untold Glory: African Americans in Pursuit of Freedom, Opportunity, and Achievement*, ed. Alan Govenar (New York: Harlem Moon, 2007), 293.

6. Miller, interview by Ross, 24.

7. Miller, interview by Bernhardt.

8. Geraldine Miller, interview by Tamar Carroll, transcript, 12, August 16, 2002, Brooklyn, NY, courtesy of Tamar Carroll. See also Miller, "Geraldine Miller: Household Technician and Social Activist," 295.

9. Quoted in Francis X. Clines, "About New York: Cleaning Women; Why Sit and Cry?," *New York Times*, June 22, 1978.

10. Miller, "Geraldine Miller: Household Technician and Social Activist," 298.

11. Clines, "About New York: Cleaning Women."

12. Miller, Saint Peter's College interview.

13. Miller, interview by Ross, 23.

14. Miller, interview by Carroll, 3.

15. Miller, Saint Peter's College interview.

16. Miller, interview by Ross, 32–33.

17. Ibid., 27.

18. Miller, "Geraldine Miller: Household Technician and Social Activist," 299.

19. Miller, interview by Bernhardt.

20. Josephine Hulett, "Profiles in Household Work," June 20, 1972, draft article for *Ms.*, Ms. Magazine Records, series 7, box 39, folder 12, Sophia Smith Collection, Smith College, Northampton, MA.

21. Carolyn Reed, interview by Robert Hamburger, 273, Robert Hamburger Transcripts and Research Materials, Schomburg Center for Research in Black Culture, New York Public Library.

22. Elizabeth Runyan to NDWUA, May 25, 1976, box 1628, folder 90, NDWU Records.

23. Dorothy Bolden, "Organizing Domestic Workers in Atlanta, Georgia," in *Black Women in White America: A Documentary History*, ed. Gerda Lerner (New York: Vintage, 1972), 237.

24. Roberts, interview by Van Raaphorst, 94.

25. Bolden, "Organizing Domestic Workers," 237.

26. Ibid.

27. Roberts, interview by Van Raaphorst, 119–20.

28. Susan B. Carter et al., *Historical Statistics of the United States: Earliest Times to the Present* (New York: Cambridge University Press, 2006), table Ba1033-1046, "Major Occupational Groups—All Persons: 1860–1990." This figure is based on Census Bureau data, which likely undercounts the number of household workers.

29. Miller, interview by Ross, 29.
30. Reminiscences of Carolyn Reed, As Interviewed by Martha Sandlin, April 15, 1980, transcript, 32, Columbia Center for Oral History, Butler Library, Columbia University, NY.
31. Miller, interview by Ross, 55.
32. Reminiscences of Carolyn Reed, 32.
33. Ibid., 18–19.
34. For more on class relations and domestic service in Orangeburg, see Kibibi Voloria Mack, *Parlor Ladies and Ebony Drudges: African American Women, Class, and Work in a South Carolina Community* (Knoxville: University of Tennessee Press, 1999).
35. Reminiscences of Carolyn Reed, 4–5.
36. Ibid., 7.
37. Ibid., 14.
38. Ibid., 10–11.
39. Ibid., 8–9.
40. Ibid., 10.
41. Ibid., 2.
42. Ibid.
43. Ibid., 14–15.
44. Ibid., 16.
45. Reed, interview by Hamburger, 270.
46. Gornick, "There Once Was a Union Maid/Who Never Was Afraid."
47. Reminiscences of Carolyn Reed, 13.
48. Ibid., 17.
49. "Housemaid's Lib Is on the Move," *Sydney Morning Herald*, May 2, 1974.
50. Reminiscences of Carolyn Reed, 2.
51. Reed, interview by Hamburger, 276–77.
52. Gornick, "There Once Was a Union Maid/Who Never Was Afraid."
53. Reminiscences of Carolyn Reed, 38–40. Mrs. Clayburgh died after Carolyn worked for the family for fourteen years.
54. Gornick, "There Once Was a Union Maid/Who Never Was Afraid."
55. Donald R. Katz, "Carolyn Reed and the Backstairs Revolt," *New York*, June 11, 1979, pp. 45–50, NUL Records, p. 50, part 3, box 449, folder 2.
56. Ibid.
57. Ron Chernow, "All in a Day's Work," *Mother Jones*, August 1976, 11.
58. The literature on the manufacturing model of union organizing is extensive. See, for example, David Brody, *Steelworkers in America: The Nonunion Era* (Cambridge, MA: Harvard University Press, 1969); David Montgomery, *The Fall of the House of Labor: The Workplace, the State, and American Labor Activism, 1865–1925* (New York: Cambridge University Press, 1987); Sean Wilentz, *Chants Democratic: New York City and the Rise of the American Working Class, 1788–1850* (New York: Oxford University Press, 1984); Sidney Fine, *Sit-Down: The General Motors Strike of 1936–1937* (Ann Arbor: University of Michigan Press, 1969).
59. For example, see Ava Baron, ed., *Work Engendered: Toward a New History of American Labor* (Ithaca, NY: Cornell University Press, 1991); Dorothy Sue Cobble, *The Other Women's Movement: Workplace Justice and Social Rights in Modern*

America (Princeton, NJ: Princeton University Press, 2004); Dorothy Sue Cobble, *Dishing It Out: Waitresses and Their Unions in the Twentieth Century* (Urbana: University of Illinois Press, 1991); Ruth Milkman, *LA Story: Immigrant Workers and the Future of the US Labor Movement* (New York: Russell Sage Foundation, 2006); Karen Brodkin Sacks, *Caring by the Hour: Women, Work, and Organizing at Duke Medical Center* (Urbana: University of Illinois Press, 1988); Robin D. G. Kelley, *Race Rebels: Culture, Politics, and the Black Working Class* (New York: Free Press, 1994); Alice Kessler-Harris, *Gendering Labor History* (Urbana: University of Illinois Press, 2006); Laurie Green, *Battling the Plantation Mentality: Memphis and the Black Freedom Struggle* (Chapel Hill: University of North Carolina Press, 2007); Michael K. Honey, *Going Down Jericho Road: The Memphis Strike, Martin Luther King's Last Campaign* (New York: Norton, 2007); Vicki Ruiz, *Cannery Women, Cannery Lives: Mexican Women, Unionization, and the California Food Processing Industry* (Albuquerque: University of New Mexico Press, 1987); Dennis A. Deslippe, *Rights, Not Roses: Unions and the Rise of Working-Class Feminism, 1945–80* (Urbana: University of Illinois Press, 2000); Annelise Orleck, *Common Sense and a Little Fire: Women and Working-Class Politics in the United States, 1900–1965* (Chapel Hill: University of North Carolina Press, 1995); Tera Hunter, *To 'Joy My Freedom: Southern Black Women's Lives and Labors After the Civil War* (Cambridge, MA: Harvard University Press, 1997); Beth Tompkins Bates, *The Making of Black Detroit in the Age of Henry Ford* (Chapel Hill: University of North Carolina Press, 2012); Robert Korstad, *Civil Rights Unionism: Tobacco Workers and the Struggle for Democracy in the Mid-20th-Century South* (Chapel Hill: University of North Carolina Press, 2003); Eileen Boris and Jennifer Klein, *Caring for America: Home Health Workers in the Shadow of the Welfare State* (New York: Oxford University Press, 2012).

60. See Mary Poole, *The Segregated Origins of Social Security* (Chapel Hill: University of North Carolina Press, 2006), and Ira Katznelson, *Fear Itself: The New Deal and the Origins of Our Time* (New York: Liveright, 2013).

61. Alexander Saxton, *The Indispensable Enemy: Labor and the Anti-Chinese Movement in California* (Berkeley: University of California Press, 1971); Nayan Shah, *Contagious Divides: Epidemics and Race in San Francisco's Chinatown* (Berkeley: University of California Press, 2001); Herbert Hill, "The Problem of Race in American Labor History," *Reviews in American History* 24, no. 2 (1996): 189–208.

62. Dorothy Bolden, *Nobody Speaks for Me: Self Portraits of American Working-Class Women,* ed. Nancy Seifer (New York: Simon & Schuster, 1977), 162–63.

63. Roberts, interview by Van Raaphorst, 66–68. By 1970 she was a grandmother of seven, six boys and one girl.

64. Reminiscences of Carolyn Reed, 44.

65. Ibid.

66. Ibid., 45.

67. Ibid., 46.

68. Gornick, "There Once Was a Union Maid/Who Never Was Afraid."

69. Mary McClendon (probably), "Household Workers Organization," speech, n.d. (probably late 1972 or early 1973), box 1, folder 3, McClendon Papers; "No Union for Dial-A-Maid," *People's Voice,* newspaper article, November 1972, p. 11, box 1, folder 23, McClendon Papers.

70. They met with Benjamin McLaurin and others on August 20, 1970. "Memo: re: Household Workers," folder 26, Workers' Defense League Papers, Walter P. Reuther Library, Archives of Labor and Urban Affairs, Wayne State University, Detroit.

71. McLaurin explained, in a 1971 memo to the attendees of the Convention of the International Brotherhood of Sleeping Car Porters, that "due to the loss of membership in the brotherhood over the last several years [organizing household workers] would activate and stimulate [the brotherhood] into a bold direction which everyone agrees is long overdue." Benjamin McLaurin, "Memo to Officers, Delegates, and Members of the International Brotherhood of Sleeping Car Porters," September 2, 1971, box 74, folder 7, Workers Defense League Papers.

72. Ruth Benjamin served as executive director of the Professional Household Workers Union. Other representatives were Marjorie Archibald and Eartha Ashkar; Mary C. Strayhorn, president; Ollie Stackhouse, vice president; and Ophelia Fulwood, secretary.

73. "Resolution," Professional Household Workers Union Local #1, April 8, 1971, box 73, folder 27, Workers Defense League Papers. It is not clear if the union got concrete support from the Brotherhood of Sleeping Car Porters (BSCP). "Proposal to Unionize Professional Household Workers," April 12, 1972, box 74, folder 9, Workers Defense League Papers.

74. Miller, interview by Bernhardt.

75. Gornick, "There Once Was a Union Maid/Who Never Was Afraid."

76. "Are You Listening: Household Technicians," unedited transcript, 1977, presented by the Ford Foundation, distributed by Martha Stuart Communications, Martha Stuart Collection, Schlesinger Library, Radcliffe Institute, Harvard University.

77. Boris and Klein, *Caring for America*.

78. Julie Yates Rivchin similarly argues that the exclusions of some workers from the National Labor Relations Act fostered new kinds of labor organizing, emphasizing grassroots participation and a community orientation that has ultimately strengthened the labor movement. See Julie Yates Rivchin, "Colloquium: Building Power Among Low-Wage Immigrant Workers: Some Legal Considerations for Organizing Structures and Strategies," *NYU Review of Law and Social Change* (2004): 397.

CHAPTER 6

Social Rights, Feminist Solidarity, and the FLSA

1. Carolyn Reed, interview by Robert Hamburger, 285, Robert Hamburger Transcripts and Research Materials, Schomburg Center for Research in Black Culture, New York Public Library.

2. Reminiscences of Carolyn Reed, interview by Martha Sandlin, April 15, 1980, transcript, 23, Columbia Center for Oral History, Butler Library, Columbia University, NY.

3. T. H. Marshall, *Citizenship and Social Class* (London: Pluto Press, 1992); Premilla Nadasen, "Citizenship Rights, Domestic Work, and the Fair Labor Standards Act," *Journal of Policy History* 24, no. 1 (January 2012): 74–94.

4. Phyllis Palmer, "Outside the Law: Agricultural and Domestic Workers Under the Fair Labor Standards Act," *Journal of Policy History* 7 (1995): 416–40. See also

Evelyn Nakano Glenn, *Forced to Care: Coercion and Caregiving in America* (New York: Cambridge University Press, 2010), 128–51; and on feminist organizing in the South, Katarina Keane, "Second Wave Feminism in the American South" (PhD diss., University of Maryland, 2009).

5. Phyllis Palmer has argued persuasively that both the civil rights movement and women's movement helped reconstruct cultural ideas of work, race, and gender regarding agricultural and domestic labor. See Palmer, "Outside the Law." See also Nancy Naples, *Community Activism and Feminist Politics: Organizing Across Race, Class, and Gender* (New York: Routledge, 1998).

6. Linda Gordon, *Pitied But Not Entitled: Single Mothers and the History of Welfare* (New York: Free Press, 1994); Barbara J. Nelson, "The Origins of the Two-Channel Welfare State: Workmen's Compensation and Mothers' Aid," in *Women, the State, and Welfare,* ed. Linda Gordon (Madison: University of Wisconsin Press, 1990), 123–51; Mimi Abramovitz, *Regulating the Lives of Women: Social Welfare Policy from Colonial Times to the Present* (Boston: South End Press, 1988).

7. Alice Kessler-Harris, *In Pursuit of Equity: Women, Men, and the Pursuit of Economic Citizenship in Twentieth-Century America* (New York: Oxford University Press, 2001); Vicky Lovell, "Constructing Social Citizenship: The Exclusion of African American Women from Unemployment Insurance in the US," *Feminist Economics* 8, no. 2 (2002): 191–97; Ellen Mutari et al., "Neither Mothers Nor Breadwinners: African American Women's Exclusion from US Minimum Wage Policies," *Feminist Economies* 9, no. 2 (July 2002): 37–61; Erica C. Morgan, "Invisible Workers: The Exclusion of Domestic Workers from Protective Labor Legislation," 2008, ExpressO, http://works.bepress.com/erica_morgan/1.

8. Ira Katznelson, *Fear Itself: The New Deal and the Origins of Our Time* (New York: Liveright, 2014), argues that white southerners played a critical role in shaping New Deal politics. See also Mary Poole, *The Segregated Origins of Social Security: African Americans and the Welfare State* (Chapel Hill: University of North Carolina Press, 2006). For more on the racial politics of the campaign to regulate domestic work in this period, see Peggie R. Smith, "Regulating Paid Household Work: Class, Gender, Race, and Agendas of Reform," *American University Law Review* (1999): 851–918; Palmer, "Outside the Law."

9. Eileen Boris, "The Racialized Gendered State: Constructions of Citizenship in the United States," *Social Politics: International Studies in Gender, State, and Society* 2 (Summer 1995): 161–80; Evelyn Nakano Glenn, *Unequal Freedom: How Race and Gender Shaped American Citizenship and Labor* (Cambridge, MA: Harvard University Press, 2002).

10. Elizabeth Clark-Lewis, *Living In, Living Out: African American Domestics and the Great Migration* (New York: Kodansha, 1996); Bonnie Thornton Dill, *Across the Boundaries of Race and Class: An Exploration of Work and Family Among Black Female Domestic Servants* (New York: Routledge, 1993); Tera Hunter, *To 'Joy My Freedom: Southern Black Women's Lives and Labors After the Civil War* (Cambridge, MA: Harvard University Press, 1997).

11. Vivien Hart, *Bound by Our Constitution: Women, Workers, and the Minimum Wage* (Princeton, NJ: Princeton University Press, 1994), esp. chapter 8.

12. See Dorothy Sue Cobble, *The Other Women's Movement: Workplace Justice and Social Rights in Modern America* (Princeton, NJ: Princeton University Press,

2004); Kessler-Harris, *In Pursuit of Equity;* Poole, *The Segregated Origins of Social Security;* Katznelson, *Fear Itself.*

13. Martin Tolchin, "Mrs. Chisholm Led Fight for Domestics' Base Pay," *New York Times,* June 21, 1973.

14. Geraldine Miller, "Geraldine Miller: Household Technician and Social Activist," in *Untold Glory: African Americans in Pursuit of Freedom, Opportunity, and Achievement,* ed. Alan Govenar (New York: Harlem Moon, 2007), 300.

15. Shirley Chisholm, "Address Before Second Annual Conference of Household Technicians," transcript, NCHE Records, series 003, subseries 03, box 02, folder 10. See also "Domestics at Session Ask Gains," *New York Times,* October 10, 1972; Jeannette Smythe, "Hard Act to Follow," *Washington Post,* July 19, 1971.

16. For more on Chisholm, see Zinga A. Fraser, "Catalysts for Change: A Comparative Study of Barbara Jordan and Shirley Chisholm" (PhD diss., Northwestern University, 2014); Julie Gallagher, *Black Women and Politics in New York City* (Urbana: University of Illinois Press, 2012); Barbara Winslow, *Shirley Chisholm: Catalyst for Change* (Boulder, CO: Westview Press, 2013).

17. Willis J. Nordlund, *The Quest for a Living Wage: The History of the Federal Minimum Wage Program* (Santa Barbara, CA: Greenwood Press, 1997).

18. "House Vote Kills Legislation Raising Minimum Wage," *CQ Almanac 1972,* 28th ed. (Washington, DC: Congressional Quarterly, 1973), http://library.cqpress.com /cqalmanac/cqal72–1250683.

19. Statement of Mrs. Edith Barksdale Sloan, executive director, National Committee on Household Employment, *Hearings Before the General Subcommittee on Labor, Committee on Education and Labor, House of Representatives,* March 15, 1973, p. 3, NCHE Records, series 003, subseries 01, box 11, folder 04.

20. David Katzman, *Seven Days a Week: Women and Domestic Service in Industrializing America* (New York: Oxford University Press, 1978); Kathy Peiss, *Cheap Amusements: Working Women and Leisure in Turn-of-the-Century New York* (Philadelphia: Temple University Press, 1986).

21. Reminiscences of Carolyn Reed, 24.

22. Statement of Mrs. Edith Barksdale Sloan, executive director, and Mrs. Josephine Hulett, field officer, NCHE, *Hearings Before the General Subcommittee on Labor, Committee on Education and Labor, on HR 10948,* August 13, 1970, p. 3, NCHE Records, series 003, subseries 01, box 11, folder 06.

23. Mary McClendon, "Household Workers Organization," informational leaflet, n.d., box 2, folder 13, McClendon Papers.

24. Patricia Mulkeen, "Private Household Workers and the Fair Labor Standards Act," *Connecticut Law Review* 5 (1973): 626.

25. Ibid.

26. Statement of Barksdale Sloan and Hulett.

27. Robert T. Thompson, US Chamber of Commerce, *Statement Before the General Subcommittee on Labor, Committee on Education and Labor, House of Representatives,* 1973, p. 228.

28. Peter Brennan, Secretary of Labor, *Statement Before the General Subcommittee on Labor, Committee on Education and Labor, House of Representatives,* April 10, 1973, p. 264.

29. Peter Brennan, Secretary of Labor, *US Senate, Hearings Before the Subcommittee on Labor of the Committee on Labor and Public Welfare,* June 1973, pp. 330–31.

30. Geneva Reid, Household Technicians of America, *Statement Before the General Subcommittee on Labor, Committee on Education and Labor, House of Representatives,* 1973, p. 205.

31. Miller, interview by Ross, 35.

32. Reed, interview by Hamburger, 284. See also Anastasia Hardin, "'Making the Dignity of Our Labor a Reality': Household Worker Organizing in New York City, 1960–1980" (MA thesis, Rutgers University, 2013).

33. Mary McClendon, "Meaningful Work and Adequate Compensation," August 1975, box 2, folder 13, McClendon Papers.

34. Aletha Vaughn, interview by Mary Yelling, in Susan Tucker, *Telling Memories Among Southern Women: Domestic Workers and Their Employers in the Segregated South* (Baton Rouge: Louisiana State University Press, 2002), 207.

35. Judith Rollins, *Between Women*; Phyllis Palmer, *Domesticity and Dirt.*

36. Dorothy Roberts, "Racism and Patriarchy in the Meaning of Motherhood," *American University Journal of Gender and Law* 1, no. 1 (1993): 1–38. Judith Rollins, Phyllis Palmer, and Mary Romero call the reliance on domestic workers a "contradiction" in feminism because of the way paid household labor re-creates the system of race, class, and gender oppression.

37. Betty Friedan, *The Feminine Mystique* (New York: Norton: 1963), 121.

38. Donald R. Katz, "Carolyn Reed and the Backstairs Revolt," *New York,* June 11, 1979, p. 50, NUL Records, part 3, box 449, folder 2.

39. National Leadership Convention, "NCHE Program Priorities for 1976 and 1977," May 1976, p. 1, box 58, folder 1124, Peterson Papers.

40. Premilla Nadasen, "Expanding the Boundaries of the Women's Movement: Black Feminism and the Struggle for Welfare Rights," *Feminist Studies* 28, no. 2 (Summer 2002): 271–301; Robyn C. Spencer, "Engendering the Black Freedom Struggle: Revolutionary Black Womanhood and the Black Panther Party in the Bay Area, California," *Journal of Women's History* 20, no. 1 (March 2008): 90–113.

41. *NYRF Newsletter* 3, no. 11 (November 1973), flyer, "Speak-Out on Jobs of Working-Class Women," October 1973, https://archive.org/details /NewYorkRadicalFeministsConsciousness-raisingAboutWork3Of3.

42. Pat Mainardi, "The Politics of Housework," in *The Politics of Housework,* ed. Ellen Malos (London: Allston and Busby, 1980): 99–104; Maria Mies, *Patriarchy and Accumulation on a World Scale: Women in the International Division of Labour* (London: Zed Books, 1998); Sylvia Federici, "The Restructuring of Housework and Reproduction in the United States in the 1970s," in Sylvia Federici, *Revolution at Point Zero: Housework, Reproduction, and Feminist Struggle* (Oakland, CA: PM Press, 2012).

43. Selma James, "A Woman's Place," in her *Sex, Race, and Class, the Perspective of Winning: A Selection of Writings, 1952–2011* (Oakland, CA: PM Press, 2012).

44. Reminiscences of Carolyn Reed, 28.

45. For a critique of the Wages for Housework movement, see Angela Davis, *Women, Race, and Class* (New York: Random House, 1981), chapter 7.

46. Gail Sheehy, "A Woman Who Took Control of Her Life," *Boston Globe*, March 25, 1980.
47. Betty F. Edwards, Maids' Honor Day Nomination for Lula Morrison, May 1976, box 1628, folder 90, NDWU Records.
48. Davis, *Women, Race, and Class*, 243.
49. Pierrette Hondagnue-Sotelo makes the argument that domestic workers enabled wealthier women to "purchase release from their gender subordination in the home." Pierrette Hondagnue-Sotelo, *Doméstica: Immigrant Workers Cleaning and Caring in the Shadows of Affluence* (Berkeley: University of California Press, 2001): 22–23. See also Joan Tronto, "The 'Nanny' Question in Feminism," *Hypatia* 17, no. 2 (Spring 2002): 34–51. For more on efforts to end discrimination in the workplace, see Nancy MacLean, *Freedom Is Not Enough* (Cambridge, MA: Harvard University Press, 2006); Alice Kessler-Harris, *In Pursuit of Equity: Women, Men, and the Pursuit of Economic Citizenship in Twentieth-Century America* (New York: Oxford University Press, 2001).
50. Ellen Roberts, "Women and Work: The Household Workers Fight," *Essence*, April 1974.
51. Mary McClendon (probably), "Household Workers Organization," speech, n.d., box 1, folder 3, McClendon Papers.
52. As Phyllis Palmer has so persuasively argued, the FLSA victory was in large part due to feminist activism that drew attention to the home as workplace.
53. Josephine Hulett, interview by Janet Dewart, "Household Help Wanted: Female," *Ms.*, February 1973, 46.
54. Ron Chernow, "All in a Day's Work," *Mother Jones*, August 1976, 16.
55. Hulett, interview by Dewart, 106.
56. Ibid.
57. Anne B. Turpeau, "NCHE Resource Development Proposed Work Plan," September 28, 1976, NCHE Records, series 003, subseries 01, box 06, folder 05.
58. NCHE, "Fair Labor Standards Campaign," December 7, 1977, box 446, folder 1, NUL Records.
59. Reed, interview by Hamburger, 289.
60. Sam Roberts, "One Who Shaped Domestic Issues," *New York Times*, April 12, 1993.
61. NDWUA, "A Proposal: To Research Techniques of Assistance in Developing a Training Program for Household Employees," n.d. (probably late 1968), box 1625, folder 52, NDWU Records.
62. NCHE, "NCHE Program Priorities for 1976 and 1977," May 1976, box 58, folder 1124, Peterson Papers.
63. NDWUA, "Training Program for Domestic Workers," n.d. (probably 1977), box 1, NDWU Records.
64. NCHE, "Minimum Wage Coverage for Domestics: At Last!!!," press release, April 8, 1974, NCHE Records, series 003, subseries 01, box 11, folder 7.
65. William Forbath, "Civil Rights and Economic Citizenship: Notes on the Past and Future of the Civil Rights and Labor Movements," *University of Pennsylvania Journal of Labor and Employment Law* 2, no. 4 (2000): 697–718; Nancy MacLean, *Opening of the American Workplace*.
66. Evelyn Nakano Glenn, "From Servitude to Service Work: Historical Continuities in the Racial Division of Paid Reproductive Labor," *Signs* 18, no. 1 (Autumn

1992): 1–43; Venus Green, "Flawed Remedies: EEOC, AT&T, and Sears Outcomes Reconsidered," *Black Women, Gender, and Families* 6, no. 1 (Spring 2012): 43–70; Kessler-Harris, *In Pursuit of Equity*, chapter 6; Cobble, *The Other Women's Movement*, chapter 6; Kimberle Crenshaw, "Demarginalizing the Intersection of Race and Sex: A Black Feminist Critique of Antidiscrimination Doctrine, Feminist Theory, and Antiracist Politics," *University of Chicago Legal Forum* 140 (1989): 139–47.

67. Eileen Boris, "Where's the Care?," *Labor* 11, no. 3 (Fall 2014): 43–47.
68. Nadasen, *Welfare Warriors*; Orleck, *Storming Caesars' Palace*; Kornbluh, *The Battle for Welfare Rights*.
69. Margaria Fichtner, "Household Help Seeks New Status," *Miami Herald*, July 21, 1971, box 2, folder 9, McClendon Papers.
70. This strategy enables the rethinking of notions of equality in terms of care work rather than the political sphere, as Eva Kittay calls for in Eva Feder Kittay, *Love's Labor: Essays on Women, Equality, and Dependency* (New York: Routledge, 1999).
71. Roberts, interview by Van Raaphorst, 102.
72. Eileen Boris, *Home to Work* (New York: Cambridge University Press, 1994).
73. Eileen Boris and Jennifer Klein, "Making Home Care: Law and Social Policy in the US Welfare State," in *Intimate Labors: Cultures, Technologies, and the Politics of Care*, ed. Eileen Boris and Rhacel Salazar Parrenas (Stanford, CA: Stanford University Press, 2010), 187–203.
74. For more on the critique of state regulation and institutionalization, see Wendy Brown, *States of Injury: Power and Freedom in Late Modernity* (Princeton, NJ: Princeton University Press, 1995).
75. Statement of Barksdale Sloan and Hulett, 8.
76. *NCHE News* 5, no. 10–11 (October–November 1974), Schlesinger Library, Radcliffe Institute, Harvard University.

CHAPTER 7
Women, Work, and Immigration

1. Lewis A. Coser, "Servants: The Obsolescence of an Occupational Role," *Social Forces* 52, no. 1 (September 1973): 31–40.
2. See Suzanne M. Bianchi, Melissa A. Milkie, Liana C. Sayer, and John P. Robinson, "Is Anyone Doing the Housework? Trends in Gender Division of Household Labor," *Social Forces* 79, no. 1 (September 2000): 191–228.
3. Geraldine Roberts, interview by Donna Van Raaphorst, transcript of oral history project, p. 114, Program on Woman and Work, Institute of Labor and Industrial Relations, University of Michigan–Wayne State University, 1978.
4. Matthew Sobek, "US Historical Statistics: New Statistics on the U.S. Labor Force, 1850–1990," *Historical Methods* 34, no. 2 (Spring 2001): 71–87. See table 8, "Labor-Force Participation Rates, by Sex, Race, and Marital Status, 1850–1990," 78.
5. Robert Self, *All in the Family: The Realignment of American Democracy Since the 1960s* (New York: Hill and Wang, 2012).
6. For a history of how child-care policies evolved, see Sonya Michel, *Children's Interests/Mothers' Rights: The Shaping of America's Child-Care Policy* (New Haven, CT: Yale University Press, 1999); Ruth Schwartz Cohen, *More Work for*

Mother: The Ironies of Household Technology from the Open Hearth to the Micro-wave (New York: Basic Books, 1983).

7. John Leonard, "About New York: Cleaning-Woman Syndrome," *New York Times*, August 18, 1976.

8. Sherry Suib Cohen, "Suburban Women and Their Maids," *Westchester Illustrated*, n.d. (probably late 1970s), 22–29, Ms. Magazine Papers, series 7, box 39, folder 12.

9. Ibid.

10. See Mary Romero, *Maid in the USA* (New York: Routledge, 1992); Hondagneu-Sotelo, *Doméstica*; Julia Wrigley, *Other People's Children* (New York: Basic Books, 1995); Cecilia Rio, "'On the Move': African American Women's Paid Domestic Labor and the Class Transition to Independent Commodity Production," *Rethinking Marxism* 17, no. 4 (October 2005): 489–510.

11. Martha J. Bailey and William J. Collins, "Wage Gains of African-American Women in the 1940s," *Journal of Economic History* 66, no. 3 (September 2006): 737.

12. Evelyn Nakano Glenn, "From Servitude to Service Work: Historical Continuities in the Racial Division of Women's Work," *Signs* 18, no. 1 (1992): 1–43.

13. Roberts, interview by Van Raaphorst, 102.

14. Angela James, David M. Grant, and Cynthia Cranford, "Moving Up, But How Far? African American Women and Economic Restructuring in Los Angeles, 1970–1990," *Sociological Perspectives* 43, no. 3 (2000): 399–420; Vicky Lovell, "Constructing Social Citizenship: The Exclusion of African American Women from Unemployment Insurance in the US," *Feminist Economics* 8, no. 2 (2002): 191–97.

15. NDWUA, "A Manpower Development, Training, and Placement Program," 1975, p. 14, box 1625, folder 53, NDWU Papers.

16. Dorothy E. Roberts, "Spiritual and Menial Housework," *Yale Journal of Law and Feminism* 51 (1997); Mignon Duffy, *Making Care Count: A Century of Gender, Race, and Paid Care Work* (Piscataway, NJ: Rutgers University Press, 2011); Evelyn Nakano Glenn, "Cleaning Up/Kept Down: A Historical Perspective on Racial Inequality in Women's Work," *Stanford Law Review* 43, no. 6 (July 1991): 1333–56.

17. Eileen Boris and Jennifer Klein, *Caring for America: Home Health Workers in the Shadow of the Welfare State* (New York: Oxford University Press, 2012).

18. Mary McClendon v. City of Detroit, Circuit Court for the County of Wayne, no. 77 704 376, April 18, 1980, p. 20, box 2, folder 30, McClendon Papers.

19. Mae Ngai, *Impossible Subjects: Illegal Aliens and the Making of Modern America* (Princeton, NJ: Princeton University Press, 2004).

20. Margo Fischer, "How to Hire a Maid," *Saturday Evening Post*, June 8, 1957, 64. See also Evan McLeod Wylie and Robert Paul Sagalyn, "The Flood of Innocents from Abroad," *Life*, May 5, 1961.

21. See Maura I. Toro-Morn, "Gender, Class, Family and Migration: Puerto Rican Women in Chicago," *Gender and Society* 9, no. 6 (December 1995): 712–26; Carmen Theresa Whalen, *From Puerto Rico to Philadelphia: Puerto Rican Workers and Post-War Economies* (Philadelphia: Temple University Press, 2001); Carmen Theresa Whalen and Victor Vasquez Hernandez, eds., *The Puerto Rican Diaspora* (Philadelphia: Temple University Press, 2008); Mérida M. Rúa, *A Grounded Identidad: Making New Lives in Chicago's Puerto Rican Neighborhoods* (New York: Oxford University Press, 2012).

22. Leonard C. Lewin, notarized statement, December 20, 1946, section 4, Presidente del Senado, series 2, Gobierno Ensular, subseries 9B, Employment and Migration Bureau, folder 277, document 17, Archivo Histórico Fundación Luis Muñoz Marín, San Juan, Puerto Rico.

23. Elena Padilla, "Puerto Rican Immigrants in New York and Chicago: A Study in Comparative Assimilation" (PhD diss., University of Chicago, 1947).

24. They earned fifteen dollars a week; African American women earned twenty-five dollars a week and white women domestics earned thirty-five to forty dollars a week.

25. Lewin, notarized statement.

26. See, for example, "Maid Problem," *New Republic*, April 28, 1947, 116.

27. Carmen Isales, draft, "Report on the Cases of Puerto Rican Laborers Brought to Chicago to Work as Domestics and Foundry Workers Under Contract with Castle, Barton and Associates," March 22, 1947, section 4, Presidente del Senado, series 2, Gobierno Ensular, subseries 9B, Employment and Migration Bureau, folder 277, document 16, Archivo Histórico Fundación Luis Muñoz Marín. See also Nicolas De Genova and Ana Y. Ramos-Zayas, "Latino Rehearsals: Racialization and the Politics of Citizenship Between Mexicans and Puerto Ricans in Chicago," *Journal of Latin American Anthropology* 8, no. 2 (June 2003): 18–57; Edwin Maldonado, "Contract Labor and the Origins of Puerto Rican Communities in the United States," *International Migration Review* 13, no. 1 (Spring 1979): 103–21; Lilia Fernandez, "Of Immigrants and Migrants: Mexican and Puerto Rican Labor Migration in Comparative Perspective, 1942–1964," *Journal of American Ethnic History* 29, no. 3 (Spring 2010); Maura I. Toro-Morn, "A Historical Overview of the Work Experiences of Puerto Rican Women in Chicago," *Centro Journal* 13, no. 2 (Fall 2001): 24–43.

28. The Bureau of Employment and Migration was formed in 1947 and initiated this program in conjunction with the Office of the Governor of Puerto Rico. In 1952 the bureau became part of the Puerto Rican Department of Labor.

29. Emma Amador, "Training Migrant Domestics: Migrant Household Workers, Labor Reformers, and the Puerto Rican Government After 1930," Conference Paper, Berkshire Conference of Women's Historians, 2014, Toronto, Canada, courtesy of Emma Amador. See also "Puerto Rican Maids to Get Aid on English," *New York Times*, March 2, 1948.

30. Frances Green Employment Agency, information about hiring policies, n.d. (circa 1967), box 57, folder 1114, Peterson Papers.

31. Ibid.

32. HWO, *Household Workers Employment News*, n.d. (probably 1970), box 1, folder 31, McClendon Papers.

33. This involves depersonalization and dehumanization. Shellee Colen, "'Just a Little Respect': West Indian Domestic Workers in New York City," in *Muchachas No More: Household Workers in Latin America and the Caribbean*, ed. Elsa M. Chaney and Mary Garcia Castro (Philadelphia: Temple University Press, 1989), 176. For more on the early history of Caribbean women's migration, see Terry A. Repak, *Waiting on Washington: Central American Workers in the Nation's Capital* (Philadelphia: Temple University Press, 1995); Rhacel Parrenas, *Servants of Globalization: Women, Migration, and Domestic Work* (Stanford, CA: Stanford University Press, 2001); Tamara Mose Brown, *Raising Brooklyn: Nannies,*

Childcare, and Caribbeans Creating Community (New York: New York University Press, 2011); Linda Carty, "Not a Nanny: A Gendered, Transnational Analysis of Caribbean Domestic Workers in New York City," in *Decolonizing the Academy: African Diaspora Studies*, ed. Carole Boyce Davies (Trenton, NJ: Africa World Press, 2003): 269–82; Irma Watkins-Owens, "Early Twentieth-Century Caribbean Women: Migration and Social Networks in New York City," in *Islands in the City: West Indian Migration to New York*, ed. Nancy Foner (Berkeley: University of California Press, 2001), 25–51.

34. Mary Romero, *Maid in the USA* (New York: Routledge, 1992). See Vicki L. Ruiz, "By the Day or Week: Mexicana Domestic Workers in El Paso," in *To Toil the Livelong Day: America's Women at Work, 1780–1980*, ed. Carol Groneman and Mary Beth Norton (Ithaca, NY: Cornell University Press, 1987): 269–83; Vicki Ruiz and Susan Tiana, eds., *Women on the US-Mexico Border: A Response to Change* (Boston: Allen and Unwin, 1987); Chad Richardson and Cruz C. Torres, "'Only a Maid': Undocumented Domestic Workers in South Texas," in *Batos, Bolillos, Pochos, and Pelados: Class and Culture on the South Texas Border*, ed. Chad Richardson (Austin: University of Texas Press, 1999).

35. Betty Liddick, "Plight of the Foreign Domestic: A Critical Game of Hide and Seek," *Los Angeles Times*, June 8, 1973, NCHE Records, series 003, subseries 01, box 09, folder 07.

36. Ibid. See also Romero, *Maid in the USA*; Hondagneu-Sotelo, *Doméstica*; Michael J. Wishnie, "Emerging Issues for Undocumented Workers," *University of Pennsylvania Journal of Labor and Employment Law* 6, no. 3 (2004): 497–524; Keith Cunningham-Parmeter, "Redefining the Rights of Undocumented Workers," *American University Law Review* 58 (2009): 1361–1415.

37. Isabel Eaton, "Special Report on Negro Domestic Service," Supplement to W. E. B. Du Bois, *The Philadelphia Negro: A Social Study* (New York: Schocken Books, 1967), first published 1899, p. 485.

38. Andrew Urban, "Irish Domestic Servants, 'Biddy" and Rebellion in the American Home, 1850–1890," *Gender and History* 21, no. 2 (August 2009): 263–86; Danielle Phillips, "Who Wants to Be an 'English' Mother? Irish and Southern African American Domestic Workers in New York, 1865–1935," *Journal of Motherhood Initiative* 2, no. 1 (2011): 226–41; Margaret Lynch-Brennan, *Irish Bridget: Irish Immigrant Women in Domestic Service in America* (Syracuse, NY: Syracuse University Press, 2009).

39. NCHE, "The Low Income Woman's IWY Action Plan," Report Prepared for the Sixth Annual Conference, October 1978, p. 13, NCHE Records, series 003, subseries 03, box 03, folder 04; Julianne Malveaux, "From Domestic Worker to Household Technician: Black Women in a Changing Occupation," in *Black Women in the Labor Force*, ed. Phyllis A. Wallace, 85–98 (Cambridge, MA: MIT Press, 1980); Vertamae Grosvenor, *Thursdays and Every Other Sunday Off: A Domestic Rap* (Garden City, NY: Doubleday, 1972).

40. Ellen Roberts, "Women and Work: The Household Workers Fight," *Essence*, April 1974. See also Trudier Harris, *From Mammies to Militants: Domestics in Black American Literature* (Philadelphia: Temple University Press, 1982); Abigail Bakan and Daiva Stasiulis, *Not One of the Family: Foreign Domestic Workers in Canada* (Toronto: University of Toronto Press, 1997); Geraldine Pratt,

"Stereotypes and Ambivalence: The Construction of Domestic Workers in Vancouver, BC," *Gender, Place, and Culture* 4, no. 2 (1997): 159–77.

41. Danielle Taylor Phillips, "Moving with the Women: Tracing Racialization, Migration and Domestic Workers in the Archive," *Signs* 38, no. 2 (Winter 2013): 379–404.

42. Charles Grutzner, "City Puerto Ricans Found Ill-Housed," *New York Times*, October 4, 1949. Only a small percentage of Puerto Rican migrants were ever employed as domestic workers. In 1960 most Puerto Rican women worked in garment or needle trades or in agricultural sectors. For more on how Puerto Ricans were cast by the media as better workers than African Americans, see Gina Perez, *The Near Northwest Side Story: Migration, Displacement, and Puerto Rican Families* (Berkeley: University of California Press, 2004).

43. Carty, "Not A Nanny," 275; Wrigley, *Other People's Children*, 10.

44. All box 58, folder 1119, Peterson Papers: NCHE press release, February 10, 1970; Elva Ruiz, "Memo to the Board of Directors," n.d.; Various Mexican-American Organizations, Statement, "For Immediate Press Release," n.d.; Anna R. Halsted, "Memo to Members of the Board of Directors" March 19, 1970.

45. Household Technicians of America, minutes, board of directors meeting, April 12, 1972, NCHE Records, series 003, subseries 01, box 08, folder 18.

46. Edith B. Sloan to Mrs. Francisca Flores, September 8, 1971, NCHE Records, series 003, subseries 01, box 15, folder 08.

47. Various translated items in folder as well as a letter verifying translation from Maria de la Luz Moreno to Edith Sloan, November 9, 1973, box 449, folder 10, NUL Records.

48. Memo from Curt Moody, NCHE Western Regional field officer, to NCHE executive board, February 2, 1973, "Re: Report of the Western Field Operations," and Curt Moody, "September Narrative of Activities," 1972 (?), box 444, folder 5, NUL Records.

49. Curt Moody, NCHE Western Regional field officer, to Edith Sloan, November 28, 1972, box 444, folder 5, NUL Records.

50. Miller, interview by Ross, 26.

51. NCHE, "Legal and Illegal Immigrants," program priorities for 1976 and 1977, adopted and ratified at the Fourth National Leadership Convention of NCHE, May 28–30, 1976, St. Louis, p. 1, NCHE Records, series 003, subseries 03, box 03, folder 01.

52. NCHE, "Household Employment: Employer's Market—Worker's Nightmare," press release, May 29, 1976, NCHE Records, series 003, subseries 03, box 03, folder 01.

53. Shelton, a graduate of Howard University who worked previously with the National Council of Negro Women and the National Urban League, replaced Edith Barksdale Sloan as NCHE executive director in 1976.

54. Anita Shelton, speech transcript, NCHE's Fourth National Conference, May 28–30, 1976, St. Louis, box 445, folder 1, NUL Records.

55. NCHE, *Program Priorities for 1976 and 1977*, May 28–30, 1976, NCHE Records, series 003, subseries 03, box 03, folder 01; "Legal and Illegal Immigrants," p. 1.

56. Ibid., 3.

57. Reminiscences of Carolyn Reed, 43.

58. *Household Employment News* 13, no. 1 (March 1981), Schlesinger Library, Radcliffe Institute, Harvard University.

59. Janet Ochs Wiener, "Careers: Standing Up for Household Technicians," *Washington Post*, September 30, 1980.

60. *Household Employment News* (September/October 1982), Schlesinger Library, Radcliffe Institute, Harvard University.

61. *Household Employment News* (April/May 1982), Schlesinger Library, Radcliffe Institute, Harvard University.

62. Josephine Hulett, "Profiles in Household Work," June 20, 1972, draft article for *Ms.*, Ms. Magazine Records, series 7, box 39, folder 12, Sophia Smith Collection, Smith College, Northampton, MA.

63. Miller, interview by Bernhardt.

64. "Bi-Weekly Report of the Special Programs Officer," January 28–February 22, 1974, NCHE Records, series 003, subseries 01, box 15, folder 20.

65. Miller, interview by Bernhardt.

66. NCHE, press release, no title, September 27, 1978, box 445, folder 3, NUL Records.

67. Roberts, interview by Lumumba, 14; Lisa Materson writes about a similar transnational, cross-racial solidarity in an earlier period. See Lisa Materson, "African American Women's Global Journeys and the Construction of Cross-Ethnic Racial Identity," *Women's Studies International Forum* 32 (2009): 35–42.

68. Edith Barksdale Sloan, Memo to Affiliates of NCHE, August 22, 1975, NCHE Records, series 003, subseries 01, box 15, folder 10.

69. Testimony of Gil Foon Hong, September 5, 1974, box 449, folder 11, NUL Records; Marlene Cimons, "Bottom of the Ladder, No Place to Go," *Los Angeles Times*, September 8, 1975; *NCHE News* 6, no. 8 (Fall 1975), Schlesinger Library, Radcliffe Institute, Harvard University.

70. Edith Barksdale Sloan, Statement Transcript, Speak-Out for Economic Justice, September 5, 1975, p. 3, NCHE Records, series 003, subseries 01, box 15, folder 11.

71. National Committee on Household Employment, *NCHE News* 8 (October 1977). NUL Records, part 3, box 3, folder 449.

72. NCHE, "The Low-Income Woman's IWY Action Plan," Report Prepared for the Sixth Annual Conference, October 1978, NCHE Records, series 003, subseries 03, box 03, folder 04.

73. DC Professional Service Workers Association, informational leaflet, NCHE Records, series 003, subseries 01, box 06, folder 12.

74. "Report of the Executive Director to the Annual Meeting of Members," December 18, 1975, NCHE Records, series 003, subseries 03, box 01, folder 05.

75. *NCHE News* 9 (April 1978).

76. "Upstairs, Downstairs Revisited: The Dwindling Ranks of Domestics Gain New Respect," *Time*, November 13, 1978, p. 112, box 449, folder 2, NUL Records.

77. NCHE, press release, September 27, 1978, box 445, folder 3, NUL Records.

78. Roberts, interview by Van Raaphorst, 113.

79. Reed, interview by Hamburger, 294.

80. Hondagneu-Sotelo, *Doméstica*; Grace Chang, *Disposable Domestics: Immigrant Women Workers in the Global Economy* (Cambridge, MA: South End Press, 2000); Parrenas, *Servants of Globalization*; Maria De La Luz Ibarra, "Mexican Immigrant

Women and the New Domestic Labor," in *Women and Migration in the US-Mexico Borderlands: A Reader*, ed. Denise Segura and Patricia Zavella (Durham, NC: Duke University Press, 2007), 286–305; Saskia Sassen, *The Global City: New York, London, Tokyo* (Princeton, NJ: Princeton University Press, 1991); Terry A. Repak, *Waiting on Washington: Central American Workers in the Nation's Capital* (Philadelphia: Temple University Press, 1995). See also Christina Mendoza, "Crossing Borders: Women, Migration, and Domestic Work at the Texas-Mexico Divide" (PhD diss., University of Michigan, 2009); Sharon Harley, ed., *Women's Labor in the Global Economy: Speaking in Multiple Voices* (New Brunswick, NJ: Rutgers University Press, 2007); Monika Batra, "Organizing in the South Asian Domestic Worker Community: Pushing the Boundaries of the Law and Organizing Project," in *The New Urban Immigrant Workforce: Innovative Models for Labor Organizing*, ed. S. Jayaraman and I. Ness, 119–41 (Armonk, NY: M. E. Sharpe, 2005); Linta Varghese, "Sites of Neoliberal Articulation: Subjectivity, Community Organizations, and South Asian New York City" (PhD diss., University of Texas, 2007); Luis L. M. Aguiar and Andrew Herod, eds., *The Dirty Work of Neoliberalism: Cleaners in the Global Economy* (Oxford, UK: Basil Blackwell, 2006); Doreen Mattingly, "The Home and the World: Domestic Service and International Networks of Caring Labor," *Annals of the Association of American Geographers* 91, no. 2 (2001): 370–86; Encarnacion Gutierrez Rodriguez, "Hidden Side of the New Economy: On Transnational Migration, Domestic Work, and Unprecedented Intimacy," *Frontiers: A Journal of Women's Studies* 29, no. 3 (2007): 60–83.

81. See Janice Fine, *Worker Centers: Organizing Communities at the Edge of the Dream* (Ithaca, NY: Cornell University Press, 2006), and Jennifer Gordon, *Suburban Sweatshops: The Fight for Immigrant Rights* (Cambridge, MA: Harvard University Press, 2005); Ai-Jen Poo and Eric Tang, "Domestic Workers Organizing in the Global City," in *The Fire This Time: Young Activists and the New Feminism*, ed. Vivien Labaton, Dawn Lundy Martin, Rebecca Walker, and Wilma Mankiller (New York: Random House, 2004); Vanessa Tait, *Poor Workers Unions: Rebuilding Labor From Below* (Cambridge, MA: South End Press, 2005); Saskia Sassen, "Incompleteness and the Possibility of Making: Towards Denationalized Citizenship," *Cultural Dynamics* 21, no. 3 (2009): 227–54; Charles Lee, "Tactical Citizenship: Domestic Workers, the Remainders of Home, and Undocumented Citizen Participation in the Third Space of Mimicry," *Theory and Event* 9, no. 3 (2006); Christiane Harzig, "Domestics of the World (Unite?): Labor Migration Systems and the Personal Trajectories of Household Workers in Historical and Global Perspective," *Journal of American Ethnic History* 25, nos. 2/3 (2006): 48–73; *Gendered Citizenship: Transnational Perspectives on Knowledge Production, Political Activism, and Culture*, ed. Kia Lilly Caldwell, Reyna K. Ramirez, Kathleen Coll, Tracy Fisher, Lok Siu (New York: Palgrave Macmillan, 2009); Bridget Jane Anderson, *Doing the Dirty Work? The Global Politics of Domestic Labour* (London: Zed Books, 2000).

82. Information based on author interview with Barbara Young, October 2, 2014, New York City.

83. For more on this, see Harmony Goldberg, "Our Day Has Finally Come: Domestic Worker Organizing in New York City" (PhD diss., CUNY Graduate Center, 2014), chapter 4.

84. Young, interview by author.

85. Ai-Jen Poo for Domestic Workers United, *Organizing with Love: Lessons from the New York Domestic Workers Bill of Rights Campaign* (Ann Arbor: Center for the Education of Women, University of Michigan, June 2010), p. 10, http://www.cew.umich.edu/sites/default/files/Organizingwithlove--FullReport-Cover_0.pdf.

86. For more on contemporary organizing, see Harmony Goldberg, "Our Day Has Finally Come: Domestic Worker Organizing in New York City" (PhD diss., CUNY Graduate Center, 2014); Sheila Bapat, *Part of the Family? Nannies, Housekeepers, and Caregivers in the Battle for Domestic Worker Rights* (New York: Ig Publishing, 2014); Monisha Das Gupta, *Unruly Immigrants: Rights, Activism, and Transnational South Asian Politics in the United States* (Durham, NC: Duke University Press, 2006); Hondagneu-Sotelo, *Doméstica*; Hina Shah and Marci Seville, "Domestic Worker Organizing: Building a Contemporary Movement for Dignity and Power," *Albany Law Review* 75, no. 1 (2012): 413–47; Eileen Boris and Premilla Nadasen, "Domestic Workers Organize!" *Working USA: The Journal of Labor and Society* 12, no. 1 (2009): 413–37; Premilla Nadasen, "Sista' Friends and Other Allies: Domestic Workers United," in *New Social Movements in the African Diaspora: Challenging Global Apartheid*, ed. Leith Mullings (New York: Palgrave MacMillan, 2009), 285–98; Fine, *Worker Centers*; Terri Nilliasca, "Some Women's Work: Domestic Work, Class, Race, Heteropatriarchy, and the Limits of Legal Reform," *Michigan Journal of Race and Law* 16 (2011); Ai-Jen Poo, "A Twenty-First-Century Organizing Model: Lessons from the New York Domestic Workers Bill of Rights," *New Labor Forum* 20, no. 1 (Winter 2011): 50–55.

87. *NCHE News* 7, no. 2 (Fall/Winter 1976), Schlesinger Library, Radcliffe Institute, Harvard University.

88. Katz, "Carolyn Reed and the Backstairs Revolt," 46.

89. Videotape, Bethune Museum opening, 1979, National Council of Negro Women Records, National Archives for Black Women's History, 001, Series 15, Subseries 7, Folder 09, Item 256.

90. Miller, "Geraldine Miller: Household Technician and Social Activist," 307.

91. See Gerda Lerner, *Living with History: Making Social Change* (Chapel Hill: University of North Carolina Press, 2009), 52–69.

92. Bonita Johnson, "'There's No More Gettin' on Their Knees': An Historical Overview of Household Employment in the US," MA thesis, Sarah Lawrence College, 1982.

93. Reminiscences of Carolyn Reed, 42.

94. "Linking Household Workers," *Off Our Backs* 11, no. 1 (January 31, 1981): 15; *Household Employment News* 12, no. 2 (August 1980), Schlesinger Library, Radcliffe Institute, Harvard University.

95. Janet Ochs Wiener, "Self-Help: Dusting Off New Priorities in the Union of Household Workers," *Washington Post*, November 19, 1980.

96. *Household Employment News* 12, no. 2 (August 1980), Schlesinger Library, Radcliffe Institute, Harvard University.

INDEX

founding of the Bronx Household
Technicians, 112; interest in labor
rights, 107; interest in the theory
and practice of feminism, 178; job
training initiatives, 98; relationship
with the women's movement, 134; on
the structure of employer-employee
negotiation, 108–9; use of public
spaces for organizing efforts, 111;
view of McLaurin's work, 121; worker
organizing efforts, 104–5
Milliken, William, 83
minimum wage campaign: alliance
between middle-class feminists and
household workers, 124–25, 215n5;
enforcement problem, 141, 177;
exclusion of household labor from
the benefits of economic citizenship, 126, 127, 130; FLSA amendments
and, 127–29, 142–43; ideology of, 130;
importance of, 125, 130; leveraging of
the gendered middle-class conflict
around household labor, 133–34; lobbying for passage of a congressional
bill, 125, 127–30; male politicians'
anti–minimum wage argument,
130–33; the New Deal's fostering of
inequality, 126; racialized inequality
under labor laws, 126, 215n8; social
citizenship concept and, 126–27, 130;
storytelling's role in, 128, 177; strategic alliance developed to pass the
FLSA amendments, 138–39, 218n52;
support from the women's movement, 140
Minnesota Commission on the Status of
Women, 209n50
Miss America Pageant and bra burning, 2
Mitchell, Margaret, 13
Montgomery bus boycott: black domestic workers' role in, 19–20, 25–27, 31–
32, 194n32; black women's bus-riding
experiences, 26–27, 33–34; carpool

arrangements and support, 28–30;
cross-class alliance, 21; fed-up attitude
of working-class bus riders, 23, 24–25,
27; Gilmore's Club from Nowhere
and, 29–31, 196n68; mass meetings,
28–29; politics of respectability during, 22–23, 195nn43–45; retaliations
by white employers, 30; sentiment
of household workers at the start of,
20–22; white employers' beliefs about
the origins of the boycott, 23–24
Montgomery Improvement Association
(MIA), 28
Moody, Curt, 162
Ms. (magazine), 165

NAACP, 14, 53
National Archives for Black Women's
History, 178
National Association of Colored
Women's Clubs, 64
National Black Feminist Organization,
134
National Committee on Household
Employment (NCHE): advocacy
for domestic workers, 61–62, 77, 80;
argument for reforming domestic
work, 64, 67–68, 204n68; change in
the character of domestic work in the
1950s, 65–66; codes of employment
standards adopted by workers, 96,
209n50; designing of programs to
meet employers needs, 70; efforts to
include Mexican Americans, 161–63;
efforts to upgrade the status of the
occupation, 68–70; forming of, 64;
hiring of Hulett, 73–74; history of
African American women and household labor and, 73, 80, 177–79; HTA
and (*see* Household Technicians of
America); immigrant workers' impact
on the labor dynamics, 163; involvement in the campaign for economic
rights, 166–68; leadership of Sloan,

dignity, 103; impetus for organizing domestic workers, 51–52; inclusion of noncitizens, 224n67; involvement in civil rights movement, 50–51, 53–54; on the lowering of standards for cleanliness, 149; origins of her political sensibility, 55–56; personal insecurities, 53; politicization of, 48; stepping back from her leadership role, 171; use of the power of loyalty to win demands, 109; view of organized labor, 118, 213n63; view of worker exploitation as a legacy of slavery, 51; views on forms of address used by employers, 94

Roberts, James, 45
Robeson, Paul, 8
Robinson, Lewis G., 48, 50
Rollins, Judith, 210n76, 217n36
Romero, Mary, 151, 217n36
Ruiz, Elva, 162

Sarah Lawrence College, 178, 179
Saulsberry, Johnnie, 87
SCLC (Southern Christian Leadership Conference), 37
Scott, Louise, 43
Service Employees International Union (SEIU), 122
Sheehy, Gail, 137
Shelton, Anita, 163, 223n53
Simms, Benjamin, 31
Sixteenth Street Baptist Church, Birmingham, Alabama, 60
"Slave Market," 4, 14, 15f, 16, 58, 59, 62, 99, 107, 157, 176, 193
slavery and domestic work: similarity between, 4, 5, 10, 11–12, 13, 14–15, 51, 58–59, 73, 80, 89–90, 91, 92, 95, 99, 102, 107, 158, 174, 192n13; slave market for domestics, 4, 14, 15f, 16, 58, 59, 62, 99, 107, 157, 176, 193
Sloan, Edith Barksdale: background and education, 59–60; campaign for

economic rights, 167; connection to the history of domestic-worker exploitation, 58, 59; efforts to include Mexican Americans in NCHE, 162; exit from the NCHE, 169; impetus for joining the civil rights movement, 60; leadership of the NCHE, 61, 71–73; lobbying for passage of a minimum wage bill, 129; professionalization of the occupation goal, 96; on the struggle for equality, 147

Sloan, Ned, 60
Smith, Mary Louise, 22
SNCC (Student Nonviolent Coordinating Committee), 37, 39–40
social citizenship concept, 126–27, 130, 144–45, 219n70
Social Security, 62, 69, 93, 99, 101, 120, 126, 137, 142
Sojourners for Truth and Justice, 16
Sophie (maid), 86
South Africa, 165, 181
Southern Christian Leadership Conference (SCLC), 37
Southern Negro Youth Congress, 15
Spanish Catholic Center, 164
Spock, Benjamin, 65
Stackhouse, Ollie, 214n72
Stanford, Max, 200n70
Steinem, Gloria, 124, 139, 140–41
Stephen E. Howe Elementary School, Glenville, Ohio, 49
Stinson, Charles, 42
storytelling and domestic work: creation of the domestic workers movement and, 3–4, 58–59, 61, 73, 76, 78, 103, 136, 176–77, 183; employer-needs bias in Maids' Honor Day, 87; political purpose of stories of social movements, 2–3; role in labor organizing, 174, 176; role in minimum wage campaign, 177; slavery's significance in individual experiences (*see* slavery and domestic work); stories told in *Like One of*